# Transforming
# Higher Education

*SRHE and Open University Press Imprint*
*General Editor*: Heather Eggins

# Transforming Higher Education

Lee Harvey
and
Peter T. Knight

The Society for Research into Higher Education
& Open University Press

Published by SRHE and
Open University Press
Celtic Court
22 Ballmoor
Buckingham
MK18 1XW

and 1900 Frost Road, Suite 101
Bristol, PA 19007, USA

First published 1996

A catalogue record of this book is available from the British Library

ISBN 0 335 19589 X pbk     0 335 19590 3 hbk

*Library of Congress Cataloging-in-Publication Data*
Harvey, Lee, 1949–
    Transforming higher education / Lee Harvey and Peter T. Knight.
        p.  cm.
    Includes bibliographical references and index.
    ISBN 0–335–19590–3  ISBN 0–335–19589–X (pbk.):
    1. Education, Higher—Great Britain.   2. Education, Higher—Great
Britain—Administration.   3. Higher education and state—Great
Britain.   4. Educational change—Great Britain.   I. Knight, Peter,
1950–  .  II. Title.
LA637.H37   1996
378.41—dc20                                                    96–8124
                                                                    CIP

Typeset by Graphicraft Typesetters Limited, Hong Kong
Printed in Great Britain by St Edmundsbury Press,
Bury St Edmunds, Suffolk

# Contents

# Acknowledgements

Our thanks are due to the thousands of people who participated in *QHE* research, to all those who helped by distributing questionnaires and organizing discussion groups, and to the members of the Steering Committee whose help and advice will be sorely missed. A special thanks to Professor Diana Green who inaugurated the project and who has been a source of inspiration throughout.

Our thanks are also due to Dary Erwin and Georgine Loacker for their help with the case studies in Chapter 8. These studies were made possible thanks to grants from Lancaster University's Research, Staff Development, and Innovation in Higher Education funds. Peter also thanks Jo Tait for help with these studies and for general support, advice and encouragement throughout.

Lee is also indebted to Lesley Plimmer, Vicki Geall and Sue Moon at the Centre for Research into Quality for all their help and support at the final drafting stage of the book. Last, but by no means least, thanks to Morag MacDonald for once again being so supportive and understanding during the making of this book and to Stephanie and Julie who sometimes had to put up with a grumpy dad.

# Preface

Several, apparently contradictory forces have been at work on higher education since the mid-1980s. The pressure to cut unit costs continues and forces institutions to look at ways of teaching more students with the same or fewer resources and numbers of staff. Yet, at the same time, government has launched a plethora of quality assurance measures, intended to ensure that cost-cutting does not compromise quality but, ideally, is accompanied by enhanced quality. Thirdly, increasing attention is being paid to universities' teaching functions, with the Enterprise in Higher Education (EHE) initiative, for example, fostering a greater range of learning outcomes and of teaching, learning and assessment methods, again against this backdrop of cost-cutting. These issues are not confined to the British higher education system: declining unit of resource, more accountable universities and massification of higher education are issues being faced by higher education systems across the world.

The theme of this book is that the drive for quality in Britain and the concurrent moves to reform teaching and learning processes have not been connected, organizationally or in practice. Our case is that quality needs to be understood as a transformative process, which means that it cannot be addressed separately from issues to do with assessment, learning and teaching. Drawing upon a major, national research project into quality in higher education (the Quality in Higher Education Project), we illustrate the variety of meanings that have attached to 'quality', revealing that a tension has emerged between quality-as-accountability and quality-as-transformation. The predominance of the former meaning has led to a 'compliance culture', such that emphasis on quality is not, in fact, producing the transformation in students that is called for in our view. This is developed by drawing international comparisons to show that the issues facing higher education systems are not unique to the United Kingdom.

We shall explore the nature of recent and future changes in higher education and assess the way higher education must respond to ensure appropriate learning in the twenty-first century.

Transformation lies at the heart of this book as the title implies. The deliberate pun in the title is intended to highlight both the need to transform higher education for the twenty-first century and that higher education is itself a major transformative process.

The worldwide impetus to expand higher education, by increasing participation rates, is driven in great measure by a future vision of the world economy. Competitive advantage in the global economy is seen as dependent upon having a well-educated workforce. The world is changing rapidly and there is a growing perception that there is a need for people who can accommodate and initiate change. As technology, competition and social upheaval transform the world at an accelerating pace so higher education is increasingly seen as crucial in producing an adequately educated population.

If higher education is to play an effective role in education for the twenty-first century then it must focus its attention on the transformative process of learning. A prime goal should be to transform learners so that they are able to take initiative, work with independence, to choose appropriate frames of reference, while being able to see the limitations of those frameworks and to stand outside them when necessary. To be an effective transformative process, higher education must itself be transformed, we argue, so that it produces transformative agents: critical reflective learners able to cope with a rapidly changing world. Throughout this book we shall explore the nature of such higher education and consider how the system of higher education needs to adapt to deliver it.

In Chapter 1 we explore the concept of quality in higher education and focus on 'transformation', which is central, we argue, both to quality and to learning in higher education. In so doing we explore the relationship between quality and standards.

In Chapters 2 and 3, the pragmatic views on quality of different stakeholders in higher education are explored to see to what notions of quality underpin them. The analysis addresses the extent to which conceptualizations of quality are linked to student learning. Chapter 2 focuses on internal stakeholders – students, teaching staff, non-teaching staff and managers – and Chapter 3 concentrates on the perceptions of a major external stakeholder – employers.

In Chapter 4 we assess higher education policy in Britain and other countries since the mid-1980s. We suggest that a paradigm shift has occurred in the move from élite to mass higher education. Policy in many countries has responded pragmatically to that shift, mainly driven by the costs of a mass higher education and the need to sustain economic competitiveness in a global economy. We show that in Britain and elsewhere, issues of quality have been kept at arm's length from issues of student learning, despite attempts to reconceptualize the purpose of higher education and the new emphasis on outputs.

Higher education policy has been driven by the desire to increase universities' accountability. A key element of this has been an emphasis on output indicators. We demonstrate that the use of such things as performance indicators have been primarily for purposes of accountability rather than the improvement of the student experience of education. In other words, the drive for accountability has not been directly concerned to enhance the quality of student learning, let alone to promote the idea of learning as transformation.

In Chapter 5 we consider another key aspect of higher education policy – external quality monitoring (EQM). We assess the purposes, principles and role of external quality monitoring and consider EQM procedures in the light of policy initiatives. Different approaches to EQM internationally are assessed and we demonstrate a convergence with a predominant accountability-led model. The dominant model is explored in terms of its link to student learning. The link between internal and external quality monitoring is examined and we undertake an initial evaluation of the impact of each on the improvement of the student experience.

In Chapter 6 an alternative improvement-led approach, which links external monitoring to transformative quality, is proposed. Our argument is that the key to quality improvement lies in empowering academic staff to undertake a process of continuous quality improvement in relation to student learning. This theme is developed across the following four chapters.

In Chapter 7 we offer a view of learning and examine how transformation relates to existing research into students' learning. Although this is a well-ploughed field, researchers have jibbed at drawing organizational implications from it. We, on the contrary, argue that if this notion of quality is to prevail, then it is necessary for universities, as organizations, to respond to learning theories and associated research. We suggest how ways of organizing learning can become transformative rather than replicative. Three areas of potential transformation are addressed: the discipline, general achievements and meta-critiques. If such transformations are to be sought, then higher education institutions will need to be transformed.

Chapter 8 proposes that the assessment of student learning is a powerful element in the development of transformative learning. Assessment tasks have the power to reinforce the goals of transformation or to subvert them completely. Transformed higher education needs transformed and transforming assessment. Two case studies from North America are used to illustrate the transformative use of assessment of learning.

In Chapter 9 we examine teaching and argue that, despite the complexity of learning and the impact of assessment, there are some underlying principles associated with teaching that facilitate and encourage transformative learning.

Chapter 10 proposes that if students are to be transformed during their undergraduate careers, then first universities need to transform themselves, moving from the rituals of teaching to the mysteries of learning. We argue that professional development of staff is a key element in that transformation.

Our conclusion is that, in recent years, there is evidence of much change in higher education, both in the United Kingdom and elsewhere. However, that change has been driven by the search for efficiency and by a quest for greater, bureaucratic accountability. Whatever the merits of these developments, we argue that they have not been directly concerned to improve the quality of student learning. We argue not just that student learning ought to be at the centre of discussions about quality enhancement, but that the goal ought to be transformation: transformation of universities with a view to transforming learners.

# 1

# Quality and Learning

## Quality

We can no longer take quality for granted in higher education. We can no longer presume we all know what we mean by a 'quality' higher education. Quite the contrary. The ambiguity of 'quality' in higher education has served a useful purpose. 'Quality', appropriated by an autonomous, non-accountable, élite, university sector, has been part of the defensive wall behind which the academy has been able to hide. However, it is irresponsible to continue with a view that quality is too ambiguous to be pinned down.

Taken-for-granted concepts of quality have to be reassessed in the light of the changing rationale and purpose of higher education. Quality and purpose are interrelated aspects of the new higher education and if we fail to recognize that, we simply create *ad hoc* categories, devise convenience measures and produce meaningless ratings that have more to do with traditional conceptions of higher education than a reappraisal of the purpose of higher education for the twenty-first century.

Quality in higher education is being assessed throughout the world. Quality is being operationalized in some way or another for the purposes of these assessments. However, it appears that far too often, quality assessment and assurance processes have started by determining how quality is to be assessed or reviewed rather than by asking what it is that is to be assessed. Equally, it is not clear that the reasons for fudging quality by taking *this* as an indicator rather than *that* have always been suitably defended.

There are widely differing conceptualizations of quality in use in education (for example, Richardson, 1992; Dill, 1993; NUS, 1993). However, these can be grouped into five discrete but interrelated ways of thinking about quality (Harvey and Green, 1993). Quality can be viewed as *exceptional*, as *perfection* (or consistency), as *fitness for purpose*, as *value for money* and as *transformation* (Table 1.1).

## *Quality as exceptional*

The exceptional notion of quality sees it as something special. There are three variations on this: first, the traditional notion of quality as distinctive;

*Table 1.1*   Approaches to quality

---

1. Quality as exceptional
    Traditional notion of quality
    Excellence (exceeding high standards)
    Checking standards

2. Quality as perfection or consistency
    Zero defects
    Quality culture

3. Quality as fitness for purpose
    Fitness for purpose 1 – customer specification
    Meeting requirements
    Fitness for purpose 2 – mission
    Quality assurance
    Customer satisfaction

4. Quality as value for money
    Performance indicators
    Customer charters

5. Quality as transformation
    Enhancing the participant
    Value added
    Empowering the participant

---

second, a view of quality as exceeding very high standards (or 'excellence'); and third, a weaker notion of exceptional quality, as passing a set of required (minimum) standards.

*Traditional notion of quality*
Traditionally, the concept of quality has been associated with the notion of distinctiveness, of something special or 'high class'. The traditional notion of quality implies *exclusivity*: for example, the supposed high quality of an Oxbridge or Ivy League education (Pfeffer and Coote, 1991). Quality is not determined through an assessment of what is provided but is based on an assumption that the distinctiveness and inaccessibility of an Oxbridge education is of itself 'quality'. This is not quality as a set of criteria but *the* quality, separate and unattainable for most people.

The traditional notion of quality does not offer benchmarks against which to measure quality. It does not attempt to define quality (Church, 1988). It is useless when it comes to *assessing* quality in education because it provides no definable *means* of determining quality.

*Excellence: exceeding high standards*
Excellence is often used interchangeably with quality (Ball, 1985). In this sense quality is seen in terms of 'high' standards (CVCP, 1986; Moodie, 1986a). It is similar to the traditional view but identifies the constituents of

excellence, while at the same time ensuring that these are difficult to attain. It is élitist in as much as it sees quality as only possibly attainable in limited circumstances. In the education context, if you are lectured by Nobel prize-winners, have a well-equipped laboratory with the most up-to-date scientific apparatus and a well-stocked library, then you may well produce excellent results.

The excellence notion of quality in education thus tends to focus on input and output. An institution that takes the best students, provides them with the best resources, both human and physical, by its nature excels. Whatever the process by which students learn, the excellence remains.

Excellence, with its emphasis on the 'level' of input and output, is an absolutist measure of quality (Astin and Solomon, 1981; Moodie, 1988; Miller, 1990). The notion of 'centres of excellence' in higher education is frequently based on this notion of quality (DTI/CIHE, 1989). It can be seen in the United Kingdom in the Research Councils' criteria for long-term funding of research centres.

### Checking standards

The final notion of quality as exceptional dilutes the notion of excellence. A 'quality' product in this sense is one that has passed a set of quality checks, which are based on attainable criteria that are designed to reject 'defective' items. The 'pass mark' for coursework and examinations is an everyday example of standards checking in higher education.

'Quality' is thus attributed to all those items that fulfil the *minimum* standards set by the manufacturer or monitoring body. Quality is thus the result of 'scientific quality control'. This threshold approach is applied, for example, by bodies controlling access to professional occupations (Harvey and Mason, 1995). A minimum degree of practitioner knowledge and competence is required to gain admission to the profession.

At any given moment there will be an 'absolute' benchmark (or standard) against which the product is checked and those that satisfy the criteria will pass the quality threshold. The benchmarks may be set internally by academics (albeit monitored by peers) or externally by commentators or analysts, often in the form of consumer league tables. Checking for quality may be pass/fail or it may be on a scale. League tables are such quality ratings, as are final classifications awarded on most undergraduate programmes of study in higher education institutions. A product that meets a higher than minimum standard is a higher quality product.

The 'checking standards' approach to quality implicitly assumes that 'standards' are 'objective' and static (Walsh, 1991). However, as we demonstrate, standards are negotiated and subject to continued renegotiation in the light of changed circumstances.

## Quality as perfection or consistency

A second approach to quality sees it in terms of consistency. It focuses on process and sets specifications that it aims to meet perfectly (Ingle, 1985).

This is encapsulated in two interrelated dictums: *zero defects* and *getting things right first time.*

### Zero defects

The 'zero defects' approach redefines quality as *conformance to specification* rather than exceeding high standards (Halpin, 1966; Crosby, 1979; Harrington, 1988). This is also, in manufacturing circles, referred to as 'excellence' but should not be confused with the notion of excellence as exceeding high standards.

In this approach there is a distinction between quality and standards. Quality is that which conforms to a particular specification. The product or service is judged by its consistency or, in some cases, by its reliability (Carter, 1978; Garvin, 1988). Excellence thus becomes 'perfection' as measured by the absence of defects. A quality product or service is one which conforms exactly to specification and a quality producer or service provider is one whose output is consistently free of defects.

Zero defects is not just about conforming to specification. It embodies a philosophy of *prevention* rather than inspection (Peters and Waterman, 1982). The focus is on ensuring that, at each stage, faults do not occur, rather than relying on final inspection to identify defects.

This notion of quality as perfection or consistency may be applicable to administrative tasks such as the maintenance of student records but it does not fit well with the idea of discovery learning.

### Quality culture

A culture of quality is one in which everybody in the organization, not just the quality controllers, is responsible for quality (Crosby, 1986). A central feature of such organizations is that each worker or team of workers is both a customer of, and supplier to, other workers in the organization: they form a chain of internal customers and suppliers. It is the responsibility of each unit to ensure the quality of their own work.

The emphasis is on ensuring that things are 'done right first time' (Crosby, 1984; Oakland, 1992). When they are not, then the process that has led to an unsatisfactory output is analysed so that corrections can be made in the *process* to ensure that the problem does not arise again. In a quality culture, there is no need to check final output. Indeed, to do so is to shift responsibility away from those involved at each stage.

As we shall demonstrate in Chapters 6 and 10, developing an appropriate quality culture, especially through delegation of responsibility for quality, is essential for an effective, responsive quality improvement process. However, it is a culture of delegated responsibility for continuous improvement rather than a culture dedicated to producing a consistent product.

## Quality as fitness for purpose

A third approach to quality argues that quality only has meaning in relation to the *purpose* of the product or service (Ball, 1985; CVCP, 1986; HMI,

1989a, 1989b; Crawford, 1991). This notion is quite remote from the idea of quality as something special, distinctive, élitist, conferring status, or difficult to attain. If something does the job for which it is designed, then it is a quality product or service. Every product and service has the potential to fit its purpose and thus be a quality product or service, unlike the exceptional notion of quality, which, by definition, must be exclusive (even in the weaker standards-checking approach).

Fitness for purpose has emerged as the fashionable way to harness the drive for perfection. The ultimate measure of perfection, 'zero defects', may be excellent as a definition of quality but runs the fatal risk of being perfectly useless. If the product does not fit its purpose then its perfection is irrelevant.

Although straightforward in conception, 'fitness for purpose' is deceptive (Moodie, 1986b), for it raises the issue of *whose purpose* and *how is fitness assessed*? Fitness for purpose offers two alternative priorities for specifying purpose. The first puts the onus on the customer, the second locates it on the provider.

*Fitting-the-customer-specification*
Quality as fitting-the-customer-specification requires that the outcome of a process matches the specified requirements. This requires, first of all, that customer requirements are precisely identified and second that the outcome conforms to those requirements. The producer or service provider is, in theory, merely the instrument in fulfilling customer needs. Some advocates of fitness for purpose argue that providers can, or indeed should (Deming, 1982), be more pro-active by anticipating consumer desires.

Fitting-the-customer-specification is also developmental as it recognizes that purposes may change over time thus requiring constant re-evaluation of the appropriateness of the specification.

However, the idea that the customer determines the specification is an idealization. In practice, customers rarely specify their individual requirements. On the contrary, the manufacturer of mass-produced artefacts or provider of standardized services assesses what the customer is prepared to buy. Not only do providers anticipate needs but, through massive marketing departments, they attempt to mould requirements to match the product. Ford's 'everything we do is driven by you' campaign for their cars uses a pun to exploit the inevitable differential between customer requirement and mass-produced output while at the same time giving the impression that 'you', the idealized consumer, have determined the product.

This raises fundamental questions about the fitness-for-purpose definition of quality as 'meeting customer requirements'. This is a problem that, for two reasons, is further exacerbated in the context of education. First, the notion of 'customer' is itself a tricky, indeed contentious, concept in education (CIHE, 1987; Harvey, 1995a). Is the customer the service user (the students) or those who pay for the service (government, employers, parents)? Second, the customer, the student for example, is not always able, nor necessarily in a position to, specify what is required (Elton, 1992).

Fitness for purpose, therefore, leaves open the question of who should define quality in education and how it should be assessed.

### Mission-based fitness for purpose

An alternative view of fitness for purpose avoids the issue of determining who are higher education's customers by returning the emphasis to the *institution*. In this case, quality is defined in terms of the institution fulfilling its own stated objectives or 'mission' (Green, 1993). Quality becomes fitness for, and performance in, the market as defined by the institution.

This view of quality underpins the approach of the British Government which (post-1992) seeks to ensure that the new funding arrangements for teaching should safeguard the best of the distinctive missions of individual institutions (DES, 1991a) and pervades the methodology underpinning the two main external checks on quality, audit and assessment. For example, the approach to teaching quality assessment adopted by the Scottish and English Funding Councils relies on making judgements about the quality of provision within the context of the individual institution's stated mission.

As we shall see in Chapter 5, this is a significant element of the dominant model of external quality monitoring in many countries.

### Customer satisfaction

The previous two approaches converge if the institutional mission is responsive to the needs or expectations of stakeholders (students, employers, government, society). In practice, this institutional responsiveness involves monitoring 'customer satisfaction' (usually student or employer satisfaction) with the 'service' offered. Customer satisfaction is indicative of fitness-for-purpose quality.

In practice, the *post hoc* investigation of student satisfaction is the most likely arbiter of *fitness* for the mission-determined purpose: educational institutions 'need to be careful that they base their quality standards upon an analysis of customer wants and needs and not just upon their own definitions' (Sallis and Hingley, 1992: 3). However, it is unlikely, even with increased competition and the encouragement of market niches, that there will be a completely 'free market' in education in which the corrective of customer satisfaction will operate to readjust missions (Ishikawa, 1985; Shores, 1988).

Customer perceptions of satisfaction are not irrevocably tied to fitness-for-purpose models. Indeed, as we shall suggest in Chapter 6 in particular, participant feedback and consequent action is central to a process of continuous quality improvement of the student learning experience.

## Quality as value for money

A populist notion of quality equates it with value for money (Ball, 1985). 'Quality at a price you can afford' implies a 'high standard' specification at reduced cost (Schrock and Lefevre, 1988). The British Government, along with many others, has made use of this populist view of quality. It has linked the quality of education to value for money through its demand for efficiency and effectiveness.

Since the mid-1980s, there has been growing pressure on higher education institutions in Europe, Australia, the USA and elsewhere to demonstrate their efficiency and effectiveness, among other things, by managing expansion without a comparable increase in resources and with no decline in quality (or standards). In countries such as Britain, Australia and Denmark the link between quality and value for money has been overtly and controversially expressed in the methodologies adopted for funding teaching which reward quality and penalize unsatisfactory provision (an issue explored in detail in Chapter 5).

Value for money is, thus, a market view of quality linked to accountability. The use of performance indicators, customer charters and league tables are an attempt to operationalize and legitimate this notion of quality by creating a pseudo-market designed to effect change through competition. The British Government, for example, 'believes that the real key to achieving cost effective expansion lies in greater competition for funds and students' (HM Government, 1991: para 17). The impact of value-for-money indicators on the quality of the student experience is explored in Chapter 4.

## *Quality as transformation*

The transformative view of quality is rooted in the notion of 'qualitative change', a fundamental change of *form*. Ice is trans*formed* into water and eventually steam if it experiences an increase in temperature. While the increase in temperature can be measured, the transformation involves a qualitative change. Ice has different qualities from those of steam or water. It is made up of the same molecules but reacts very differently with its environment.

Transformation is not restricted to apparent or physical transformation but also includes cognitive transcendence. This transformative notion of quality is well established in Western philosophy and can be found in the discussion of dialectical transformation in the works of Aristotle, Kant, Hegel and Marx. It is also at the heart of transcendental philosophies around the world, such as Buddhism and Janism. More recently, it has been entertainingly explored in Pirsig's (1976) *Zen and the Art of Motorcycle Maintenance.*

This transformative notion of quality raises doubts about the relevance of product-centred approaches such as fitness-for-purpose. There are problems, as we have seen, in translating product-based notions of quality to the service sector. This becomes particularly acute when applied to education (Elton, 1992).

Education is a participative process. Students are not products, customers, consumers, service users or clients – they are participants. Education is not a service *for* a customer (much less a product to be consumed) but an ongoing process of transformation *of* the participant.

There are two elements of transformative quality in education, enhancing the participant and empowering the participant.

*Enhancing the participant*
A quality education is one that effects changes in the participants and, thereby, enhances them. Value-added notions of quality provide a measure of enhancement (Astin, 1985, 1991; Kogan, 1986; Barnett, 1988; CNAA, 1990a; PCFC, 1990d).

Value added is a 'measure' of quality in terms of the extent to which the educational experience enhances the knowledge, abilities and skills of students. A high-quality institution would be one that greatly enhances its students (Astin, 1991). Oxbridge may produce some 'brilliant' first-class graduates but having brilliant school leavers in the first place they may not have added very much. However, exactly how much is added depends on the methodology and what is defined as being of value in the first place (Barnett, 1988; CNAA, 1990a).

*Empowering the participant*
The second element of transformative quality is empowerment. Empowering students is a concept that has grown in prominence since the start of the 1990s. There are those for whom empowering students lies at the heart of a radical reappraisal of higher education and underpins any assessment of educational quality. There are others for whom empowering students is a contradiction in terms or merely empty rhetoric. Students cannot possibly know what's good for them, nor should they demand more time, effort and resources from a hard-pressed intellectual élite.

We claim that empowering students involves giving power to participants to influence their own transformation. It involves students taking ownership of the learning process. Furthermore, the transformation process itself provides the opportunity for self-empowerment, through increased confidence, self-awareness, and so on.

There are four main ways of empowering students (Harvey and Burrows, 1992). First, empowering students via *student evaluation* – that is, giving students the opportunity to comment on the education they are receiving. Some institutions require that student evaluation reports are included in annual course reports and review and validation documents. In the United States, student evaluation of teaching has been an integral part of college life for decades. However, students will only be empowered if action results from their evaluation. Even so, it is a limited form of empowerment for two reasons. First, in most cases students are reacting to agendas set by academic or administrative staff rather than their own agendas for improvement. Second, even where the agenda is set by students (Moon, 1995), it rarely deconstructs the transformative process of learning.

A second form of empowerment is to *guarantee students minimum standards of provision* and give them responsibility for monitoring it, for example, through student charters. In Britain, there is a Student Charter for both further and higher education systems. Universities and colleges have produced local versions and in some cases faculties within a university produce their own. This is also a limited form of empowerment for the same reasons. 'Charterism' in education rarely involves students in policy formulation at the national or even institutional level. The Student Satisfaction Approach at the University of Central England in Birmingham is a rare example of an action cycle based on student perceptions impacting on institutional strategic management. The Copenhagen Business School is relatively unique in involving students directly in the development of its quality policies and practices.

Third, give students *more control over their own learning*. This ranges from allowing students to select their own curriculum to students entering into a learning contract. The selection of a curriculum usually means, in practice, choosing which teaching programmes they attend and thus which assessment they undertake. While superficially liberating, this does not necessarily empower the student. The American experience from the 1960s suggests the contrary. An unstructured collection of small units which the student selects from a sometimes bewildering array of available options, with little or no guidance, can ill-equip them for the post-educational experience (Ratcliff and associates, 1995). The problem with the open 'cafeteria' approach is that while units are accumulated there is often no identifiable progression or conceptual development . Similar concerns are being voiced about the growing trend to unitize learning in Britain through the introduction of semesterized modular schemes.

The development of a learning contract, while apparently more restrictive, has a much greater potential to empower students. The student does not simply choose which teaching programmes to attend but negotiates a learning experience. The student controls how they learn and when and how it is assessed.

The fourth approach to empowerment is to *develop students' critical ability*, that is, their ability to think and act in a way that transcends taken-for-granted preconceptions, prejudices and frames of reference. Critical thinking is not to be confused with 'criticism', especially the common-sense notion of negative criticism. Developing critical thinking involves getting students to question the established orthodoxy and learn to justify their opinions. Students are encouraged to think about knowledge as a process in which they are engaged, not some 'thing' they tentatively approach and selectively appropriate.

Developing critical ability is about students having the confidence to assess and develop knowledge for themselves rather than submitting packaged chunks to an assessor who will tell them if it is sufficient or 'correct'. A critical ability enables students to self-assess, to be able to decide what is good quality work and to be confident when they have achieved it (Wiggins, 1990). In short, an approach that encourages critical ability treats students as intellectual performers rather than as compliant audience. It transforms teaching and learning into an active process of coming to understand. It enables students to easily go beyond the narrow confines of the 'safe' knowledge base of their academic discipline to applying themselves to whatever they encounter in the post-education world. This requires that students are treated as intellectual performers and that any system of assessment is clear, public, and an integral part of the learning process, not an 'add-on' (Paskow, 1990: 4).

This fourth approach, thus, attempts to empower students not just as 'customers' in the education process but for life. Empowering students for life requires an approach to teaching and learning that goes beyond requiring students to learn a body of knowledge and be able to apply it analytically. Developing critical ability involves encouraging students to challenge preconceptions, their own, their peers' and their teachers'. This form of empowerment is at the heart of the dialectical process of critical transformation.

## Critical transformation

Transformation is a process of transmutation of one form into another. In the educational realm this refers, in part, to changes in the knowledge and abilities of students – the development of domain expertise – but it also refers to the process of coming to understand.

Where work is highly structured, as it is in some schools and in some universities, learners are constrained by this structure to the extent that one can say that they are on the nursery slopes of critical activity. Where the work is less structured, then they can be seen as advanced beginners, well able to ski on marked-out *pistes*. However, we contend, higher education is about more than just producing skilled acolytes, important though that undoubtedly is. It is also about producing people who can lead, who can produce new knowledge, who can see new problems and imagine new ways of approaching old problems. Higher education has a role to prepare people to go beyond the present and to be able to respond to a future which cannot now be imagined.

This sounds vaguely utilitarian, as though higher education is to be justified by the utility of its outcomes alone. Yet, there is a long history of higher education being seen as something valuable in its own right because of its effects upon the individual, effects that might show through in the world of wealth generation but which might equally show through in the people's conceptions of themselves, life and the world.

Our point is that both cases call for people who can go beyond the givens: people who can draw upon a variety of explanatory frameworks and who can also stand outside them to the extent of recognizing their limitations and the degree to which any framework limits, as well as enables, thinking and feeling.

This takes us closer to the idea of critical transformation. It stands in relation to critical thinking in the same way that metacognition stands in relation to cognition. Just as metacognition involves being aware of our thinking processes, of their limitations and possibilities, so too critical transformation depends upon understanding the limits of our frameworks of understanding, an appreciation of when and where they might be profitably

*Table 1.2* Elements of the transformation perspective on higher education

**Expertise within a domain**
Knowledge of structure, principles and procedures in a domain
Ability to use new data to reshape old concepts and form new ones
  (accommodation)
Skill at general operations (for example, oral communication)
Metacognitive awareness (see Chapter 7)

**Transformation**
Independence as a learner
Commitment to continued learning, especially through reflection,
  construction and deconstruction
Use of a range of frames of reference or of explanatory apparatus
Recognition that frames of reference empower and limit
Interplay between own values and values in professional settings –
  continuous refinement of own values and sense of self (reflective
  practitioner)
Development of critical, dialectical thinking

used, as well as an insight into ways in which they constrain thought, values
feeling and action.

Critical transformation sees quality in terms of the extent to which the
education system transforms the *conceptual* ability and *self-awareness* of the
student. Table 1.2 identifies elements in critical transformative learning.

Critical transformative action involves getting to the heart of an issue
while simultaneously setting it in its wider context. It is a matter of conceptually shuttling backwards and forwards between what the learner already
knows and what the learner is finding out, between the specific detail and
its broader significance, and between practice and reflection.

Transformative learning involves a process of deconstruction and reconstruction. Abstract concepts need to be made concrete and a core or essential concept identified as a pivot for deconstructive activity. Deconstruction
gets beneath surface appearances; be they traditional modes of working,
taken-for-granted attitudes, embedded values, prevailing myths, ideology
or 'well-known' facts. The core concept is used to 'lever open' the area of
investigation. That is, the relationship between the core concept and the
area of enquiry is investigated at both an abstract and a concrete level to
explore whether underlying abstract presuppositions conflict with concrete
reality. Not all concepts will provide a suitable lever – indeed, critical reflective activity involves a constant process of exploration and reflection until
the appropriate lever is located. It is like trying to lever the lid off a tin by
using and discarding a number of likely tools until one does the job. Then
it is time to sort out the contents.

Take housework, for example.[1] What is it? Who does it? And should it be
a paid activity? If so, by whom? The taken-for-granted approach sees housework as a set of tasks done in the home for no pay. Traditionally, in many
societies, it is women's work because they were the homekeepers. But there

is an inconsistency here, because the same set of tasks done in someone else's home is paid work. And if we take the case, for example, of farmwork done on a domestic setting, some of it is economically accountable as it adds value (such as butchering some livestock), yet cooking it for the family to eat is non-accountable, free domestic labour.

A more useful way to view housework, which addresses these anomalies, is to deconstruct it as a relation of production. It is not a set of tasks, and to attempt to analyse the notion of housework in those terms will answer no fundamental questions. Housework is essentially a work *relationship*. Housework is unremunerated work done by one family member *for* another. To discuss it as a set of tasks reflects a patriarchal ideology that conceals the actual nature of the exploitative relationship. To see it as a work relationship provides a meaningful context for questions about paying for housework. It also sets housework in a broader sphere, takes it out of the 'merely' domestic as it questions the interrelationship between domestic exploitation the wider economic system. To see domestic labour as a set of tasks does not even begin to address such questions.

Critical transformative learning is thus deconstructive. It is also reconstructive. It is not just a matter of taking things apart and it certainly is not a matter of blowing them up. Once the concept has been deconstructed an alternative conceptualization, or conceptualizations, needs to be built to enable sense to be made of experience. To deconstruct the task-set notion of housework is one thing, but unless an alternative is proposed, such as housework is a work relationship, the learner has become trapped by criticism in a cage of someone else's making. However, having reconstructed an alternative conceptualization is not the end of the story. The process is continuous: the reconstructed alternative becomes the subject of further critical transformative learning.

So, transformation is not just about adding to a student's stock of knowledge or set of skills and abilities. At its core, transformation, in an educational sense, refers to the evolution of the way students approach the acquisition of knowledge and skills and relate them to a wider context. This is developed further in Chapter 7. While this view will dominate our discussion of higher education, we wish here to note that higher education can have other transformative effects.

### Higher education and self-actualization

By self-actualization we mean 'that the individual develops those qualities peculiar to mature and well-adjusted people ... [becoming] for example, realistic, independent, creative, problem-centred rather than self-centred, and with a ready appreciation both of other people and of the world' (Fontana, 1981: 213). In other words, we are associating self-actualization with an aspect of transformation that is associated with the qualities valued by stakeholders in higher education (see Chapter 3).

At this point it is important to ask whether higher education does make a difference in such areas. Obviously, graduates have gained specialized knowledge, but do they also develop in other ways? This is a hard question to answer, since it needs to be established that any change to their critical reasoning, moral thinking, self-esteem or personal adjustment is related to participation in higher education, rather than to maturation. Yet it is a question that we need to address, since we have argued that transformative higher education should be about cognitive development as well as about encouraging personal development or self-actualization.

The massive review of the effects of higher education published in 1991 by Pascarella and Terenzini provides some answers that are mainly drawn out of North American research. There appear to be small, positive effects on self-esteem; a reduction in authoritarian, dogmatic and ethnocentric thinking; greater personal adjustment and psychological well-being; an enhanced belief that one has control over one's own fate; and an increase in the complexity and reflectiveness of students' thinking. Moreover, the limited and somewhat flawed research on this topic, which Pascarella and Terenzini (1991) reviewed, 'is consistent in indicating that college attendance has a unique impact on students' aesthetic, cultural, and intellectual attitudes, values, and interests' (p. 284). A 'modest, net effect on social conscience and humanitarian values' (p. 287) has been discerned, along with a small increase in political activism and general interest in politics, including a tendency for studies to find 'a net positive college effect on support for civil rights and liberties' (p. 290) and for students to hold more egalitarian views of gender roles. Some rather slender evidence suggests that college attendance may also be associated with the development of more secular attitudes. Moreover,

> attaching importance to civil liberties and due process of law; freedom from the constraints of arbitrary laws in personal, social, economic, and political spheres; and humanitarian conduct towards others represented a profile of values most pronounced among individuals who had gone to college. This profile distinguished college from non-college respondents even when a number of demographic characteristics (including age, race, and social class) were taken into account... [it seems that] a general humanization of values and attitudes concerning the rights and welfare of others is associated with college attendance.
> (Pascarella and Terenzini, 1991: 347)

In sum, there is North American evidence that higher education is associated with changes in students that are additional to those changes that occur through the natural process of growing up. These effects are seldom large, although this raises the question of how large a change needs to be before it is *educationally*, as opposed to statistically, significant.

An interesting finding is that 'the net impact of attending (versus not attending) college tends to be substantially more pronounced than any differential impact attributable to attending different kinds of college' (Pascarella and Terenzini, 1991: 588). At first sight this seems to invalidate the thrust of our argument, for we have been claiming that certain educational processes promise to make bigger differences than others. Yet here is evidence that the institution attended has not been found to be a significant variable. However, this is not the same as saying that there are no variations: rather, Pascarella and Terenzini imply that the variations are hidden by analyses at the whole-institution level. At the departmental and programme level they are discernible and the quality of student interaction with faculty (teaching staff) and other students is seen as a key factor. Residential arrangements also play a part, with effects being most pronounced for students who are resident on campus.

Two qualifications need to be noted. First, the within-college effects are generally smaller than the overall effect of attending college. Secondly, 'Students are not simply the recipients of institutional effects. They bear a major responsibility for the impact of their own college experience . . . it is the individual student who perhaps most determines the extent to which college makes a difference' (Pascarella and Terenzini, 1991: 611). How, then, are students to be mobilized to interact, rather than to receive?

That said, Pascarella and Terenzini argue that 'in noncognitive areas, the organization and interpersonal climate of the department may well have a significant influence' (Pascarella and Terenzini, 1991: 652). Arguing that departmental climates may be deliberately shaped, they also point to the importance of extended and contexted orientation programmes for new students, by means of which expectations may be appropriately shaped. In other words, a conclusion that might be drawn from this authoritative review is that higher education does have an effect on students' non-cognitive development and that this effect is related to the departmental climate, which can be moulded by faculty action. We suggest that the approach to learning, teaching and assessment that we outline in later chapters is consistent with a departmental climate that, through respecting students and interacting with them (rather than talking at them), promotes non-cognitive development, or self-actualization.

Given the importance that stakeholders attach to the quality of learning, it is incumbent upon us to suggest ways in which this priority might be reflected in mechanisms for quality improvement, as well as to indicate, in some detail, how learning quality might be enhanced at departmental, course and module levels. This latter concern shapes the Chapters 7 to 9, which analyse learning in order to offer suggestions for the improvement of assessment procedures and teaching. Necessarily, this leads us to consider issues of personal and professional development, which occupy Chapter 10. First, though, we need to return to the theme of quality and to associate this complex notion of transformation with it.

*Transformation as meta-quality*
The transformative notion of quality presupposes a fundamental purpose of higher education. It assumes that higher education must concern itself with transforming the life-experiences of students, by enhancing or empowering them. The transformative conception is, in effect, a meta-quality concept. Other concepts, such as perfection, high standards, fitness for purpose and value for money, are *possible* operationalizations of the transformative process

rather than ends in themselves (Harvey, 1994b: 51). They are, though, inadequate operationalizations, often dealing only with marginal aspects of transformative quality and failing to encapsulate the dialectical process.

For example, seeing quality in terms of perfection ('zero defects' or 'getting things right first time') might be a useful way to cut down the costs of production and monitoring of output but it is indifferent to any absolute evaluation of the attributes of the product and embodies a reductionist view of the nature of the production process. When shifted from the production of inanimate objects to the realms of education, perfectionist approaches to quality have not only little to say about 'standards' but also devalue the transformative process. This devaluation occurs on two fronts. First, a reductionist focus on the minutiae of the chain of customer–supplier interfaces deflects attention from the educative process as a whole. Second, and related to the first, the emphasis on 'zero defects' is incompatible with the learning process and the development of knowledge. Learning and the development of knowledge is fundamentally a process of critique and reconceptualization, which is the opposite of a defect-free, right-first-time, mechanistic approach to problem solving (Kolb, 1984; Harvey, 1990). In short, a perfectionist process is at variance with a transformative process.

At best, 'right-first-time' or 'zero-defects' may offer an operationalization of some aspect of the transformative process. Such operationalizations tend to be specifications to be met in codified customer–supplier arrangements (both internally and externally). For example, it has been used as a tool of delegated administrative responsibility, in which the time-consuming process of checking on the typing output of a subordinate in an administrative section is replaced by an approach which requires the introduction of methods that ensure the output is self-monitored and unflawed (Porter and Oakland, 1992). However, this is somewhat peripheral to the transformation process at the heart of educational quality. Where the approach has been used somewhat closer to the staff–student interface, such as the specification of the turnaround time for assessed student work (Geddes, 1992), the emphasis has been on the mechanics rather than the content of the feedback.

Similar analyses can be applied to 'fitness-for-purpose' and 'excellence' approaches to quality. They offer a *possible* means by which aspects of transformative quality might be operationalized but are no substitute for getting to grips with the transformative process.

## Standards

What of standards in all this? How do standards relate to these different notions of quality? 'Standard' is a strange word, meaning both excellent (high standard) and ordinary (standard procedure), being both an identification of uniqueness (regimental flag) and measure by which conformity is judged (standard weights and measures). In education, the term 'standard' is equally elusive but usually relates to three areas of activity:

- academic standards;
- standards of competence;
- service standards.

## Academic standards

Academic standards measure ability to meet specified levels of academic attainment. In relation to teaching and learning, this refers to the ability of students to fulfil the requirements of the programme of study, through whatever mode of assessment is required. This usually requires demonstration of knowledge and understanding. Implicitly, other skills are assessed, such as communication skills. Sometimes 'higher level' skills, such as analysis, comprehension, interpretation, synthesis and critique are explicitly assessed. In essence, standards relate to the development of domain expertise (see Table 1.2). A single level of attainment may be set (pass or fail) or a graded set of levels identified, against which to measure 'degree of excellence'.

## Standards of competence

Standards of competence measure specified levels of ability on a range of competencies. Competences may include general transferable skills required by employers and skills required for induction into a profession.

Standards of competence are more often assessed in terms of threshold minimums than degrees of excellence. Obtaining a professional qualification, for example, involves conforming to minimum standards of practitioner competence.

Standards of competence may be stated or inferred as part of taught course objectives. They may be an implicit part of the expectations of competences to be achieved by research students.

Standards of competence begins to overlap with academic standards, when higher-level skills and abilities are explicitly identified as intrinsic to competence, as in professional education, where, for example, reflection and critique may be an element in the attainment of an award. The distinction between academic standards and standards of competence is, to some extent, pragmatic. For some definitions of quality, such as the 'exceptional' approach, the distinction between academic standard and standard of competence is more pronounced than, for example, in the 'transformative' approach (see Table 1.3).

## Service standards

Service standards are measures devised to assess identified elements of the service or facilities provided by higher education institutions. Student Charters tend to be primarily concerned with service standards and set 'contractual' benchmarks specifying minimum levels of service. Such standards may include turnaround times for assessing student work, maximum class sizes, frequency of personal tutorials, availability of information on complaints procedures, time-lag on introducing recommended reading into libraries, and so on. Benchmarks tend to be quantifiable and restricted to measurable items, including the presence or absence of an element of service or a facility. *Post hoc* measurement of 'customer' opinions (satisfaction) are frequently used as indicators of service provision. Thus, service standards in higher education parallel consumer standards.

## *Interrelationship between quality and standards*

The interrelationship between quality and standards depends on the approach to quality and the particular notion of standard. With five 'definitions' of quality and three 'definitions' of standards there are fifteen interrelationships (see Table 1.3).

The exceptional approach to quality emphasizes the maintenance of academic standards, through the summative assessment of knowledge. It presumes an implicit, normative 'gold-standard' both for learning and for research. It continues to advocate élitism, even within a mass education system. It prioritizes knowledge over skills, other than 'high-level skills' or professional competence. The approach presumes that service standards are dependent on inputs such as well-qualified staff, well-stocked libraries, well-equipped laboratories and students with good entry qualifications. There is a reluctance to expose professional (teaching) competence to scrutiny.

The perfection approach emphasizes consistency in external quality monitoring of academic, competence and service standards. Its emphasis on a consistent process producing a defect-free output is inconsistent with the exploratory nature of higher learning. Its principal focus within institutions is on flawless and accessible administrative support systems.

The fitness-for-purpose approach relates standards to specified purpose-related objectives. Therefore, in theory, it requires criteria-referenced assessment of students. However, purposes specified in mission statements or course aims often include a comparative element so criteria-referencing is mediated by norm-referenced criteria. The approach tends towards explicit specification of skills and abilities and requires clear evidence by which to identify threshold standards. Professional competence is primarily assessed in terms of threshold minimums against professional-body requirements for practice. Purposes usually specify or imply minimum service standards for such things as professional standards of competence of service providers, support for students, both academic and pastoral, and the interrelationship of teaching, scholarship and research.

The value-for-money approach places emphasis on a 'good deal' for the customer or client, usually government, employer, student or parents. It requires the maintenance or improvement of academic standards, of both graduate abilities and research output, for the same (or declining) unit of resource. It also expects the maintenance of the supply of competent

*Table 1.3* Relationship between quality and standards

| | Academic standards | Standards of competence | Service standards |
|---|---|---|---|
| | *Definition* | | |
| | The demonstrated ability to meet specified level of academic attainment. For pedagogy, the ability of students to be able to do those things designated as appropriate at a given level of education. Usually, the measured competence of an individual in attaining specified (or implied) course aims and objectives, operationalized via performance on assessed pieces of work. For research, the ability to undertake effective scholarship or produce new knowledge, which is assessed via peer recognition. | Demonstration that a specified level of ability on a range of competencies has been achieved. Competencies may include general transferable skills required by employers; academic ('higher level') skills implicit or explicit in the attainment of degree status or in a post-graduation academic apprenticeship; particular abilities congruent with induction into a profession. | Are measures devised to assess identified elements of the service provided against specified benchmarks. Elements assessed include activities of service providers and facilities within which the service takes place. Benchmarks specified in 'contracts' such as student charters tend to be quantified and restricted to measurable items. *Post hoc* measurement of customer opinions (satisfaction) are used as indicators of service provision. Thus, service standards in higher education parallel consumer standards. |

| Quality | Definition | | | |
|---|---|---|---|---|
| Exceptional | A traditional concept linked to the idea of 'excellence', usually operationalized as exceptionally high standards of academic achievement. Quality is achieved if the standards are surpassed. | Emphasis on summative assessment of knowledge and, implicitly, some 'higher-level' skills. Implicit normative gold-standard. Comparative evaluation of research output. Élitism: the presupposition of a need to maintain pockets of high quality and standards in a mass education system. | Linked to professional competence; emphasis mainly on traditional demarcation between knowledge and (professional) skills. | Input-driven assumptions of resource-linked service/facilities. Good facilities, well-qualified staff, etc. 'guarantee' service standards. Reluctance to expose professional (teaching) competence to scrutiny. |
| Perfection or consistency | Focuses on process and sets specifications that it aims to meet. Quality in this sense is summed up by the interrelated ideas of zero defects and getting things right first time. | Meaningless, except for an idealistic notion that peer scrutiny of standards or quality will be undertaken in a consistent manner. | Expectation of a minimum prescribed level of professional competence. Problem in assessing for 'zero defects'. | Primary relevance in ensuring service-standard based quality – mainly in relation to administrative processes (accuracy and reliability of record keeping, timetables, coursework arrangements, etc.) |

Table 1.3 (cont.)

| Quality | Definition | Academic standards | Standards of competence | Service standards |
|---|---|---|---|---|
| Fitness for purpose | Judges quality in terms of the extent to which a product or service meets its stated purpose. The purpose may be customer-defined to meet requirements or (in education) institution-defined to reflect institutional mission (or course objectives). | Theoretically, standards should relate to the defined objectives that specify the purpose of the course (or institution). Summative assessment should be criteria referenced, although as purposes often include a comparative element (e.g., in mission statements) these are mediated by norm-referenced criteria. | Explicit specification of skills and abilities related to objectives. Evidence required to, at least, identify threshold standards. Professional competence primarily assessed in terms of threshold minimums against professional-body requirements for practice. | The purpose involves the provision of a service. Thus, process is assessed in terms of (minimum) standards for the purpose – usually in terms of teaching competence, the link between teaching and research, student support (academic and non-academic) and so on. |

| Quality | Definition | | |
|---|---|---|---|
| Value for money | Assesses quality in terms of return on investment or expenditure. At the heart of the value-for-money approach in education is the notion of accountability. Public services, including education, are expected to be accountable to the funders. Increasingly, students are also considering their own investment in higher education in value-for-money terms. | Maintenance or improvement of academic outcomes (graduate standards and research output) for the same (or declining) unit of resource. That is, ensure greater efficiency. Similarly, improve the process-experience of students. Concern that efficiency gains work in the opposite direction to quality improvement. Provide students with an academic experience (qualification, training, personal development) to warrant the investment. | Maintain or improve the output of generally 'employable' graduates for the same unit of resource. Similarly, ensure a continual or increasing supply of recruits to post-graduation professional bodies. Provide students with an educational experience that increases competence, in relation to career advancement, which ensures a return on investment. | Customer satisfaction analyses (student, employers, funding bodies) to assess process and outcomes. Students and other stakeholders are seen as 'paying customers'. Customer charters specify minimum levels of service (and facilities) that students (parents, employers) can expect. |

*Table 1.3* (cont.)

| Quality | Definition | Academic standards | Standards of competence | Service standards |
|---|---|---|---|---|
| Transformation | Sees quality as a process of change, which in higher education adds value to students through their learning experience. Education is not a service for a customer but an ongoing process of transformation of the participant. This leads to two notions of transformative quality in education: enhancing the consumer and empowering the consumer. | Assessment of students in terms of the standard of acquisition of transformative knowledge and skills (analysis, critique, synthesis, innovation) against explicit objectives. Focus on adding value rather than gold standards. As transformation involves empowerment, formative as well as summative assessment is required. Transformative research standards are assessed in terms of *impact* in relation to objectives. | Provide students with enhanced skills and abilities that empower them to continue learning and to engage effectively with the complexities of the 'outside' world. Assessment of students in terms of the acquisition of transformative skills (analysis, critique, synthesis, innovation) and the transformative impact they have post-graduation. | Emphasis on specification and assessment of standards of service and facilities that enable the process of student learning *and* the acquisition of transformative abilities. |

*Source*: Harvey (1995d)

recruits to post-graduation professional bodies and suitably skilled gradu-ates for employment. Similarly, the approach expects that the teaching and learning experienced by students does not significantly decline and, in-deed, that innovations improve the experience in relation to clearly speci-fied objectives. Minimum service standards are frequently specified in student charters. Students expect that the academic standard of their course and the competencies they acquire will have currency outside the institution and will be an adequate return on their investment of time and money. The value-for-money approach prioritizes efficiency and accountability to 'cli-ents' and 'customers'.

The transformative approach uses standards to assess the enhancement of students both in terms of academic knowledge and a broader set of transformative skills, such as analysis, critique, lateral thinking, innovation and communication. As transformation involves empowerment, formative as well as summative assessment is required. Service standards emphasize the specification facilities that enable the process of student learning and the acquisition of transformative abilities.

In Chapters 2 and 3 we explore the extent to which students, staff and employers see learning as a transformative process.

# Note

1. This example draws heavily on the exposition of critical social research in Harvey (1990: 19–32), which makes use of Christine Delphy's (1985) study of housework.

# 2

# Students and Staff

It could be argued that higher education, rather than operate with a clear concept of quality, approaches the issue in an entirely pragmatic way. Students and staff in higher education institutions, if not exactly knowing quality when they see it, approach it in terms of a set of operational criteria, against which they judge the adequacy of the provision. Students may judge the 'quality' in terms of how accomplished the lecturers are at teaching, whether the library meets their learning needs or whether the sports facilities are adequate. Staff might assess quality in terms of the entry qualifications of the students, the research profile of the institution or the adequacy of staff rooms and lecture theatres. All sorts of specific criteria might be employed in different contexts as a basis for assessing quality. While it is possible to see these as operationalizations of particular notions of quality, they are frequently employed in a taken-for-granted way or in response to specific evaluations, such as requirements for professional validation of a programme of study.

## *QHE* survey of staff and students

To assess the pragmatic notion of quality employed in UK higher education, a substantial survey of student and staff views of quality criteria was undertaken, in 1992, as part of the research of the Quality in Higher Education Project (*QHE*). The survey encompassed a total of 4000 staff and students in a diverse sample of 16 universities and polytechnics (Harvey, Burrows and Green, 1992b). The results revealed a high degree of agreement across the entire sample.

### *Agreement*

The data show high levels of agreement on criteria for assessing quality. This agreement transcends institutional, sector, subject, staff and student boundaries. The mean scores for each sub-group on all 111 items correlated very highly and reflect a consensus between staff and students in general about the main criteria for assessing quality (Harvey, Burrows and Green, 1992b).

The respondents were broken down into three broad subject areas: sciences, social sciences and arts. This breakdown is fairly crude but it was expected that it would show some differences. In the event, the level of agreement between the three broad subject areas was very high. The lowest level of agreement was between sciences and arts but this still resulted in a correlation in excess of 0.9. The level of agreement is also high across more narrowly defined disciplines: all correlations are significant at the 1 per cent level and the *lowest* correlation is $r = 0.81$, between business and humanities. Furthermore there was an equally high level of agreement across sectors (0.96) and between institutions: again the lowest correlation is $r = 0.82$ (Harvey, Burrows and Green, 1992b).

Variations in the criteria for assessing quality between sectors and across disciplines, reflecting traditional ways of working and differing priorities, were expected. It was a surprise that the diverse sample concurred about the most important criteria for assessing quality.

## *The total student experience*

The results also clearly indicated that the key factor in the assessment of quality in higher education is the student experience. This is not restricted to the student experience in the classroom but to the *total student experience.*

Given the opportunity to comment on possible criteria of quality, staff and students identified the vast majority of the 111 items as of some importance when judging the quality of higher education. Only 5 items were seen as irrelevant by more than 10 per cent of respondents. Conversely 45 items were seen as essential by more than half the respondents.

Despite most items being seen as important, the results showed that some items were considered more important than others. There was marked variation in the extent to which respondents regarded items as essential: ranging from 85.1 per cent for '*the aims of the programme are understood by staff*' down to just 10 per cent of the respondents who rated '*assessment of prior experience*' as essential in judging quality (Harvey, Burrows and Green, 1992b). The responses thus indicated the *relative* rather than absolute importance attached to criteria.

A significant feature of the results was that some taken-for-granted aspects of quality were seen as relatively less important than is often presumed. Such things as entry standards, low drop-out rates and high percentages of good class degrees are often seen as important indicators of quality. Similarly, quality is often linked to the research profile of the institution. Relatively speaking, none of these were regarded as important.

This apparent abandonment of 'traditional' indicators of quality was, initially, a rather surprising result. What appears to have occurred is that criteria for judging the quality of higher education prioritize the student experience. This does not mean that research, input and output indicators

*Table 2.1*  Highest rated items for the entire *QHE* sample

| Highest rated criteria | Percentage essential | Mean | Rank |
|---|---|---|---|
| *Teaching* | | | |
| The aims and objectives of the programme are understood by staff. | 85 | 93 | 1 |
| | | | |
| *Institutional resources* | | | |
| There is adequate access to library facilities (time and location). | 83 | 93 | 2 |
| The library has adequate resources to cater for the learning demands of students. | 83 | 93 | 3 |
| The library has adequate resources to cater for the teaching demands of staff. | 75 | 90 | 5 |
| There are sufficient and adequately equipped workshops and laboratories. | 71 | 88 | 12 |
| There are sufficient staff to support effective use of the library. | 68 | 87 | 14 |
| There is adequate access to information technology facilities. | 67 | 87 | 16 |
| There are accessible technical and support staff to assist information technology and laboratory users. | 60 | 84 | 25 |
| | | | |
| *Assessment* | | | |
| Assessment methods are valid, objective and fair. | 80 | 91 | 4 |
| There are clear criteria for assessment that are understood by staff and students. | 74 | 89 | 8 |
| Students receive useful feedback from assessed work. | 72 | 89 | 10 |
| Assessment tests whether the aims and objectives of the programme have been met. | 63 | 85 | 23 |
| | | | |
| *Content* | | | |
| The academic standard or level of the programme is appropriate to the award. | 76 | 90 | 6 |
| The content is designed to achieve programme aims and objectives. | 70 | 88 | 13 |
| The programme content inspires students and gives them confidence. | 67 | 87 | 15 |
| The programme content has a coherent sequence and structure. | 65 | 86 | 18 |
| | | | |
| *Knowledge skills and attitudes* | | | |
| The ability to communicate effectively (written and oral). | 74 | 89 | 7 |
| Independent judgement (critical thinking). | 72 | 89 | 9 |
| Ability to solve problems. | 64 | 86 | 19 |
| Analytic skills. | 63 | 85 | 20 |
| Enquiry and research skills. | 60 | 84 | 24 |

*Table 2.1* (cont.)

| Highest rated criteria | Percentage essential | Mean | Rank |
|---|---|---|---|
| *Learning* | | | |
| The aims and objectives of the programme are understood by students. | 72 | 88 | 11 |
| Students are encouraged to be actively involved in the learning process. | 66 | 86 | 17 |
| *Management* | | | |
| A commitment to quality is part of the ethos and culture of the institution. | 65 | 85 | 21 |
| *Equal opportunities* | | | |
| There is adequate access to buildings for the disabled. | 65 | 85 | 22 |

*Source*: Harvey, Burrows and Green (1992c)

are not regarded as important *per se* but that the focus of attention in judging quality of higher education is on the learning process experienced by students. A clear set of priorities emerged across the sample that emphasized the importance of the *total* student experience.

In one respect, it is not surprising that the majority of items were rated quite highly as they all derived from various 'expert' opinion as to how quality in higher education should be assessed. However, based on detailed analysis of the survey, it is possible to identify a *single* group of criteria from the list of 111 regarded as the most important by all groups of respondents.

The highest rated criteria are dominated by resource, programme content, assessment, and knowledge, skills and attitude items that relate to the total student experience of learning (Table 2.1).

*Teaching and learning*
A teaching item tops the list of criteria. Surprisingly, however, it is not the kind of item, such as 'guaranteed small group tuition', that is often suggested as an essential element of a student charter (Meikle, 1991).

Staff understanding of the programme's aims and objectives emerged as the most important teaching item. Similarly, the most important learning criterion is that students understand the programme aims and objectives. This concern with aims and objectives is further reinforced by the inclusion in the highest rated items of '*the content is designed to achieve programme aims and objectives*' and '*assessment tests whether the aims and objectives of the programme have been met*'.

A focus on aims and objectives of courses and the way content and assessment relates to these, reflects a concern with the student experience of learning. Having a clear and coherent structure, of which students and staff are aware, provides a framework for the student experience, both in terms of course content and the assessed work that they undertake.

The emphasis is clearly on learning not teaching. Items that relate to small group tuition, a balance between lectures and seminars, and effective use of audio-visual aids were seen as of less importance in judging quality than the encouragement of students to be involved in the learning process. This is further reinforced by the high rating given to resource, assessment and content items.

*Learning resources*
Library provision, access to libraries, workshops and laboratories, and availability of information-technology facilities were seen as very important factors in assessing the quality of higher education. The early 1990s witnessed a rapid expansion in higher education which placed enormous pressure on library provision (HEFCE, 1992). Libraries became overcrowded and noisy and students found it hard to obtain books (Lloyd, 1992). The prominence of learning resources in quality thinking in 1992 may have been a product of the timing of the survey, although there is no reason to believe that pressure on university libraries has lessened since then (Harvey *et al.*, 1995).

Respondents considered that library support of teaching and learning was a more important indicator of quality than support of research and scholarship (*'the library has adequate resources to cater for the research demands of staff'* is ranked 31st overall as a criterion of quality). Support for research scores lower, on average, than all the other aspects of the library, even among the academic staff. It is the only aspect of the library where staff and students diverge in terms of the relative importance of the item as an indicator of quality (Table 2.2).

The very high importance attached to institutional resources reflect a concern with the provision of an adequate environment for student learning. These were seen as much more important than, for example, items related to the general environment and facilities. Attractive surroundings, halls of residence, well maintained grounds and buildings and adequate sports facilities rated very poorly as indicators of quality. The only environmental item that appears in the top half of the ranked criteria was *'teaching rooms provide a supportive teaching and learning environment'*, which is ranked 40th overall.

*Assessment*
Practices and procedures for the assessment of student work are also considered to be of major importance when assessing the quality of higher education. Respondents were asked to rate ten assessment-related items, about half of which addressed the student experience of doing the assignment, being graded, receiving feedback and appeals procedures (Table 2.3).

Valid, objective and fair assessment with clear criteria that results in useful feedback for students are items that are rated very highly. Indeed these are all in the top ten of the 111 quality items. Students, especially, give very high priority to *useful* feedback, ranking it the most important assessment

*Table 2.2* Importance ratings of five library items as indicators of quality

| Item no. | Item | All | Students | Teaching staff | Non-teaching staff | Science | Social science | Arts |
|---|---|---|---|---|---|---|---|---|
| S91 | There is adequate access to library facilities (time and location) | **93** | 92 | 94 | 92 | 92 | 93 | 93 |
| S92 | Adequate resources to cater for the learning demands of students | **93** | 92 | 94 | 92 | 92 | 93 | 94 |
| S93 | Adequate resources to cater for the teaching demands of staff | **90** | 88 | 92 | 90 | 89 | 90 | 92 |
| S95 | There are sufficient staff to support effective use of the library | **87** | 86 | 88 | 88 | 85 | 87 | 89 |
| S94 | Adequate resources to cater for the research demands of staff | **83** | 79 | 87 | 83 | 83 | 83 | 83 |

Table 2.3  Importance ratings of ten assessment items as indicators of quality

| Item no. | Item | All | Students | Teaching staff | Non-teaching staff | Science | Social science | Arts |
|---|---|---|---|---|---|---|---|---|
| S51 | Assessment methods are valid, objective and fair | **91** | 90 | 93 | 92 | 91 | 90 | 92 |
| S48 | Clear criteria for assessment that are understood by staff and students | **89** | 88 | 90 | 91 | 88 | 89 | 91 |
| S53 | Students receive useful feedback from assessed work | **89** | 90 | 88 | 88 | 87 | 89 | 92 |
| S47 | Assessment tests whether the aims and objectives of the programme have been met | **85** | 81 | 86 | 88 | 83 | 85 | 84 |
| S49 | Clear and unambiguous regulations governing assessment and appeals | **82** | 79 | 84 | 85 | 80 | 82 | 86 |
| S56 | External examiner reports are routinely used to assess standards | **78** | 73 | 81 | 82 | 76 | 78 | 80 |
| S50 | A range of assessment methods is used | **73** | 73 | 73 | 73 | 71 | 73 | 75 |
| S52 | Assessment standards are set high | **72** | 69 | 74 | 73 | 70 | 73 | 75 |
| S54 | Where appropriate, assessment is undertaken in the work environment | **56** | 59 | 51 | 59 | 55 | 57 | 54 |
| S55 | There are arrangements for assessing experience prior to the programme | **49** | 49 | 44 | 55 | 44 | 51 | 44 |

item and the fifth most important criterion for assessing quality overall. Linking assessment to aims and objectives also emerges as important. The high rating of these four assessment criteria endorses an approach to quality that prioritizes an active and transparent learning process. This is further discussed in Chapter 8.

Two of the three items to do with 'justice' and 'standards' – clear regulations and the use of external examiner reports – were also quite important, although marginally more for staff than students. The third item – high assessment standards – was seen as relatively unimportant. Students, in particular, seemed relatively uninterested in standards of assessment as a touchstone of quality and instead highlighted the learning utility of assessment. Standards issues, on the one hand, and the availability of a range of assessment methods, on the other, were seen as far less important than feedback and fairness. However, students indicated elsewhere in the survey that they thought it very important for the content of the course to reflect the standard of the award.

The remaining items concerned work-based assessment and assessment of prior learning. These were both regarded as unimportant in assessing the quality of the student experience. Even where appropriate, workplace assessment was not regarded as important in assessing quality. However, with the development of a 'skills' orientation in higher education (AGR, 1995), assessment in the work situation may gain in importance. The existence of arrangements for the assessment of experience prior to the programme (designed, in Britain, to give people credit for relevant experience that might count towards an award or towards entry qualifications for a programme) was seen as the least important criterion for judging quality, ranked 111th overall. It may be that the low rating was due to very few staff and students having been involved in such procedures at the time of the survey and that few formal mechanisms were in place. Nevertheless, with few exceptions, assessment of prior learning remains a peripheral activity.

The results that emerge about assessment from the *QHE* survey emphasize the *learning* role of assessed work, which is explored further in Chapter 8. Students want assessed work to be useful to them. They want feedback and they want what they produce to be related to the aims and objectives of the course. If they are going to be graded they want the system to be fair and they want to know what criteria are being used to assess their work.

*Programme content*
Apart from achieving aims that both staff and students understand, programme content that is coherent and structured, that inspires students and gives them confidence and that is at a standard that reflects the award, are all considered as important indicators of quality in higher education.

Interestingly, the specific nature of the content, whether it relates to advances in the subject, to specialist knowledge or to a broadly-based education, was regarded as less important. Overall, content items that relate to the *learning process* were rated as more important in assessing quality than items that related to what is learned.

This is reflected in the high rating of some knowledge, skills and attitude items. In particular, it was considered important, in assessing quality, that the programme should develop in students effective communication, independent judgement (critical thinking), problem solving and analytic skills (Table 2.4).

Three-quarters of the sample (74 per cent) thought it essential that '*the programme of study should develop in students the ability to communicate effectively*' and only 4 per cent regarded it as of little or no importance (Harvey, Burrows and Green 1992b). Developing independent judgement (72 per cent essential) was also highly rated as a quality indicator, as were the development of problem-solving (64 per cent) and analytic skills (63 per cent). Other learning and exposition skills (research, argument and decision-making) were also highly rated across subject areas and by both staff and students. The emphasis on individual learning is reflected in the relatively low importance rating of teamworking. However, there are indications that teamworking has grown in importance over the last three years, with increasing amounts of team-based assessment on programmes of study.

Variations between broad discipline areas were evident in the importance of the ability to use information technology and numeracy. Science-based respondents gave higher ratings to these items than did arts or social science respondents.

A hotly disputed result is the relatively low rating of the development of specialist subject knowledge. When discussing the results, this has caused a good deal of consternation and, inevitably, the research instrument has been called into question. The most usual explanation is that academics take the subject knowledge for granted. However, this is not consistent with a fifth (19 per cent) of them indicating that it was of little or no importance and less than a third (32 per cent) saying it is essential. Another comment suggests that emphasis may have been placed on 'specialist' rather than 'subject' knowledge by respondents and that this may have implied esoteric knowledge which may not been seen as essential as an indicator of quality. This indeed may have been the case but the relatively low rating of '*the programme develops within students specialist subject knowledge*' (mean = 70, rank 80th) is echoed by the equally poor rating of the separate item '*the programme concentrates on providing specialist knowledge*' (mean = 56, rank 106th).

The mean score of 70 and the fact that half the academics (49 per cent) thought specialist knowledge desirable suggests that they regard it as fairly important in *absolute* terms. However, that it was given a low *relative* rating by academics suggests that it was seen as less important than other attributes.

Overall, then, the outcomes of the *QHE* student and staff survey prioritize the student learning experience rather than what is learned.

The outcomes of this research can be compared with two other well-publicized studies to assess the robustness of the conclusion that the fundamental focus of quality for internal stakeholders in higher education is the total learning experience of students. The first of these is a Canadian study, conducted in the early 1990s, that uses an entirely different methodology to determine quality criteria. The other is the annual Student

Table 2.4  Importance ratings of 15 knowledge, skill and attitude items as indicators of quality

| Item no. | Item | All | Students | Teaching staff | Non-teaching staff | Science | Social science | Arts |
|---|---|---|---|---|---|---|---|---|
| S44 | The ability to communicate effectively (written and oral) | 89 | 88 | 91 | 90 | 88 | 89 | 93 |
| S36 | Independent judgement (critical thinking) | 89 | 86 | 92 | 89 | 87 | 89 | 93 |
| S35 | Ability to solve problems | 86 | 83 | 88 | 87 | 88 | 84 | 84 |
| S32 | Analytic skills | 85 | 81 | 90 | 85 | 85 | 85 | 88 |
| S34 | Enquiry and research skills | 84 | 81 | 87 | 86 | 83 | 84 | 87 |
| S40 | Logical argument | 84 | 80 | 88 | 83 | 83 | 83 | 85 |
| S33 | Decision-making skills | 80 | 81 | 79 | 82 | 81 | 81 | 87 |
| S41 | Self-skills (self-awareness, self-confidence, self-management) | 80 | 81 | 78 | 80 | 77 | 81 | 81 |
| S37 | Imagination and creativity | 78 | 75 | 80 | 78 | 75 | 77 | 85 |
| S42 | Flexibility and adaptability | 76 | 76 | 76 | 77 | 73 | 77 | 77 |
| S46 | The ability to relate a subject to the wider social and economic context | 74 | 76 | 73 | 74 | 67 | 78 | 78 |
| S43 | The ability to work in a team | 72 | 75 | 69 | 73 | 72 | 74 | 69 |
| S39 | The ability to use information technology | 71 | 71 | 70 | 75 | 74 | 61 | 63 |
| S45 | Specialist subject knowledge | 70 | 68 | 72 | 71 | 69 | 70 | 75 |
| S38 | Numeracy | 69 | 66 | 70 | 73 | 75 | 67 | 59 |

Satisfaction survey at the University of Central England (UCE) in Birmingham, which not only assesses student satisfaction with provision but also identifies the importance that students place on different elements of their experience.

## Canadian project on quality criteria

A project was set up in Canada to 'identify criteria and indicators of quality and excellence in Canadian colleges and universities' (Nadeau, 1993: 1). It focused on six areas: teaching staff (faculty), students, institutional managers (administrators), programmes of study, institutional environment and external context or factors. The research was designed to investigate the levels of consensus among various panels, numbering about 250 experts in total.

Coincidentally, the Canadian study also identified 111 important criteria of quality, although, given its remit, these did not cover the same range as the *QHE* study. For example, the Canadian study did not include specific statements about types of student assessment, workload, appeals procedures and so on. Conversely, it included many more statements on the competence of 'administrators' and had specific items on such things as public support for higher education, which were beyond the parameters of the *QHE* study.

None the less, the Canadian study, despite its very different methodology and the fact that it was undertaken on a different continent, shows a remarkable similarity in priorities. The most important criteria in the Canadian study included: teacher knowledge, competence and learning facilitation; student commitment to learning, development of independent learning, effective study skills and basic as well as 'higher level' skills; and programmes of study with clear objectives, coherent content and appropriate standards (Table 2.5).

In addition the vision, competence, leadership ability and the commitment to quality of 'administrators' (senior managers), along with clear institutional mission, a climate of openness, a commitment to review and evaluation, student satisfaction and public support for post-secondary education, all rated highly.

The research productivity of teaching staff and their ability to obtain research funds were given very low importance ratings, as were many of the elements that linked academia to the outside world, such as service of teaching staff to the profession and the community, responsiveness of the programmes to job opportunities, developing job-related skills, obtaining private-sector funding and adapting programmes for wider access, all of which echo the *QHE* results. Ironically, the low rating of 'job-related skills' is at variance with the high rating given to most of the things that employers would regard as job-related skills, which suggests a breakdown in communication as evident in Canada as it is in Europe. These are issues we develop in Chapter 3.

*Table 2.5*   Canadian study of quality criteria: most important items

| Item no. | Item | Area | Mean score |
|---|---|---|---|
| 1 | Teaching competence of staff | teaching staff | 4.6 |
| 3 | Teaching staff have effective communication skills | teaching staff | 4.6 |
| 23 | Interpersonal skills and leadership abilities of administrators | administrators | 4.6 |
| 31 | Administrators' concern for quality, excellence | administrators | 4.6 |
| 2 | Teaching staff up-to-date in subject matter | teaching staff | 4.5 |
| 71 | Students' commitment to learning | students | 4.5 |
| 18 | The planning and innovating abilities of administrators | administrators | 4.4 |
| 22 | Decision-making ability of administrators | administrators | 4.4 |
| 76 | Ability of students to analyse, synthesize and think critically | students | 4.4 |
| 19 | Commitment of administrators to institutional goals and objectives | administrators | 4.3 |
| 46 | Clarity of institutional mission and goals | institutional context | 4.3 |
| 92 | Development of independent learning on programmes | programme of study | 4.3 |
| 24 | Administration and management skills of administrators | administrators | 4.2 |
| 25 | Visionary educational leadership of administrators | administrators | 4.2 |
| 33 | Public support for postsecondary education | external environment | 4.2 |
| 53 | A climate of openness | institutional context | 4.2 |
| 58 | Student satisfaction with the institution | institutional context | 4.2 |
| 67 | Basic communication skills of students | students | 4.2 |
| 78 | Students' exhibit effective study skills and habits | students | 4.2 |
| 97 | Programmes have clearly identified goals and objectives | programme of study | 4.2 |
| 4 | Student-centred teaching | teaching staff | 4.1 |
| 21 | Commitment of administrators to programme and institutional evaluation | administrators | 4.1 |
| 50 | Adequate administrative support services | institutional context | 4.1 |
| 62 | General academic preparedness of students | students | 4.1 |
| 83 | Expertise of students at the end of the programme | students | 4.1 |
| 104 | Programmes have appropriate performance standards | programme of study | 4.1 |
| 106 | Programmes have periodic review and evaluation | programme of study | 4.1 |
| 111 | Programme content is coherent | programme of study | 4.1 |

*Note*: Adapted from Nadeau (1993), Tables, pp. 3–10. Mean scores in this study range from 2.5 to 4.6 on a scale from 0 to 5.

*Table 2.6*  The most important items in the 1995 Student Satisfaction survey at UCE

| Item | Area | Mean 1994 | Mean 1995 |
|------|------|-----------|-----------|
| The academic/professional understanding of the subject matter by teaching staff | teaching staff | 6.6 | 6.6 |
| Availability of recommended reading material | library | 6.4 | 6.5 |
| Up-to-dateness of books | library | 6.4 | 6.5 |
| Range of books | library | 6.4 | 6.5 |
| Approachable teaching staff | teaching staff | 6.4 | 6.3 |
| The enthusiasm of the teaching staff | teaching staff | 6.4 | 6.3 |
| Reliability of the teaching staff (i.e. do not cancel classes) | teaching staff | 6.3 | 6.3 |
| Develop a broader understanding of the subject | self-development | 6.2 | 6.3 |
| Multiple copies of core books | library | 6.0 | 6.3 |
| Usefulness of tutors' formal feedback on assessed work | assessment | 6.2 | 6.2 |
| Knowing what is expected of you as a student | information | 6.2 | 6.2 |
| Opening hours of the library | library | 5.7 | 6.2 |
| Cleanliness of the refectories | refectories | 5.5 | 6.2 |
| Range of topics covered in your syllabus | course organization | – | 6.2 |
| Number of car-park spaces provided for students | university environment | – | 6.2 |
| The clarity of teaching in taught group sessions | teaching and learning methods | 6.6 | 6.1 |
| Teachers encourage effective learning | teaching staff | 6.3 | 6.1 |
| Teachers treat students as mature individuals | teaching staff | 6.3 | 6.1 |
| Usefulness of tutors' informal feedback on assessed work | assessment | 6.2 | 6.1 |
| Accessibility of information about your course | information | 6.1 | 6.1 |
| Promptness of feedback on assignments | assessment | 6.0 | 6.1 |
| The usefulness of tutorials (i.e. tutor with 1 or 2 students) | teaching and learning methods | 5.7 | 6.1 |
| Adequacy of workspace in the library | library | 5.4 | 6.1 |
| Noise levels in the library | library | 5.2 | 6.1 |
| The suitability of placements | teaching and learning methods | 4.6 | 6.1 |
| The balance between coursework and examinations | assessment | – | 6.1 |
| Knowing what you can expect from your course and your tutors | information | – | 6.1 |
| Level of expertise of support staff in practical sessions | teaching and learning methods | – | 6.1 |
| Extent to which teaching staff are sympathetic and supportive to students' needs | teaching staff | – | 6.1 |
| User-friendliness for people with disabilities | university environment | – | 6.1 |

*Table 2.6* (cont.)

| Item | Area | Mean 1994 | Mean 1995 |
|------|------|-----------|-----------|
| *Total number of items: universal items* | | 106 | 154 |
| *Subgroup items* | | (33) | (48) |
| *Sample size* | | 1753 | 2191 |

*Note*: The items in this table only include 'universal items' that is, those which the vast majority of students comment on. There were a number of other items that were specific to sub-groups of students that scored 6 or more which have not been listed, such as the computing and printing facilities in the central word processing facility and student services both used by less than 20 percent of students.

## Student Satisfaction at UCE

The emphasis on the student learning experience as the primary focus of quality in higher education is also reflected in the Student Satisfaction surveys undertaken at the University of Central England (UCE) on an annual basis. Although not a survey setting out to determine the importance of quality criteria, it does ask a large sample of students to rate the importance of a set of 'satisfaction' items identified as significant by student focus groups. As we have seen in Chapter 1, 'satisfaction' is but one aspect of quality. Customer satisfaction is closely linked to fitness-for-purpose models of quality, which, in higher education, tends to be a mission-based fitness for purpose. In such circumstances, the provider asks students to indicate satisfaction or dissatisfaction with those aspects of provision that are linked to the mission of the institution, department or programme of study. However, if the satisfaction questionnaire is based not on the provider view but on the perspective of the participant and focuses on the participant experience, then it also offers insights into transformative quality.

Analysis of the 1995 Student Satisfaction results allows us to identify the 30 items that had the highest mean importance rating across the university (Table 2.6 – 1994 scores for equivalent items are included to illustrate consistency over time). The importance scores range from 1 (low importance) to 7 (high importance) for any individual response.

This set of priorities again reveals an emphasis on the student experience of learning. Four library items, relating to bookstock, are among the top ten ranked items. Opening hours, workspace and noise levels in the library also feature as very important, giving a clear indication of the centrality of this learning resource to student perception of their experience at university.

Staff are also seen as important, and here they show up more noticeably than in the 1992 *QHE* study. However, the most important aspects of teaching staff are their knowledge, enthusiasm, reliability and approachability, along with their effectiveness as learning facilitators and the way they treat students rather than how they organize and perform in taught sessions.

Apart from the clarity of teaching in group sessions (lectures, seminars, and so on) the most important teaching and learning methods items are geared to *learning*, including items that relate to the usefulness of individual tutorials, the suitability of placements and the expertise provided by support staff in practical sessions.

Assessment of students is another important area and the high ratings for the *usefulness* of tutors' formal and informal feedback on assessed work also places a firm emphasis on learning facilitation. Useful comments are regarded as more important than the promptness of feedback, although this too is among the most important items. The importance of information items, particularly those that relate to what is expected from students and what can be expected from the programme of study and from tutors, also suggests that communication about learning is a major issue.

Opportunities for personal development were also seen as important in the annual Student Satisfaction survey. Developing a broader understanding of the subject was rated most important and, although it was the only such item in the top thirty, developing learning skills, discussing ideas with others, increasing self-confidence and developing practical skills all achieved a mean satisfaction score of 6.0.

## Conclusion

The evidence in this chapter suggests that staff and students alike focus on the student learning experience when making judgements about quality. It, thus, seems curious that there has not been a closer link between quality policy and innovation in higher education in Britain, or indeed in most countries that have introduced external quality monitoring procedures (this is explored in more detail in Chapters 4 and 5). It is not easy to identify the reasons for this lack of convergence between quality policy and innovation in teaching and learning, although the following may be contributory factors.

First, the development of quality policy and practice in the United Kingdom has been a pragmatic procedure guided by political imperatives. The political imperative that has overridden all others is the ideological commitment to accountability in the public sector. This has meant that the government has imposed a value-for-money framework on quality monitoring, with higher education being accountable for the resources provided by the state. As part of this, artificial competition has been introduced along with increased constraints on the strategic options open to institutional managers.

Second, it has been assumed by the government and many of its agencies that increasing accountability will increase quality. On this view, quality improvement is a mere by-product of the drive for accountability. However, as we shall argue in Chapter 5, increased accountability requirements may lead to increased compliance rather than to significant improvement.

Third, a real improvement-oriented approach, a point at which innovation and quality policy would come together, poses some threat to established interests. The establishment in Britain of the Academic Audit Unit (subsequently a division of the Higher Education Quality Council (HEQC) ) was designed to ensure not only sector ownership of the monitoring body but also an approach that minimized the threat to institutional and individual academic autonomy. Academic Audit, while forcing institutions to address their system of quality monitoring, made no comment about the quality of provision at the institutional level, and made no significant impact at the level of the taught programme of study.

In the event, the funding councils, instructed by ministers, put in place an approach that included direct observation of the activities of academic staff in the teaching and learning situation. Yet even so, apart from some tenuous and underfunded links to staff development programmes, no serious attempts were made to link quality to innovation in higher education. In a sense, dissemination of good practice comes too close to direct criticism of an academics' professionalism if it is pitched at the level of the learning situation. The situation is complicated because these teaching quality assessors have not demonstrably been selected for their skill in teaching (by which we mean all staff activities, including planning activities, that contribute to learning), let alone for expertise in the field of pedagogy.

It is striking that the assessment of teaching quality in various disciplines was not better linked to teaching and learning innovation. This very remoteness is indicative of the accountability and compliance approach of the government rather than an improvement and agenda-setting approach, which is explored further in Chapter 5. It is indicative of the ideological blindness of an accountability approach irrespective of maximizing improvement potential. It also betokens a certain intransigence and dogmatism amongst some academics, who, despite rarely being trained as teaching professionals, defend their right to teach as they think fit, irrespective of its efficacy. This we consider further in Chapter 10 when exploring professional development.

Yet the empirical studies examined above cry out for a learning orientation. The preferred criteria that emerge from these studies are unlikely to be fixed for all time: quality is dynamic and priorities will change. However, the *QHE* research showed clearly that quality in higher education should relate to the whole learning experience of the student. Hence we coined the term 'Total Student Experience' as an antidote to the evangelical promotion of Total Quality Management as the panacea for higher education (Harvey, Burrows and Green, 1992b; Harvey, 1994c). A transformative approach to quality is about enhancing and empowering students, which requires a focus on the total *learning* experience – all aspects of students' experience that impact upon their learning. It means concentrating on student learning rather than staff teaching. This is easier said than done, as will be demonstrated in Chapter 9, but nevertheless, we argue, focusing on learning is both necessary and desirable. And focusing on transformative learning is, we repeat, more desirable still.

## Transparency, integration and dialogue

Enabling transformative learning requires, among other things, a *transparent*[1] process that provides a coherent and *integrated* learning experience based on *dialogue* between participants and providers (Harvey, 1995c).

Transparency, in this sense does not mean that you can see through the education but that the process of learning is not clouded by intellectual mysticism. Transparency means being explicit, clear and open about the *aims* of the programmes, the *processes* of teaching and learning, the modes of and criteria for *assessing* students, and the intended student *attainments*. Transparency is more than being explicit; a teacher can be explicit about wanting a well argued essay but that does not make the process of achieving one transparent to the student!

*Integration* requires that these elements are linked together into a cohesive whole so that the aims are reflected in the transformative outcomes and the teaching/learning and assessment process works explicitly towards enhancing and empowering students. Research in the USA (Ratcliff and associates, 1995) has argued that integration is important if quality learning is to ensue. Here we signal a problem that receives further attention in Chapters 7 and 9. Whatever the case for allowing students to choose easily in a cafeteria of short modules or courses, it has enormous power to threaten the integration of their learning. Arguing that this integration should come from the student has some force but it fails to recognize that there may be integrating themes, principles and procedures that will readily escape the novice. Moreover, choice of modules may be such that integration will be hard since modules may have little in common. Conversely, they may have too much in common, all of them fortuitously promoting a similar selection of goals at similar levels.

*Dialogue* involves discussions with learners about the nature, scope and style of their learning. For example, discussing the relevance of knowledge and skills, agreeing on appropriate and meaningful assessments, exploring suitable teaching and learning approaches, giving and receiving feedback on graded and other assessed work and so on.

Dialogue also requires teachers to talk with each other about the teaching and learning process. Accepting that teaching and learning is not a private affair between consenting adults (teacher and students). It is a process that should be open and responsive to new ideas and external pressures, not secretive and defensive.

Transparency, integration and dialogue go to the heart of the traditional process and challenge the locus of power in higher education. Such notions are not universally popular. Some academics, for example, are sceptical about explicit procedures because they say it makes the educational process too prescriptive. Similarly, as we have noted, it can be said that integration is part of the intellectual work that students must do, not something for academics to hand them on a plate! And, for some academics, dialogue with students is ridiculous, 'if they knew what's best for them they would not be students'. Besides, there is insufficient time for a dialogue when some academics find it hard to find the time for their monologues.

A retort might be that perhaps transparency, integration and dialogue are not welcomed by all academic staff because they require work and clear thinking to identify what it is the students are getting from a programme. It is understandable if people under pressure are reluctant to take on more teaching work in such stressful times, especially when 'clear thinking' may involve reconceptualizing one's beliefs about teaching, let alone about learning. It is much easier to take a producer view and supply a 'product' (for example, a programme of study), irrespective of user views. Until recently academics working in higher education have tended to disregard 'user' views. Whether this orientation can continue is a political question. It would probably be foolish to anticipate its early death. Yet, such disdain is unsustainable once students are seen not as users but as *participants* in a transformative process. As such, they are entitled to a *responsive* process that is explicit and integrated and based on dialogue.

We explore the nature of transformative teaching and learning in Chapters 7, 8 and 9.

# Note

1. In common-sense usage, something that is transparent is something that we look through, ideally without noticing that the transparent object is there. This is not what we have in mind when we commend transparency. Our sense is of being enabled to see to the heart of the matter, of that core not being hidden by the opacity that characterizes many assessment, teaching and learning methods.

# 3

# Employers

In this chapter we explore employer views of higher education. Employers are a major, but by no means the only, external stakeholder concerned with the quality of higher education. Other major stakeholders, including validating and accrediting agencies, such as professional bodies, quality assurance and assessment organizations, funding bodies and the government are considered elsewhere. Employers differ from most of these as they are 'end-users' of higher education rather than charged with any responsibility for monitoring it.

However, employers are more than 'clients' or 'consumers' of an end product, be it graduates or the research outcomes of higher education. They are often partners, working on joint research, sponsoring professorships, developing joint programmes of study, including work-based learning accredited by universities, developing tailor-made training programmes, and so on.

Employers provide a useful reference point from which to assess higher education, in particular the extent to which it develops transformative learning. Employers are predominantly concerned with the outcomes of higher education, especially when it comes to employing graduates. Their observations provide a useful resource in identifying the parameters for the transformation of higher education.

We saw in Chapter 2 that vested interests and government ideology have inhibited the convergence of quality policy and teaching and learning innovation. For employers, the preoccupation of academia and government with such things as the nature and structure of external and internal quality monitoring merely deflects attention from the central problem: how to improve teaching and learning in higher education so that it produces graduates who can work in a modern organization.

## Higher education and economic development

Higher education is seen as having an important future economic rôle because all forecasts predict profound and rapid changes in technology and society with far-reaching alterations to the framework conditions of economic activity (Meyer-Dohm, 1990). Higher education is expected to be a major constituent in transforming society to cope with change.

> The policy debate on the role of higher education in a changing world has to be based on a judicious balance between the preservation of those features which should remain as part of the educational and cultural heritage and the changes which are essential to the role society accords to higher education. The aim should be to make higher education more responsive to the general problems facing humanity and the needs of economic and cultural life, and more relevant in the context of the specific problems of a given region, country or community.
>
> (UNESCO, 1995: 24, para 51)

If higher education is to do this it must itself face up to change (Ball and Eggins, 1989). The opening remarks of the British Minister of State for Employment at the 1993 *QHE* 24-Hour Seminar emphasize the importance that must continue to be accorded change.

> Ladies and gentlemen, we live in a world of rapid change. It affects industry. It affects career opportunities for graduates. It affects – perhaps you don't need me to remind you of this – higher education itself. We are all learning to live with such change. It is part of a continuum. It is exacting for us all. It is fundamental.
>
> (Widdecomb, 1993: 29)

Higher education institutions, it is argued, need to be aware of this world-wide context of change, to ensure that they are geared up to dealing with it and that they produce graduates who are capable of coping with it. 'It is important for industry to have an adaptable and flexible workforce, one that is capable of acquiring whatever skills may be relevant to the changing times and environment' (Bailey, 1990: 68).

For more than a decade there has been a concern about the rôle and function of higher education in a modern industrial society (Cannon, 1986; Teichler, 1989; Gungwu, 1992; OCUA, 1994). The contribution of higher education to economic growth has been called into question as has the match of higher education outputs to the skills needs of industry and commerce (IRDAC, 1990; BT, 1993).[1] The European Community (EC) has been urging member countries to develop higher education because it will be crucial in ensuring the future competitiveness of the Community in the world market:

> Higher education has a vital role to play in providing a supply-led boost for economic development and in equipping all members of the labour force and young people with the new skills needed to meet the rapidly changing demands of European enterprises.
>
> (EC, 1991: 5)

The Industrial Research and Development Advisory Committee (IRDAC, 1990) of the Commission draw a direct link between the development of human resources and the attainment of economic objectives, claiming that the output of education and training systems (including, in particular, higher education) is the prime determinant of a country's level of industrial productivity and hence competitiveness.

A joint report by the Department of Trade and Industry and the Council for Industry and Higher Education (DTI/CIHE, 1990) noted that chief executives of many companies point to their need for highly educated and skilled people to ensure the success of their business. The Council was subsequently of the view that 'those charged with overseeing the "quality" of higher education should seek employers' views not only on the skills they immediately need but on the long-term demands of employment, including flexibility and adaptability, which students must be prepared to meet' (CIHE, 1992: 1). Echoing this, both the English and Scottish higher education funding councils have linked aspects of quality assessment to employer views (SHEFC, 1992a, 1992b; HEFCE, 1993a, 1993b; Davies, 1993).

Analysis of the relationship between higher education and the labour market has led to allegations that there is a gap between the needs of an industrially developed, or developing, society for certain types of output from education and their supply (Lindley, 1981; O'Leary, 1981; TUC, 1989; PSI, 1990; IOD, 1991; Khawaja *et al.*, 1991; IRDAC, 1994).

> One feature of current skills shortage is the *widespread lack of important generic skills* and social skills such as quality assurance skills, problem-solving skills, learning efficiency, flexibility and communication skills. These are in addition to *shortages of critical scientific and technological skills*. In the 1990s the skills content of work is expected to increase. There will be a greater proportion of workers needing communications, language, management and organizational skills. More polyvalent forms of education and training will be necessary in order to enable workers to contribute to the objectives of successful innovation, high quality products and processes, flexibility in meeting consumer needs and adaptability to new technologies, new forms of industrial organization and higher productivity.
>
> (EC, 1991)

While this 'human capital' view of the relationship between higher education and economic well-being has not gone unchallenged (Murphy, 1993a, 1993b), it would be politically naïve to ignore the consensus that higher education is in the business of promoting achievements that are widely seen to be crucial to national well-being.

## The *QHE* research on *Employer Satisfaction*

The *QHE* research on employer views (Harvey with Green, 1994) set out to establish the priorities of employers and the extent to which higher education is matching their requirements.[2] The empirical study, supported by extensive secondary sources, included focus group discussions and a questionnaire that asked employers not only how important they rated each of a set of 62 graduate qualities but also how satisfied they are with the abilities of their graduate recruits.

There is a significant body of research into the criteria that employers use when recruiting graduates (for example, Fergus, 1981; Caswell, 1983; Wingrove and Herriot, 1984a, 1984b; Green, S., 1990). There is rather less research on the satisfaction of employers with graduates (De Winter Hebron, 1973; Bacon, Benton and Gruneberg, 1979; Gordon, 1983; NBEET, 1992). Most research on employer views tends to be at the local level, either geared towards perceptions of particular courses (such as, Heath, 1988) or of specific institutions or groups of institutions (such as Baseline Market Research, 1991; Meanwell and Barrington, 1991). Most such studies focus on employer reaction to what is provided by institutions. Some have addressed the issues of the importance attached by employers to aspects of graduate attainment as well as satisfaction (Richardson, 1989; Binks, Grant and Exley, 1993).

Previous research has suggested that there are likely to be differences in views between manufacturing and service industries and government agencies. The size of employer organizations is also likely to have an impact on views as is the educational status of the respondent (Cannon, 1986; Burrows, Harvey and Green, 1992a; Johnson and Pere-Vergé, 1993; Johnson, Pere-Vergé and Hanage, 1993).

There are also international differences, not least the degree of involvement of commerce and industry in higher education. In the United States, for example, there is a longer tradition of industrial involvement with major universities (such as the University of Chicago) being established and heavily sponsored by prominent industrialists (Bulmer, 1984; Harvey, 1987). In Britain, there has tended to be more distancing of industry from higher education (Lowe, 1990). In addition, there is unlikely to be a homogeneity of views *within* an organization. Senior executives, graduate recruiters and line-managers are likely to have different requirements of graduates (Cannon, 1986; Mansergh, 1990) and employer views about higher education as a whole may be very different to views about graduates from a particular university course.

## Why employ graduates?

It is often taken for granted that organizations employ graduates because they want 'bright' (CUCD, 1990) or 'brainy' (Darby, 1993) people and a degree provides credentials to that effect. However, employing graduates involves costs as well as benefits. Graduates have tended to command higher salaries and there are training costs to be incurred as most graduates have little or no industrial or commercial experience. Graduate recruitment is a gamble as most have no history of practical achievement and there is no guarantee that the investment in graduates will pay-off: a particular concern to small and medium employers (SMEs).

*Figure 3.1*   Enhancement continuum

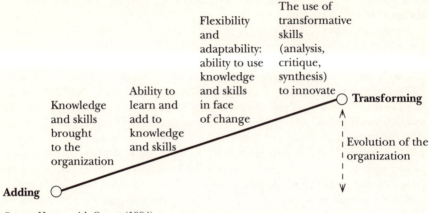

*Source*: Harvey with Green (1994)

Benefits to employers, apart from 'intelligence', include such things as flexibility, ambition, logical thinking, analysis, creativity, innovation, ability to learn quickly and independently, well-developed communication skills, and specialist knowledge (Gordon, 1983; NBEET, 1992). Such benefits are indicative of four underlying reasons for the employment of graduates:

- the knowledge and ideas graduates bring to an organization;
- their willingness to learn and speed of learning;
- their flexibility, adaptability and ability to deal with change;
- their logical, analytic, critical, problem-solving and synthetic skills and the impact they have on innovation.

The four underlying reasons for employing graduates can be seen as lying on an 'enhancement continuum' which ranges from 'adding to an organization' at one end to 'transforming the organization' at the other (see Figure 3.1). The more that graduate employees are able to operate along the continuum, the greater the potential evolution of the organization. This is not, of course, to suggest that *only* graduates are able to contribute to the evolution of an organization. The model is suggested as a means of exploring the rationale for employing graduates and employer satisfaction with the graduates they recruit.

## Transformative potential

The enhancement continuum emphasizes the transformative potential of graduates. Earlier studies had identified the importance of graduates as change agents. For example, Gordon's (1983) respondents, mainly from large organizations, noted that graduates 'bring a fresh, creative mind to a job' and 'are quick to learn, tend to question assumptions and are therefore, more able to cope with change' Johnson, Pere-Vergé and Hanage (1993: 92–4) found that, although reticent to invest in graduates, over a quarter of the SMEs in their study saw graduates as 'potential generators of new and fresh ideas'. An earlier *QHE* study (Harvey, Burrows and Green, 1992a) also showed that employers are looking for more than just competent graduates who can do a job or who have narrowly based vocational qualifications (EPI, 1995); what they really want are graduates 'who can make an impression' on the way an organization functions.

The *Employer Satisfaction* research reaffirms the thesis that, irrespective of size, organizations that recruit graduates are looking for *transformative potential*. Employers are often criticized for not being clear about what they want from graduates. This imprecision is not surprising if employers are focusing on potential. By its very nature, transformative potential is elusive and dynamic. It is not a matter of specifying clear requirements for an unambiguous purpose, as if ordering stock from a supplier. Graduate recruitment thus has a speculative component that can only be hazily sketched and at best identified as a suite of potentially transforming skills, attributes and attitudes.

Employers want graduates who not only add value but are likely to take the organization forward in the face of continuous and rapid change. Six broad areas of graduate attributes emerge from the research as of major importance to employers:

- knowledge;
- willingness to learn;
- intellectual ability;
- ability to work in a modern organization;
- interpersonal skills;
- communication.

*Knowledge and core principles*
Employers assume that a degree brings with it a body of knowledge. Just what is expected and the importance that employers attach to knowledge is dependent on the context within which the graduate will be working. Some employers expect students to have a grounding in the principles of a particular discipline or field of study. A minority may even expect up-to-date specialist knowledge that may provide the organization with a market edge. One respondent to the *Employer Satisfaction* survey noted:

> We actually use graduates as a source of the latest techniques in some areas such as laser technology. We recruit postgraduates for the latest research but also find that undergraduate teaching is surprisingly close to the forefront of new technology.
>
> (Harvey with Green, 1994: 20)

Other organizations are much more interested in whether graduates can apply their basic theoretical or academic knowledge to 'real-world' situations

(BT, 1993: 10). For others, general knowledge and an awareness of the world are all that is expected or of relevance to the employer.

The earlier *QHE* study (Harvey, Burrows and Green, 1992a) revealed that employers rated 'specialist subject knowledge' as least important of 15 broad categories (see Table 3.1). The Australian study for the Business-Higher Education Round Table (1992: Part 2) produced similar results. The development of thinking and decision-making skills and the learning of communication skills were regarded by both employers and university academics as being of greater importance than the achievement of knowledge objectives (broad general knowledge at secondary school and professional knowledge at university). This, in turn, was considered as being more important than learning knowledge and skills directly related to the workplace.

The poor ratings for subject knowledge that was found in 1992 were replicated in the more detailed *Employer Satisfaction* study (Harvey with Green, 1994). Overall, specialist factual knowledge was ranked 59th out of the 62 attributes (Table 3.2). Nearly a third of the sample (31 per cent) rated it as unimportant. SMEs tended to rate it as significantly more important than large employers although ranking it only slightly higher in the list of attributes (53rd compared to 59th).[3] There was no notable difference in the importance attributed to specialist factual knowledge by the industrial and service sectors.

Where specialist factual knowledge was identified as necessary for the graduate recruit, not surprisingly, it scored a higher average score than when it was seen as irrelevant, where it was ranked last. However, even where it was relevant, the overall ranking of specialist subject knowledge *vis-à-vis* other items was still low at 47th out of 62 attributes, mainly because such knowledge has a short shelf-life (see also NBEET HEC, 1992; NAB/UGC, 1984).

What many employers want in areas where degree subject matters is an understanding of core principles rather than subject knowledge. In the *Employer Satisfaction* study, 'understanding core principles' was ranked 16th for the group of employers for whom subject knowledge was required but 43rd for those not interested in the degree subject. In both groups, the ranking for core principles was higher than that for subject knowledge. SMEs regard core principles (6th) as significantly more important than do larger organizations (36th). Often technical competence and problem solving are equated with an understanding of core principles and rated as more important than knowledge.

Many employers are prepared to 'trade-off' knowledge for potential. For example, 20 per cent of respondents, in a recent study, who maintained they had subject preferences admitted that personal qualities of graduates were more important when recruiting (Rigg *et al.*, 1990). Similarly, in the *Employer Satisfaction* study, respondents admitted 'we look for a relevant qualification if possible but general qualification is equally acceptable if our other selection criteria are well met' and 'knowledge is not necessarily important for an organization that trains its staff but ability is vital' (Harvey with Green, 1994: 22–3).

*Table 3.1*  The importance attached by employers to fifteen knowledge, skills and attitude items: *QHE* (1992)

| Knowledge, skills and attitudes | Irrelevant (%) | Unimportant (%) | Desirable (%) | Essential (%) | Employer mean | Manufacturing mean | Service mean | Government mean |
|---|---|---|---|---|---|---|---|---|
| Effective communication | 0.0 | 0.8 | 17.7 | 76.6 | 93 | 87 | 98 | 92 |
| Team work | 0.8 | 0.8 | 23.7 | 74.6 | 91 | 87 | 95 | 89 |
| Ability to solve problems | 0.0 | 1.7 | 36.4 | 61.9 | 87 | 89 | 89 | 82 |
| Analytic skills | 0.8 | 1.7 | 39.0 | 58.5 | 85 | 82 | 87 | 86 |
| Flexibility and adaptability | 0.8 | 2.5 | 39.0 | 57.6 | 85 | 79 | 87 | 87 |
| Self-skills (confidence, etc.) | 0.8 | 2.5 | 44.1 | 52.5 | 83 | 77 | 88 | 82 |
| Decision-making skills | 0.8 | 1.7 | 51.7 | 45.8 | 81 | 78 | 82 | 82 |
| Independent judgement | 0.8 | 4.2 | 52.5 | 42.4 | 79 | 79 | 80 | 79 |
| Numeracy | 0.0 | 9.3 | 49.2 | 41.5 | 78 | 81 | 78 | 74 |
| Logical argument | 0.8 | 7.6 | 56.8 | 34.7 | 75 | 69 | 78 | 80 |
| Enquiry and research skills | 0.0 | 14.5 | 55.6 | 29.9 | 72 | 70 | 70 | 77 |
| Imagination and creativity | 1.7 | 14.4 | 66.1 | 17.8 | 67 | 64 | 65 | 73 |
| Use information technology | 3.4 | 17.8 | 59.3 | 19.5 | 65 | 69 | 58 | 71 |
| Relate to wider context | 5.9 | 25.4 | 58.5 | 10.2 | 58 | 50 | 57 | 68 |
| Specialist subject knowledge | 10.2 | 28.0 | 44.1 | 17.8 | 57 | 62 | 43 | 70 |
| *Sample size* | | | | | 124 | 35 | 47 | 34 |

*Table 3.2*  Importance scores of 62 items as rated by employers

| Attribute | Mean | Rank |
| --- | --- | --- |
| Willingness to learn | 92.77 | 1 |
| Commitment | 88.29 | 2 |
| Dependability/reliability | 88.10 | 3 |
| Self-motivation | 87.81 | 4 |
| Team work | 87.40 | 5 |
| Communication skills (oral) | 86.89 | 6 |
| Co-operation | 85.83 | 7 |
| Communication skills (written) | 85.66 | 8 |
| Drive/energy | 84.52 | 9 |
| Self-management | 84.50 | 10 |
| Desire to achieve/motivation | 84.33 | 11 |
| Problem-solving ability | 84.02 | 12 |
| Analytic ability | 82.99 | 13 |
| Flexibility | 82.94 | 14 |
| Initiative | 82.85 | 15 |
| Can summarize key issues | 82.47 | 16 |
| Logical argument | 82.28 | 17 |
| Adaptability (intellectual) | 81.35 | 18 |
| Numeracy | 80.99 | 19 |
| Adaptability (organizational) | 80.36 | 20 |
| Can cope with pressure/stress | 79.96 | 21 |
| Time management | 79.96 | 21 |
| Rapid conceptualization of issues | 79.33 | 23 |
| Enquiry and research skills | 79.10 | 24 |
| Self-confidence | 78.31 | 25 |
| Persistence/tenacity | 78.20 | 26 |
| Planning ability | 78.07 | 27 |
| Interest in life-long learning | 77.29 | 28 |
| Ability to use information technology | 77.25 | 29 |
| Understanding of core principles | 76.98 | 30 |
| Organizational skills | 76.86 | 31 |
| Critical ability | 76.79 | 32 |
| Can deal with large amounts of information | 76.77 | 33 |
| Consideration for others | 76.45 | 34 |
| Leadership potential | 76.03 | 35 |
| Independent judgement | 76.02 | 36 |
| Ability to relate to wider context | 75.39 | 37 |
| Maturity | 75.00 | 38 |
| Tact | 74.79 | 39 |
| Equipped for continuous education | 74.58 | 40 |
| Innovation | 74.18 | 41 |
| Loyalty | 73.80 | 42 |
| Tolerance | 73.70 | 43 |
| Technical ability | 73.41 | 44 |
| Influencing skills | 73.14 | 45 |
| Decision-making skills | 72.95 | 46 |

*Table 3.2* (cont.)

| Attribute | Mean | Rank |
|---|---|---|
| Curiosity | 71.63 | 47 |
| Imagination | 69.47 | 48 |
| Creativity | 67.83 | 49 |
| Experience of the world of work | 67.08 | 50 |
| Leadership ability | 66.32 | 51 |
| Commercial awareness | 66.04 | 52 |
| General knowledge | 65.55 | 53 |
| Financial knowledge or understanding | 64.18 | 54 |
| Negotiation skills | 62.60 | 55 |
| Deep understanding | 61.71 | 56 |
| Relevant work experience | 57.29 | 57 |
| Problem-setting ability | 57.17 | 58 |
| Specialist factual knowledge | 55.20 | 59 |
| Knowledge of social/political issues | 49.21 | 60 |
| Knowledge of the organization | 47.52 | 61 |
| Prior knowledge of the job | 45.83 | 62 |

*Source*: Harvey with Green (1994)

*Willingness to learn*

For most employers, the willingness of graduates to learn and continually update their knowledge is far more important than a stock of knowledge: 'We are looking for people who are learning how to learn, the degree suggests they have the ability to learn' (Harvey with Green, 1994: 23).

*Willingness to learn* is for employers the single most important factor to emerge from the *Employer Satisfaction* research. None of the respondents considered it unimportant and three-quarters (72 per cent) of respondents consider it *very* important. This premier position applies to both industrial and service sectors and to large and small organizations.

The importance attributed to willingness to learn is compatible with the 'enhancement continuum' model of graduate recruitment.

Although willingness to learn is crucial, the speed of learning is also important for some employers, especially SMEs, who want graduates to 'hit the deck running'. Some organizations employ graduates because of their 'self-reliance' (Dillon, 1992) and ability to work productively at an early stage without high levels of supervision.

However, previous experience of higher education is sometimes perceived as problematic because young 'graduates have had an intensive learning programme from 11–21 years of age and they go into business where learning is much slower, the work is much more mundane and it is demotivating' thus graduates get bored as they are unused to alternative ways of learning and are not always able to 'define job satisfaction in different ways' (Harvey with Green, 1994: 23).

*Intellect and adaptability*

Employers expect graduates to exhibit a range of intellectual abilities. They want graduates who are inquisitive, innovative, logical, analytic, numerate, critical, able to deal with large amounts of information and think laterally. Employers want flexible and adaptable graduate recruits with a broad view.

Employers want graduates who see change as an opportunity rather than a threat. There is a demand, internationally, for higher education to produce 'students and employees who are accepting of change and can recognize and seek out the opportunities of change' (Business-Higher Education Round Table, 1992).

It is not just a matter of coping reactively to a situation of flux. Thus, for example, at IBM, 'recruitment is very broad and we look for other skills apart from those that might equate with management. One thing in particular, is the ability to initiate change'. Employers want graduates who are 'keen to experiment with new ideas' and who have 'an ability to question existing practice and solutions'. Generally, a 'sceptical outlook is helpful' (Harvey with Green, 1994: 29–31).

In short, employers want graduates with transformative potential, who can edge along the 'enhancement continuum' and help transform the organization.

*Working in an organization*

The culture of a modern workplace organization is quite different from traditional university culture and it is often difficult for graduates to fit in. Employers want graduates who can make an impression on an organization. Increasingly, organizations want people who can make a contribution quickly, which requires that the graduate becomes sensitized to the operation and culture of the organization as rapidly as possible.

Teamworking and co-operation are important aspects of working in an organization and represent a significant difference from the way higher education traditionally operates (Burgess, 1986). Well over half the respondents (59 per cent) rate team work as *very* important and only 2 per cent think it is unimportant. Teamworking involves flexibility and adaptability as it not only requires the ability to accommodate other points of view but also to play a variety of roles depending on the task in hand and make-up of the team.

Working in an organization involves more than just teamworking ability, personal skills, such as self-confidence, self-management, self-motivation and commitment are all important in developing an understanding of organizational culture. Self-confidence is something that recruiters look for during the selection process and it is viewed as a major factor in developing good interpersonal skills. Dependability is a particularly important attribute when working in an organization as is the ability to cope with pressure, manage stress and work to deadlines.

Although employers place little importance on graduates' knowledge of the organization or the job they do expect applicants to make an effort to find out. Commercial awareness and basic knowledge of the organization is indicative of motivation and preparedness for a job-interview, as this excerpt from a group discussion illustrates:

> I'm not so concerned that they know about British Gas, but that they have attempted to find out. When I ask them what they know about British Gas, I get really fed up when they say 'they turn the cooker on and out comes the gas' – they might as well leave there and then. Have they bothered to find out anything? It is a matter of motivation.
>
> Exactly. It is fundamental. They are trained to investigate things. This information can be located in easy sources, in a single room. It is not difficult. But not a lot of finding-out goes on.
>
> (Harvey with Green, 1994: 35–6)

*Interpersonal skills*

'Interpersonal skills' is a term that covers a variety of specific abilities but, in general, refers to those attitudes, skills and abilities that enable people to relate to others. Such skills represent an area in which employers have explicit expectations (CIHE, 1987; NBEET, 1992; BT, 1993).

Interpersonal skills are, arguably, at the heart of the problem that graduates have in adjusting to organizational culture. Employers rate 'thrusting skills', such as self-motivation and desire to achieve very highly. Those attributes that may smooth the entry of graduates into the organization, such as consideration for others, tact and tolerance are relatively less important.

*Leadership* is an attribute of graduates that a few employers rate highly. Graduates used to be employed with a view to taking on leadership roles at various levels within an organization. Although flatter organizational structures and the gradual disappearance of 'graduate jobs' has meant that the career path of graduates is less clear, there is still a sense in which graduates are expected to exhibit leadership characteristics. In an Australian study of job advertisements (NBEET, 1992) leadership skills were the 5th most frequent skill specified with 10 per cent of all advertisements requiring it of graduates.

*Communication skills*

In study after study, communication skills emerge as among the most important, if not as *the* most important quality that employers require of graduates (SCOEG, 1985; Greenwood, Edge and Hodgetts, 1987; Allen and Scrams, 1991; IMS/AGR, 1991; CBI, 1991; Harvey, Burrows and Green, 1992a; NBEET, 1992; Binks, Grant and Exley, 1993).

Communication skills is shorthand for a set of attributes including: basic competence in grammar, spelling and punctuation; the ability to write clearly for a variety of different audiences; to make oral presentations; to engage effectively in discussions in various forums; to listen effectively; to be conversant in more than one language; and to use electronic media for communication purposes. The dissatisfaction with written communication skills may seem surprising, for students tend to complain that they do little else except read and write. However, the writing is all of one register, for one audience. What employers want is markedly different from the writing skills that universities value.

In the *Employer Satisfaction* research, oral and written communication skills were seen as extremely important, use of information technology less important and language ability was rarely mentioned!

Not only are communication skills important to employers but, if the available research is anything to go by, to academics and students as well. In the earlier *QHE* study 'academics' (students, teaching staff and non-teaching staff in higher education institutions) rated effective communication as the most important of 15 knowledge, skills and attitudes items (Harvey, Burrows and Green, 1992b). The Australian Round Table Study showed that the communication skills, along with decision making, were the most important objectives for university education (Business-Higher Education Round Table, 1992).

## Satisfaction

Overall, employers express satisfaction with the graduates they have recruited. Only 4 of the 62 items on the *Employer Satisfaction* questionnaire score 'unsatisfactory' (that is, with a mean rating below 50). However, despite this apparent endorsement of graduate abilities, employers are far more satisfied with some attributes than with others. In relative terms, those attributes that caused most concern are those rated as important but unsatisfactory. Ten items fell into this category, with written communication skills being the one in which there was greatest differential between the importance and satisfaction ratings. The key areas of employer satisfaction and dissatisfaction, based on both the quantitative and qualitative data, are summed up in Table 3.3.

## Transferable or core skills?

In Chapter 7 we shall subject the notion of transferable skills to critical scrutiny but, for the moment, we wish to work on the basis that, even if difficulties with the notion of transfer are frequently overlooked, we cannot overlook the fact that many commentators believe that there are general skills, abilities and dispositions that higher education ought to foster. The *QHE* research suggests that staff, students and employers all regard the development of 'transferable skills' as an important outcome of higher education. Employers tend to seek a range and balance of skills in their recruits (Hansen, 1991; Harvey, Burrows and Green, 1992a).

The perceptions of employers involved in the *QHE* research are compatible with the notion that there are a set of generic or core skills and attitudes. The attributes that are regarded as most important are willingness to learn, team work, communication skills, problem solving, analytic ability, logical argument, ability to summarize key issues and a range of personal

*Table 3.3* Areas of employer satisfaction and dissatisfaction with graduates

Most employers are satisfied with:

- the core content of courses although some are concerned about the apparent cut-back in core principles in modular programmes;
- the willingness to learn of graduates, *the single most important factor for employers*;
- the commitment, self-motivation, drive and desire to achieve of graduates;
- graduates' ability to be analytic, logical, numerate, to conceptualize issues rapidly and to deal with large amounts of information;
- graduates' ability to work in teams and with their co-operativeness: although some employers claim that graduate recruits often 'stuck out like sore thumbs' from the rest of the workforce and were incapable of team working;
- the flexibility and intellectual adaptability of graduates;
- the dependability and organizational adaptability of graduates;
- the self-confidence of graduates: although there is a fine line drawn between arrogance and self-confidence;
- graduates' 'computer literacy': although some employers noted that graduates are often more comfortable communicating with computers than with people.

Employers are only moderately satisfied with:

- the technical ability of graduates;
- the critical ability of graduates.

Employers are somewhat dissatisfied with:

- the innovation of graduates, in part due to the insensitiveness of graduates to the implications of innovation;
- the lateral thinking and synthetic ability of graduates.

Employers are dissatisfied with:

- oral communication skills of graduates, who seem to have had little experience of making presentations or of having the attribute assessed, despite its very high importance;
- written communication skills of graduates; their range of writing abilities is limited as is their ability to write for diverse audiences: some graduates seem to have a poor grasp of the fundamentals of written communication, especially basic grammar, sentence structure and punctuation;
- the problem-solving ability of graduates, despite its importance, because of graduates' lack of 'real world' application;
- the ability of graduates to cope with pressure, time management and organizational skills;
- graduates' understanding of the culture of a modern organization and naïvety about industrial relations issues, organizational politics, knowing how to deal with people of different seniorities and recognizing other people's motivations;
- the ability of graduates to apply knowledge or understanding to practical work situations because they lack commercial awareness or an appreciation of the human or cultural context;
- the leadership qualities of graduates.

*Note*: Data refer to graduates who have been recruited and are working in firms.

attributes including commitment, energy, self-motivation, self-management, reliability, co-operation, flexibility and adaptability. Many of these are the kinds of 'core skills' that some educational and industrial bodies have been advocating for some time (Allen, 1981; NAB/UGC, 1984; CBI, 1988, 1989; FEU, 1990; BTEC, 1991).

There is growing evidence that academics agree in principle that graduates should be able to demonstrate a number of skills and abilities other than the acquisition of a body of knowledge and theory. The earlier *QHE* research (Harvey, Burrows and Green, 1992a, 1992b, 1992c) illustrated that students, teachers and employers in British higher education saw the development of a range of skills as very important outcomes of higher education. Similarly, Otter (1992) argued that there is not a great discrepancy between what graduates and employers are looking for from higher education.

Ramsden (1986) also suggested that there is a fairly high degree of consensus between academics, employers and students about the outcomes and processes of higher education. In addition to subject-specific skills and knowledge, considerable emphasis is placed on transferable skills, such as critical thinking and high-level problem solving, the testing of hypotheses against evidence and the ability to synthesize and organize complicated ideas. The Australian Government study *Achieving Quality* concludes:

> The groups [of employers and academics] consulted were as one on this issue – while discipline skills and technical proficiency were seen as important, and more so in some areas and for some purposes than others – the so-called higher level generic skills were seen as critically important, and sometimes lacking . . . While it would not be claimed that these characteristics were found only in graduates, most commentators would acknowledge that, if universities are to add value, they must take responsibility for the specific development and refinement of these skills.
>
> (NBEET HEC, 1992: 20)

Table 3.4 is a list of broad attributes (in alphabetical order) synthesized from available research and commentaries. Each attribute needs to be specified within a particular context. For example, 'leadership skills', may mean the ability to organize people in one sense and to inspire people in another. The list is not definitive but indicative of the range of attributes that a higher education experience should encourage, nurture and enhance.

That does not mean that all students should leave higher education with the same mix or level of skills. Employers do not want standardized graduates, rather they 'require a range of abilities from which to select' (Pierce, 1993: 48). The exact composition of the list of 'core', 'basic', 'transferable' or 'employability' attributes is much less important than the principle that an extensive subject knowledge is not the only outcome – indeed, to these employers, at least, that it is no longer the primary outcome of higher education study.

However, it is very important to remember that whether 'transferable' or not the acquisition of these attributes is not a one-off event. These are not

*Table 3.4* Alphabetical list of core employability attributes

---

*Attribute*

---

Ability to deal with change and uncertainty (anticipate and cope with change)
Ability to use information technology
Analytic ability
Commitment
Communication skills: presentational (oral and written), explain listen, persuade
Creative problem-solving
Critical, reflective, lateral thinking, offering a broad view
Dependable, reliable, honest, ethical and integrity
Energy, drive and enthusiasm
Enquiry and research skills: knowing how to find out
Flexibility and adaptability
Foreign-language competence
Independent learner
Innovative, using initiative, seizing opportunities
Leadership skills and potential (management of people, vision, inspiration)
Logical argument
Numeracy
Organizational awareness (political sensitivity, ability to relate to others)
Planning ability, decision-making and exercising judgement
Self-assessment and self-reflection, self-awareness
Self-confidence
Self-management, time management, stress management
Self-motivation and desire to achieve, self-promotion
Summarizing, conceptualizing and synthetic skills
Team work and co-operation
Understanding core principles of a subject area
Willingness to learn and continue learning

---

things you either have or you do not have: they are abilities and dispositions that can be developed at various levels and their acquisition is a continuous process of perfection whether through on-the-job experience or through more formal education either as part of a first degree or diploma or through continuing education (DME, 1991).

# Employer satisfaction and quality

The teaching quality assessment process in Britain makes a clear link between employer satisfaction and the quality of higher education. The implication is that if employers are satisfied then this is indicative of a 'higher quality' than if they are dissatisfied. Satisfaction is, thus, an indicator of quality. But what kind of quality?

The extent to which satisfaction is an indicator of quality depends on how quality is viewed. Where quality is seen as exceptional, as exceeding some implicit or explicit level of performance, then employer satisfaction is indicative of perceived *standards*. For many employers, maintenance of the standards of higher education is important, even if they find it difficult to specify the exact nature of such standards.

Satisfaction, in the context of a fitness-for-purpose notion of quality, is indicative of a 'delighted' employer (Deming, 1982). Satisfied employers, in this sense, have had their needs, *requirements* or desires met. Graduates fit the purpose for which they have been employed. This is an instrumental approach to quality that fits in with the notion of a skills gap and the need to decrease it.

Value-for-money notions of quality relate to employer satisfaction both at a system-wide, supply level and at the organizational-demand level. Employers, as taxpayers, have a stake in the accountability of higher education: in producing suitable graduates as efficiently as possible. They also want their own direct investment in graduates to *pay-off* in terms of benefits to the organization. Employers, especially small employers, are much more concerned about the latter than the former. Indeed, efficiencies at the system level are seen as potentially undermining the value that employers get from employing graduates. There is a feeling, among some employers, that under-resourcing of higher education is having an impact on 'standards' and thus on the benefit they gain from employing graduates.

The transformative notion of quality sees students as participants in a process that is going to enhance their capabilities and empower them for lifelong learning. Employer satisfaction, in this context, is indicative of a view that higher education produces graduates who are not only transformed but are transforming. That is, higher education produces graduates to whom value has been added through the acquisition of knowledge, abilities, skills and attitudes. These graduates, suitably enhanced, are able to subsequently add value to the employing organization by the utilization of their skills and knowledge within the organization. However, one of the reasons for employing graduates is that they bring 'higher-level skills' to an organization. It is through these higher-level skills that graduates are able to make a contribution towards *transforming* the organization. In a world of rapid change, organizations have to adapt and evolve. Graduates, as we have seen, are perceived as a major element of the strategy for dealing with change (Jones, 1994).

Thus, in relation to employer views of higher education, satisfaction implies one of four foci:[4]

- standards (excellence);
- meeting requirements (fitness for purpose);
- pay-off (value for money);
- adapting to change (transformation).

When employers say that they are satisfied it means that they are satisfied with the *standard* of graduates (even if the criteria for this are not always clearly specified) *or* that graduates fulfil the *requirements* expressed by employers *or* that employers get a *return* for the money they invest in graduate recruitment and employment *or* that graduates assist the organization to

*Table 3.5*  Satisfaction by reason for employing graduates

|  | Standards | Meeting requirements | Pay-off | Transformation |
|---|---|---|---|---|
| Knowledge | Expectations about standards | Some added value | Marginal. Understanding core principles has more potential return | Willingness and ability to learn and continue learning |
| Intellect and adaptability | No clear standards (some use of testing) | Potentially transformative | Innovation | Anticipate and cope with change |
| Ability to work in an organization | No clear standards | Graduates play effective rôle | Smooth operation of organization | Potential via ability to work effectively in teams |
| Interpersonal skills | No clear standards | Graduates interact sensitively | Smooth operation of organization | Potential via good internal communication |
| Communication | Expectation of basic standards of 'literacy' | Ability to communicate with customers and colleagues | Convincing exposition of new ideas | Evolution of organization |

*adapt to* the rapidly changing situation of the 1990s and beyond. These are not mutually exclusive and employers may judge their satisfaction by one or more of these. Furthermore, the basis for judging satisfaction for one area (such as graduate knowledge) may be different for judging satisfaction with another area (such as interpersonal skills).

Five broad areas were identified when suggesting why employers recruit graduates: the knowledge they bring, their intellectual ability, the ability of graduates to work in a modern organization, their interpersonal skills and the communication skills of graduates.

If we match satisfaction with the reasons for employing graduates we can create a matrix against which to judge the satisfaction of employers (Table 3.5).

If we consider the first of the reasons for recruiting graduates – the knowledge that graduates bring to the organization – the exceptional approach would judge satisfaction against expected standards. A fitness-for-purpose approach would perhaps expect the graduate to add some value to the organization, although this may not be an easy requirement to directly monitor. A value-for-money approach would probably expect little direct pay-off from graduate knowledge: understanding core principles offers more

potential return. It is not so much knowledge *per se* against which the transformative approach would want to judge satisfaction but the willingness of
the graduate to learn and continue to learn.

The two-dimensionality of the matrix is a useful organizational device but
analytically deceptive. In terms of the analysis developed so far it is necessary to incorporate the enhancement continuum (Figure 3.1, page 46) as
the third dimension. Satisfaction with knowledge, for example, tends to be
judged primarily in terms of added value rather than transformative potential. The body of knowledge is seen as adding only marginal value in most
cases. For some employers, though, a sound knowledge base, especially if
it incorporates an understanding of core principles, is a necessary prerequisite for any potential input into future transformation of the organization.

Much more important than knowledge is ability and willingness to continue learning so that value can be continually added. Furthermore, it is
important that graduates relate their knowledge to the development of a
practical 'real world' awareness. Thus, they effectively move along the enhancement continuum to a more flexible and adaptable use of their knowledge in the face of social, political, economic and technological change.

A similar analysis can be undertaken for the other recruitment factors.
In relation to intellect and adaptability, employer satisfaction is mainly di-
rected at innovation, flexibility and ability to cope with or anticipate change.
This focus is thus on the transformative potential of graduates.

The third and fourth areas identified were ability to work in an organization and interpersonal skills. Satisfaction was more likely to reflect the
ability of graduates to meet the requirements of employers that graduates
play an effective rôle within an organization, which means appreciating and
responding to internal protocols, co-operating and working in teams and
being able to relate to other people at all levels within the organization.

The fifth area was communication and satisfaction was based on added
value, transformative potential and standards. Good communicators add
value to the organization through their communication with outsiders,
especially customers. In this respect employers expect graduates to meet
their requirements. Within the organization, good communication skills
are necessary for the convincing exposition of new ideas and for effective
teamworking. The evolution of the organization relies heavily on effective
communication. Finally, as with knowledge, employers judge communication in terms of standards. Communication skills was one of the few areas
where base standards were alluded to when commenting on graduate ability.

Thus, employer satisfaction, is indicative of different aspects of quality
and thus it is irresponsible to suggest that client satisfaction is in any way
an indicator of a particular notion of quality, much less to suggest that it
can be used as an uncritical performance indicator, for example, of fitness
for purpose.

What the three-dimensional analysis does indicate is that undertaking
action designed to lead to enhanced client satisfaction will not necessarily improve the quality of higher education. Not only is satisfaction indirectly linked
to quality, some elements of client satisfaction can be seen as representing

short-term immediate gratification rather than longer term improvement of the total student experience or attainment.

For some academics, as we have seen, client satisfaction is not so much viewed as improving quality as jeopardizing it. This is often presented as an issue of academic freedom.

## Academic freedom

Government statements about accountability, the needs of the economy and the need for higher education to forge partnerships with industry and commerce, constitute a perceived threat to academic freedom and autonomy. Employer involvement in programme design and implementation, inclusion and assessment of skills and the use of work placements all raise substantial questions about the nature of the academic experience. 'There is a potential conflict between the often unstated educational aims of universities and the often poorly articulated staff-expertise requirements of employers' (Boucher, 1993: 44). Such questions go to the heart of the élite and detached view of the pursuit of knowledge and learning that has been seen to underpin the values and purposes of much higher education (Minogue, 1973; Birch, 1988).

It is generally taken for granted that higher education should support economic development, whether directly (through software engineering degrees) or more generally (through promoting 'enterprise' competencies in all students), but the question remains as to whether higher education should be concerned with supporting economic and business concerns, such as government policies on economic growth, and providing commerce and industry with the graduates it needs in order to be competitive in the global market (Reeves, 1988; Grover, 1989). Academics (students and staff at all levels) are particularly cautious about any notion that graduates are 'business fodder' and often openly hostile to any ideas that higher education should have any part in developing graduates whose value system includes a work ethic, which gives them a positive view of the role of business and entrepreneurship (Business-Higher Education Round Table, 1992).

Many academics are opposed to what they perceive as the priority given to employer views. Indeed, employer organizations have been relatively successful in placing their requirements on to the higher education agenda. Research in Finland, for example, indicates that the Finnish Employers' Confederation has devoted more effort to publicizing its views on educational policy than has the largest labour organization. The powerful impact of employers on educational policy rests on their ability to present their own interests as the interests of society as a whole (Kivinen and Rinne, 1992).

Many academics are also against the idea that higher education has 'customers' and 'clients', of which students are but one and no more important than employers, government or society. For most academics, this consumerist rhetoric is the language of people who do not teach. Education is not a service being sold to customers or supplied to clients, it is a process in which students are participants!

Academics are also concerned about the impact at the programme level of any responsiveness to external stakeholders, particularly employers. They regard employer requirements as potentially compromising the cohesiveness and breadth of the educational experience of students (Warnock, 1989). Employers are often seen as wanting particular skills or immediately consumable information that might give them a market edge. They are seen as having a short-term view that is not the same as the long-term needs of students and they are not perceived as having an interest in developing the critical abilities of students. Such reservations are fuelled by official and semi-official statements that imply a subversion of academic values:

> Collaboration between business and higher education can encourage the adaptation of degree courses so that the content is of greater direct relevance to the needs of business.
>
> (DTI/CIHE, 1990: 5)

> In this context it should be noted that at the end of the century some 80 per cent of the existing labour force will be active. A new partnership between higher education and economic life must evolve to meet these challenges, one that will take account of the changing skills needs of the economies, one which emphasize flexibility in the forms of delivery and education and training and in the acquisition of qualifications and one which will be marked by a greater commitment by all parties to continuing and recurrent education and training.
>
> (EC, 1991: para 15, p. 5)

The apparent emphasis being placed on employer perceptions in quality monitoring also causes concern. For example, Ron Emanuel (1994), lead assessor for chemistry in Scotland, recently suggested that amongst a number of 'acceptable norms' emerging from the assessment process was 'substantial employer involvement in processes such as programme and course design and review, and, in particular, the definition of aims'. Add to this well-meaning recommendations on how companies can become involved in and contribute to academic programmes (DTI/CIHE, 1989) and some academics begin to feel under siege.

However, as we have seen, employers are not a homogeneous group, nor are they uninterested in such 'academic' activities as critique and synthesis, nor do they all have a short-term view. Employer approaches are very different as Fisher (1994) succinctly illustrates by comparing Ford with Unipart.

> The Ford Employee and Development Programme (EDAP) is non-job related. In other words it doesn't fund welders to study welding. The rhetoric is of empowering individuals. Empowerment means courses in literacy, numeracy, losing weight, stopping smoking, starting driving and underwater photography. Ford workers are learning 27 foreign languages and 240 of them are using EDAP grants to study for degrees . . . Over 30,000 UK employees have taken part, it has cost Ford

£10 million and earned it the 1992 National Training Award. Ford does not concentrate solely on self-improvement. It promotes an Automotive Engineering Honours degree (accredited by Anglia Polytechnic University), still has 800 apprentices and is putting 2500 engineers through an Engineering Quality Improvement Programme. The latter encourages the teamworking which gradually replaces single-task production line labour.

Unipart has a mission statement and a 'group corporate aim to build the world's best lean enterprise'. Unipart's new training centre is called a 'University', its gym is the 'Lean Machine', its library the 'Learning Curve', its computer training room the 'Leading Edge' and a cadre of senior management has been dubbed Deans of Marketing, Outlets, Warehousing and so on . . . A third of the workforce has attended compulsory 'core courses' which . . . appear . . . about inculcating values [and] . . . forging anti-unionism into a business principle, calling it a 'traditional, short-term, power-based relationship'.

While academics might sympathize with the Ford approach, the 'Unipart University' exemplifies the nightmare scenario for most academics. It is this kind of approach that makes some academics think that overt development of skills has nothing to do with developing rounded, thinking individuals.

In Chapter 2 we argued that academics, irrespective of any concern about employer views, should adopt a more integrated, transparent and dialogic approach to teaching and learning so as to more readily enhance and empower students. That is, academics must be more explicitly responsible to students. This responsibility should also extend to addressing the employability of graduates. Being aware of potential employability does not constitute a compromise with academic freedom or autonomy but it does serve to sensitize the academic community to things of value that might usefully be incorporated into degree programmes without loss of academic integrity.

That it does not constitute a compromise is clear when we consider the main messages that come from employers. Employers do not want to interfere in higher education. The majority of employers do not have the time, nor inclination to get involved in higher education and would no more wish to interfere in the running of higher education than they would expect academics to interfere in the running of their organizations (Harvey with Green, 1994). By and large, they are not intending to infringe academic freedom. Employers want higher education properly resourced. They want to see good programmes of study produce good graduates. Nor do they appear to be any more critical of the quality of the teaching and learning than are those who work in higher education.

## Convergence of employer and academic expectations

The attributes desired by employers are not necessarily at variance with academic scholarship nor do they imply a loss of autonomy over the curriculum. Employers are not looking for 'trainees' (Fairclough, 1993: 15) when they employ graduates but people equipped to learn and deal with change. They want rounded, intelligent people, with a broad grounding in a subject and an understanding of core principles. Employers want graduate recruits who are adaptable and flexible, who can communicate well and relate to a wide range of people, who are aware of, but not indoctrinated into, the world of work and the culture of organizations, and who, most importantly, have inquiring minds, are willing and quick to learn, are critical, can synthesize and are innovative. In terms of outcomes, there is little here that constitutes a compromise with traditional academic values and expectations.

Indeed, some academics suggest that this concern with core or transferable skills is a lot of fuss about very little. They point out that most of the skills being identified (communication, problem-solving, analysis, critique, flexibility, adaptability, numeracy and so on) are at the heart of the academic process. Higher education has always produced all these things. There is no need to identify them as separate entities, they are implicit in, indeed the essence of, the undergraduate experience (CHE, 1963).

The biggest difference between employers and academics is not the attributes students should develop but the way they do it. Academics tend to see such attributes as 'spin-offs' from developing subject knowledge while employers want the skills and abilities as explicit outcomes of programmes of study. Making the 'academic essence' explicit would not only help reduce a communication gap but would also facilitate the development of transformative student learning (CNAA, 1990b; Harvey, 1995c).

The issue is not one of a challenge to academic autonomy or freedom by employers demanding a different curriculum that suits their short-term requirements. The issue is not about content so much as the explicitness of the learning process and its goals, as we saw in Chapter 2. Employers, if anything, are adding their weight to the growing demand that the total student experience of learning must be seriously reviewed and enhanced.

## Autonomy with responsibility

Employers, in making suggestions about graduate employability, are not suggesting that academics should abandon their autonomy. Rather, employers appear overwhelmingly to endorse the idea of autonomy with responsibility (Harvey, 1994b; Business-Higher Education Round Table, 1992).

That is, an autonomy that looks outwards rather than an introverted cloisterism. Employers are not alone in thinking that higher education should reconsider its introversion.

> The most basic consideration underlying the emergence of the current challenge to higher education, to reconcile more effectively its responsibilities to scholarship and to society, is its inherent tendency to behave as a relatively closed academic system.
>
> (Birch, 1988: 7)

'Autonomy with responsibility' is also the essence of Meyer-Dohm's (1990: 66–7) notion of 'receptiveness and detachment'. Receptiveness to the demands of industry and commerce can give grounds for mistrust and fear by academics who are afraid that 'fundamental research could be neglected or that a too-decisive shift in the direction of socio-economic utilitarianism may occur'. It is thus important that academics adopt a 'detached attitude', that is, adopt 'the requisite degree of aloofness of science from everyday problems, the more fundamental apprehension of problems and the preoccupation with questions of generality'. However, it is a mistake to confuse detachment with the ivory tower: that is not detachment but isolation. Detachment without receptiveness turns into isolation, receptiveness without detachment into a failure to carry out the scientific task. Standing aside from practicality is important provided it is done habitually for the purposes of arriving at 'balanced, unaffected, more objective judgments'.

The pressures on higher education to reappraise its nature and purpose are considerable. However, it should not simply respond to the requirements of specific employers, requirements that may be ill-defined and short term (Targett, 1993, 1995). It is important to distinguish between piecemeal responses and an approach that establishes the quality framework underpinning employer views.

From our point of view, the importance of employers' views is the contribution they make towards developing transformative learning. Employers appear to want graduates with transformative potential. Higher education should respond to this by overtly developing these higher-order *transformative* skills.

As we have seen, the transparent development of graduate attributes is not just about making clear to employers and students the skills and abilities that are being developed in students. This is a by-product. Transparency is fundamentally about empowering students. It provides them with clear aims and outcomes which enable them to develop their own learning (Barnett, 1990). Employing organizations, in order to contend with the rapid change envisaged in the next century need empowered employees who can continue to learn.

What higher education, therefore, must do is develop responsibility to its students and through them to other stakeholders. This would be a process greatly facilitated if it was appropriately encouraged through government policy. In Chapter 4 we consider the recent history of higher education policy, particularly the emergence of quality issues and show that, despite the 'consumerist' language and the development in the United Kingdom of the Student Charter, the focus has been on accountability rather than on improvement of the student experience.

# Notes

1. One has to be careful in using terms such as transferable skills, interpersonal skills, personal skills, knowledge, attitudes and abilities as each one conjures up

different notions for different people. There is no intention to propose a set of definitive categories as many skills areas cut across any particular boundary. Communication skill, for example, may be seen as a transferable skill, an inter-personal skill and an ability. It depends on the particular aspect of communica-tion that is being considered. It is thus important to try and break down taken-for-granteds and identify what respondents actually mean when they refer to general categories. As far as possible we will attempt to do this when reporting people's views but it is impossible to identify, consistently, what our respondents and those in other surveys meant when referring to various attributes of gradu-ates. Bearing this in mind, and the heterogeneity of employers, we will avoid making any *definitive* statements about employer views.

2. In this section there are a number of generalizations about employer perspec-tives of graduates, which are sustainable across a wide range of employer organ-izations. However, there is no suggestion that there is a single employer view (Cannon, 1986). While there is much agreement about many aspects of higher education, the heterogeneity of commerce and industry needs to be kept firmly in mind.

3. The cut-off point for SMEs is 250 employees. Only 17 of the 127 respondents were in this category.

4. Quality as perfection has little meaning in this context. If quality is seen as perfection – as 'right first time' – then satisfaction is indicative of *consistent* out-put. Although, this may be a notion of quality applied by employers to products, it is rarely used in the context of graduates. Rather, employers want a variety of graduates to fulfil a range of different roles. It might, though, sum up quality at the 'Unipart University'!

# 4

# Policy and Accountability

Higher education policy in Britain, and in many other countries since the mid-1980s, has increasingly focused on issues of 'quality'. Almost universally, quality has been employed in the service of accountability: an accountability predicated on budgetary constraint within the context of a highly competitive world economy (CEC, 1991; Gungwu, 1992; Green and Harvey, 1993). There are several reasons for this, including:

- a widespread concern about the size of public expenditure and the share of higher education, especially in the face of competing demands such as health and social welfare;
- a concern about the future competitiveness of the economy and hence the labour needs of a post-industrial society;
- the problem of monitoring the input, process and output of higher education in a diverse and rapidly expanding system that is constrained by a shrinking unit of resource;
- the internationalization of higher education and attempts to ensure greater explicitness about the nature and equivalence of academic and professional qualifications, especially as far as employers are concerned;
- an ideological commitment, in some countries, to making public services, including education, more efficient and more responsive to the needs of customers (Moodie, 1988; Cave and Kogan, 1990). 'Quality' provides the vehicle for expressing this ideological commitment in Britain.

'Accountability' has a variety of nuances (Vroeijenstijn, 1995) but a central feature of accountability is:

> that of 'rendering an account' of what one is doing in relation to goals that have been set or legitimate expectations that others may have of one's products, services or processes, in terms that can be understood by those who have a need or right to understand the 'account'. For this reason, accountability is usually, if not always, linked to public information and to judgements about the fitness, soundness, or level of satisfaction achieved.
>
> (Middlehurst and Woodhouse, 1995: 260)

Curiously, the drive for quality at a policy level has been almost independent of a clear assessment of the learning outcomes of higher education and implementation of procedures that are likely to lead to them. This lack of integration occurs despite concurrent innovations in teaching and learning within higher education.

As we suggested in Chapters 2 and 3, internal and external stakeholders in higher education have raised questions about the appropriateness of the outcomes of higher education. In policy terms, this concern has been translated into economic issues. At one level, it involves questions about whether the higher education system is producing sufficient graduates to enhance the growth and competitiveness of the economy. Concern in the European Union about the 'skills gap' and efforts in some countries to encourage young people into science and technology are indicative of an economic, utilitarian approach (IRDAC, 1994).

At another level, economic considerations simply reflect pressure on government budgets. With so many competing claims for budgetary consideration, higher education has had to become more accountable for the money it receives. In effect, this means that higher education must not only be explicit about where it spends the money but also must endeavour to provide good value for the money it receives.

This emphasis on accountability is the primary reason why there has been very little linkage between quality policy and the encouragement of innovative approaches to teaching and learning. Accountability focuses attention on quality as value for money, although this may be mediated by other notions of quality.[1]

What this accountability orientation overlooks is the transformative process. If quality is viewed as a process in which key stakeholders are participants, rather than as a product made available to customers or clients, then it is necessary to explore the nature, development and evolving outcomes of that transformative process. It is not very meaningful to assess a continually evolving participatory process by inspecting it at a single point in time. A transformative notion of quality requires a focus on *change*.

In essence, the failure to unite quality policy and learning development in common cause is a function of the tension between accountability and improvement that besets the quality debate. A review of the quality policy in Britain shows the nature of the accountability–improvement tension and demonstrates the failure to link quality with innovations in teaching and learning.

The tension between accountability and improvement is also indicative of an organizational tension between managerialism and collegialism. Before reviewing the policy agenda and exploring the way in which it prioritizes accountability, it is appropriate to explore the relationship between collegialism and managerialism.

## Managerialism

Managerialism in higher education refers to the tendency for professional managers, through their decision-making role, to alter academic processes on the basis of non-academic criteria amongst which financial criteria have been prominent, or in response to management theories and fashions (Bowtell, 1993; Miller, 1994). Accounting procedures dominate decision-making, finance is raised from the status of a parameter within which to work to the guiding operating principle, and financial arguments are used to manipulate political aims (Wilkins, 1994).

The rise of managerialism involves a shift towards a more formalized management structure and control at the institutional level which is reflected in more direct management of the higher education system by the government (Holmes, 1993; Trow, 1993).

Higher education, it is argued, is faced with the emergence of unelected, oligarchic managerial élites, which wield great power without accountability either externally or internally (Wilkins, 1994). In Britain, this managerialist tendency first appeared in the former polytechnic sector. Following the incorporation of the then polytechnics, there was a centralizing of control and an erosion of the contribution of academics to institutional policy-making and 'a sense of alienation from senior management began to manifest itself' (Yorke, 1993: 5). This has subsequently spread into the traditional university sector. In Europe, the professional higher education manager is still a rarity as most systems require that university rectors and deans are elected and serve relatively short terms of office. However, the system is beginning to change (Acherman, 1995).

There is a view that managerialism does not threaten academic freedom. On the contrary:

> good management of the universities is essential as a defence against further erosion of their autonomy . . . For the good of all the academic departments and for the job security of their staff, the universities need to be managed by people who understand and respect academic values but who have not only the time and expertise but the interest to do it well; who do not just see management as a regrettable distraction from their real work; and who are willing to immerse themselves in the job and to learn about it.
>
> (Rear, 1994a)

This view is possibly sustainable at the level of the university although it arguably relies on the benign paternalism of senior management. The widely publicized events relating to the vice-chancellors at the British universities of Huddersfield and Portsmouth are seen as indicative of a rather more Machiavellian approach.

> Externally, provided they balance their books they are unlikely to be challenged. Internally, in the name of 'effective management', senates and academic boards are being stripped of any worthwhile powers and greatly reduced in their breadth of representation. Governing councils provide little effective check. Appointed members owe too much to the patronage of the élite who put them there, while elected representation

is reduced . . . I do not deny the possibility of benign oligarchies and dictators. I would prefer not to be forced to rely on it.

(Wilkins, 1994: 10)

It is not the managerialism operating at the level of the institution that is the major concern. Managerialism also operates at the level of the state. It is manifest in the direct interference in higher education, in the name of accountability, of the government and its agencies, such as the funding council.

Managerialism has been linked to government control of the sector through the emergence of 'hard' as opposed to 'soft' managerialism (Trow, 1993). Soft managerialism, that advocated by John Rear (1994a, 1994b), is based on improving efficiency and sees managerial effectiveness as crucial in producing high quality at lowest cost. The hard conception, which is now central in the reshaping of British higher education, elevates system and institution management to a dominant position and focuses on 'the continual assessment of the outcomes of educational activities, and the consequent reward and punishment of institutions and primary units of education through formulas linking these assessments to funding' (Trow, 1993: 2).

Hard managerialism, in Britain, is characterized by:

- a desire to treat education as a product that can be continually improved whilst lowering the unit cost;
- withdrawal of trust by government in the academic community and academia's capacity to critically assess and improve its own activities (Annan, 1993; Mulgan, 1995).

This has led to the creation of bureaucratic machinery and formulae that are imposed on the universities from outside the higher education system. These agencies create criteria of performance and rules for accountability and apply formulae that link funding to quality to ensure the automatic improvement of efficiency and effectiveness of higher education. In effect, 'external assessment linked to funding is thus a substitute not only for trust but also for the effective competitive market which is the chief control both of quality and cost in commercial enterprises' (Trow, 1993, p. 4). Under the guise of competition, the British Government has used managerialism to impose a 'command economy' on higher education. It is not, therefore, surprising that academics are growing increasingly suspicious of quality and of the burgeoning quality industry.

## Collegialism

Higher education institutions are often assumed to embody a collegiate ethos (Moore and Langknecht, 1986; Cannon, 1994; Dearlove, 1995). A college, in one sense, is nothing more than a community of scholars. However, there is underlying 'philosophy' implicit in the notion of collegiality, which will be referred to as 'collegialism' (Harvey, 1995c).

Collegialism is characterized by three core elements:

- a process of shared decision-making by a collegial group in relation to academic matters;
- mutual support in upholding the academic integrity of members of the group;
- conservation of a realm of special knowledge and practice.

There has been a revival of interest in collegialism in the wake of managerialism of the late 1980s. Collegialism can be seen to span a continuum from 'cloisterism' to 'new collegialism' (Harvey, 1995a).

Cloisterism embodies a conservative reassertion of academic autonomy and freedom. It emphasizes the absolute right of the collegial group to make decisions relating to academic matters, regards the integrity of members as inviolable (except where exceptionally challenged from within), and considers the role of the group as that of developing and defending its specialist realm, which is usually discipline-based. Cloisterism tends to be staff-directed, producer-oriented and research-dominated. It relates to the internal concerns of the group and sees students as novices to be initiated into the mysteries of the discipline. It is effectively inward-looking. The knowledge it possesses is revealed incrementally and according to the dictates of the self-appointed 'owners'. The skills and abilities it expects students to develop are often implicit and obscure. Sometimes what is expected of students is deliberately opaque and shrouded in mystifying discourse.

New collegialism sees the collegial group as the forum for academic decision-making but is prepared to enlarge that group to allow discourse and negotiation with significant others, not least students. It emphasizes accountable professional expertise rather than inviolable academic integrity. New collegialism is outward-looking and responsive to changing circumstances and requirements. It is learning-oriented. It focuses on facilitating student learning rather than teaching, and explicitly encourages the development of a range of skills and abilities. It prefers explicitness to obfuscation. It values team work. It sees its role as one of widely disseminating knowledge and understanding through whatever learning-facilitation and knowledge-production processes are most effective. New collegialism disavows the inwardness of the cloisterist approach while retaining its scepticism of management-dominated quality assurance processes. New collegialism embodies an approach to teaching and learning that is responsible, responsive and transparent and sees quality in terms of transformation of a participant rather than attempting to fit the purpose of a customer. The core of a new-collegiate approach is the development of a quality culture of continuous improvement. Table 4.1 summarizes these distinctions.

The new collegialism is self-critical and concerned to continually improve its processes and practices rather than rest content with traditional modes of functioning. Academic autonomy in the new collegialism is manifested through ownership and control of an overt, transparent process of continuous quality improvement rather than in the retention of a non-accountable,

*Table 4.1*  Comparison of cloisterism and new collegialism

| Cloisterism | New collegialism |
| --- | --- |
| Secretive | Open |
| Isolationist | Networking |
| Individual | Teamwork |
| Defensive | Responsive |
| Traditional approach | Innovative |
| Producer-oriented | Participant-oriented |
| Clings to power | Empowering |
| Wary of change | Welcomes change |
| Élitist | Open access |
| Implicit quality criteria | Explicit quality criteria |
| Information provider | Facilitates active learning |

*Source*: Harvey (1995c)

mystifying, opaque cloisterism. In short, the new collegialism is about the development of an explicit professionalism (Elton, 1992).

# Quality in mass higher education

Quality crept on to the British political agenda for higher education in the middle of the 1980s (Burrows, Harvey and Green, 1992b). It was hardly noticed at first, and was considered to be a marginal concern. After all, by definition, universities were quality institutions (Kogan, 1986).

The mid-1980s saw the establishment of an agenda that would drive the development of higher education policy in Britain for the next decade. At root was the shift from an élite to a mass higher education system. Four interrelated themes dominated the mass higher education agenda: accountability and value for money, maintaining standards, measuring outputs, and external quality monitoring (EQM). We consider the first three in this chapter and explore EQM, in an international context, in Chapter 5.

## Accountability and value for money

Accountability takes two forms, one pitched at the level of economic planning and the other at the level of institutional efficiency. In Britain, for example, both elements have been highlighted by government policy statements.

The Jarratt Report (CVCP, 1985) on efficiency recommended that universities and the system as a whole should work to clear objectives and achieve value for money. It was suggested that the University Grants Committee (UGC) and the Committee of Vice-Chancellors and Principals of the Universities of the United Kingdom (CVCP) should jointly develop performance indicators designed for use both within individual universities and for making comparisons between universities. The recommendations for universities included: the development of rolling academic and institutional plans and the introduction of arrangements for staff development, appraisal and accountability. This requirement reflected a general requirement for the public sector to be efficient and effective ( Joseph, 1986; DES, 1987; Secretary of State for Education, 1988; Pollitt, 1990b; PCFC, 1990c). It also parallels the situation in the United States where the initial impetus for a serious re-evaluation of higher education originated from demands for more accountability (NGATF, 1986; Jennings, 1989; Cross, 1990; Hutchings and Marchese, 1990; Millard, 1991).

Accountability on the level of economic planning was evident in the United Kingdom Green Paper, *The Development of Higher Education into the 1990s* (DES, 1985) and in the ensuing White Paper *Higher Education: Meeting the Challenge* (DES, 1987). The British Government stressed the need for higher education to serve the economy more effectively and to have closer links with industry and to promote enterprise. It noted that other countries produced more qualified scientists, engineers, technologists and technicians than the United Kingdom and, therefore, wanted British higher education to develop the flexibility to be able to respond to future change. An increase in the 'age participation rate' (that is, the percentage of those in the 18–21 age group) to 18 per cent was proposed. In the United States, similar concerns were being expressed about the needs of the economy (AAC, 1985; NGA, 1986), a theme that was coming to preoccupy the European Union (IRDAC, 1990, 1994; CEC, 1991).

The White Paper also indicated that efficiency was to be increased by improvements in institutional management; changes in the management of the system and the development and use of performance indicators. Accountability was firmly established at centre-stage in higher education policy debates in Britain, prefacing similar concerns around the world (see also Chapter 5). Quality improvement, *per se*, was not on the agenda. At this stage, accountability was not wrapped up in a 'quality' cloak but was simply couched in terms of efficiency gains and of clarifying responsibility for maintaining standards. This changed somewhat the following year when institutions covered by the Polytechnics and Colleges Funding Council (PCFC) were expected to provide, in return for public funds, a method for monitoring institutional performance and assuring quality. The Secretary of State recommended that the PCFC should develop indicators of both the quality and quantity of institutions' teaching in relation to funding (Secretary of State for Education, 1988). This recommendation came to partial fruition in 1989 with the establishment of a funding 'premium' for courses of 'outstanding quality' in the PCFC sector (PCFC, 1989).

The shift from 'raw' value-for-money accountability to a more subtle quality-linked accountability went one step further in a later UK White Paper, *Higher Education: A New Framework* (DES, 1991a), which enjoined further efficient expansion in student numbers while stressing the need to maintain and enhance quality in higher education. The *Further and Higher Education Act* (HM Government, 1992) firmly linked efficiency and effectiveness to quality. It was axiomatic in the plan for an annual 5 per cent. increase in student numbers with no comparable increase in resources. In addition, efficiency concerns underpinned the link between quality assessment and funding, which rewarded good provision rather than use resources to improve inadequate provision. It was proposed that, whatever the method of quality assessment, the funding methodology should give more resource either through increased student numbers or through a funding premium to those institutions assessed as providing high quality teaching and learning in particular academic subject categories and that institutions with areas assessed as being of unacceptable quality would be warned of a possible withdrawal of funds if improvements were not put in place (PCFC/UFC, 1992a, 1992b).

Quality assessment was, at least in theory, to be based not on any absolute measure of excellence but upon the ability of an institution to deliver what it promised through its mission statement and programme aims and objectives; a recurring theme in other countries, as will be seen in Chapter 5.

## Maintaining and controlling standards

Throughout the last decade, standards have been a continuing concern of all stakeholders in higher education, although at times this has been camouflaged by the preoccupation with quality.

The sub-text of the Lindop Report (Lindop, 1985) was a concern with standards. Among other things it suggested that the best safeguard of academic standards is not external validation or any other form of external control, but the growth of the teaching institution as a self-critical academic community. It suggested a code of practice (published two years later (CVCP, 1987)) noting, in particular, that 'the external examining system is an important and currently under-exploited safeguard of academic standards'. A prolonged debate about the rôle and effectiveness of the external examiner system in Britain has ensued culminating in the predominant view that it should be retained but needs modifying (CNAA, 1992; Silver, 1993; Harvey and Mason, 1995; HEQC, 1995a; Silver, Skennett and Williams, 1995; Warren Piper, 1995).

> The external examining system is not to be dismissed as an expensive cosmetic . . . It is a vigorous system involving a high proportion of the country's leading academics and the work is undertaken with great seriousness and care. It is a necessary function if there is to be a policy of parity between awards and it confers a number of incidental benefits . . . One thing, however, seems certain – the external examiner system cannot go on as it is. It has either to be scrapped or revamped . . . External examiners can no longer fulfill their traditional function. The gap between examiner and candidate widens; fewer external examiners actually see any students and are inexorably pushed towards judging the teaching and examining system and away from judging the

candidates. This is an unplanned shift to a meta-level of quality assurance – an incidental effect of adopting modular degree structures and the progressive move to mass higher education. Indeed, the very nature of a degree program is changed to one in which an academic discipline is no longer the central organizing force giving shape and coherence to undergraduate study . . . There is a shift from the subject-based view to the academy-based view of the examiner.

(Warren Piper, 1994: 237–9)

Policy advisers and researchers in other countries, including Australia, Sweden and the United States have also explored the possibility of establishing or extending the external examiner systems to assist in the maintenance of standards (for example, Fong 1988).

The Lindop Report noted that, if academic standards were to be effectively maintained, it would be necessary to develop safeguards, other than validation, to ensure the quality of certain key factors including recruitment of staff, quality of students admitted, and professional and vocational relevance of degree courses. The traditional concern with inputs also implicitly reaffirmed an exceptional notion of quality. Indeed, it has been 'excellence' that has mediated the value-for-money requirements of subsequent legislation, rather than any concern with the effectiveness of enhancement or empowerment process in higher education. The British government has also clearly linked improved standards in higher education to the quality of teaching, while doing nothing directly to enable or motivate changes in this area.

Managers in higher education have been of the view, prompted by government requirements for efficiency gains, that there is slack in the system and that an increase in staff : student ratios and more pressure on capital and equipment will have minimal impact on the student experience. However, even here there is seen to be a practical limit:

> Government and Industry are entitled to expect universities to be innovative and efficient, but repeated annual squeezes of unit cost will not deliver the desired expansion of HE at a quality necessary to face international competition . . . The UK deserves a better policy for expansion than one based on marginal costs.
>
> (Harrison, 1991: 1)

Even the British Government has changed its position. Initially it used output statistics to legitimate its position that more does not mean worse by referring to the increased proportion of first- and upper-second class degrees to justify underfunded expansion (HM Government, 1991; PCFC/UFC, 1992a, para 251; Secretary of State for Education, 1988). According to Kenneth Clarke, then Secretary of State for Education and Science,

> The statistics speak for themselves, with the proportion of graduates in PCFC sector institutions gaining first and upper seconds having risen alongside the surge in student numbers. There are plenty of examples

from HMI to show how increasing numbers need not adversely affect quality – quite the reverse.

(DES, 1991b: 1)

However, the British Government, spurred, amongst others, by employers, professional bodies, and higher education organizations, has required a closer look at standards and asked the HEQC to develop a methodology as part of academic audit to ensure comparability of standards (HEQC, 1995b). Given that audit has a fitness-for-purpose approach to quality assurance mechanisms, it is difficult to see how an absolutist comparability will be accommodated. Furthermore, universal standards are also undermined by the further extension of competition between institutions, encouraging them to find their niche in the 'education market' (Richards, 1992; Rothblatt, 1992).

## Measuring outputs

The Green Paper, *The Development of Higher Education into the 1990s* (DES, 1985) gave notice of a shift towards output indicators. It suggested that external judgements about quality can be attempted by comparing the success of students in obtaining jobs, their relative salaries, and their reported performance in employment, and by reference to the international standing of our academic qualifications in addition to comparative judgements by external agencies.

The concern with outputs in Britain has been focused on the search for institutional and system performance indicators rather than a specific concern with the outcomes of the learning process: that is, on what students know and can do. A considerable amount of innovation in teaching and learning in higher education, backed up by research, had been developed up to the mid-1980s (Entwistle and Ramsden, 1983; Kolb, 1984; Marton, Hounsell, and Entwistle, 1984; Biggs, 1987; Ramsden, 1988). However, this was somehow disassociated from the accountability-based political imperatives despite the White Paper of 1987.

*Higher Education: Meeting the Challenge* (DES, 1987) indicated that academic standards and the quality of teaching in higher education should be judged primarily on the basis of students' achievements. It encouraged development of broader courses in some circumstances and further emphasis on transferable skills and positive attitude to enterprise. To that end, in December 1987, the Enterprise in Higher Education (EHE) initiative was launched by the Secretary of State for Employment with the support of the Secretaries of State for Education and Science, Trade and Industry, Scotland, and Wales. It was originally designed to encourage the 'development of qualities of enterprise' amongst those undertaking higher education courses but there has been a focus on the development of personal skills related to future employment (HMI, 1993), curriculum change and staff development (ED TEED, 1990, 1991; TIHR, 1990) all of which suggest that EHE has a wider rôle as an agent of institutional change (Elton, 1993).

Despite this emphasis on student achievement, output preoccupations have been mainly directed at the search for performance indicators, such as staff : student ratios, ratio of private fees to public funds, the number and mix of enrolled students by level of study and mode of attendance, wastage and completion rates, rather than any meaningful evaluation of student abilities (CVCP/UGC, 1986, 1987a, 1987b, 1988, 1989, 1990; PCFC, 1990c, 1992). Such indicators are used as crude measures of institutional (and programme) *efficiency* (HMI, 1990). Output indicators have, therefore, been used for accountability purposes and directed at a value-for-money notion of quality rather than seriously attempting to address transformation (Yorke, 1995b).

There have been some attempts to construct performance indicators that are pertinent to *learning* outcomes. However, most of these are very crude and tend to be surrogates for measuring teaching quality rather than learning. In the last resort they are based on those things that are already measured or which are easily measurable, such as graduate destinations, wastage rates and degree classifications, but which, at best, provide tenuous indicators of learning and, at worst, are completely misleading (Bourner and Hamed, 1987; Johnes and Taylor, 1990). For example, the balance of subjects in an institution will have a strong bearing on the degree classification profile. Science subjects tend to award a greater percentage of first- and upper-second class degrees (Table 4.2). Similarly, there are significant differences in the employment pattern between different occupations and different employment rates occur in different subject areas at any given time (Porrer, 1984; Brennan and McGeevor, 1988). Measures of value added and student evaluations are the only serious attempts to obtain indicators of learning.

### Value added
Approaches have been developed that attempt to measure the 'value added' to a student. These take into account the abilities of the student when entering higher education and offset some of the criticisms relating to the use of degree classifications as performance indicators.

The most significant research in the United Kingdom in this area was the jointly funded PCFC/CNAA project that evaluated a range of different approaches to calculating value added (CNAA, 1990a). The report advocates a comparative value-added approach. This approach has two stages: the calculation, on the basis of empirical evidence, of the degree classification that a student with a given set of entry qualifications could be expected to achieve, followed by a comparison with the degree classification that they actually achieve. A single score is produced, which is negative if the student achieves less than expected and positive if they achieve more. The size of the positive or negative score is relative to the size of the difference between the actual and anticipated degree classification achieved. Thus a student whose anticipated degree class is a 'third' and whose actual class is a 'first' will achieve a higher score than a student whose anticipated class was a 'third' and whose actual score was a 'lower second'.

*Table 4.2*   Honours graduates awarded first-class or 'good' degrees in universities and polytechnics in the United Kingdom (1971–86)

| Subject | First-class degrees (%) | 'Good' degrees (%) |
| --- | --- | --- |
| Physics | 17 | 45 |
| Computing and maths, physics | 17 | 43 |
| Engineering (general) | 16 | 47 |
| Chemistry | 16 | 45 |
| Chemical engineering | 13 | 46 |
| Aeronautical engineering | 13 | 40 |
| Mechanical engineering | 12 | 42 |
| Electrical engineering | 12 | 41 |
| Mining engineering | 11 | 46 |
| Metallurgy | 11 | 44 |
| Technology (general) | 11 | 44 |
| Industrial engineering | 10 | 47 |
| Art and design | 10 | 47 |
| Civil engineering | 10 | 39 |
| Biology | 8 | 48 |
| Philosophy | 7 | 50 |
| Health studies | 7 | 46 |
| Pharmacy | 7 | 46 |
| English | 7 | 46 |
| Theology | 7 | 43 |
| Combined science | 7 | 37 |
| History | 6 | 50 |
| Modern languages | 6 | 44 |
| Environmental sciences | 6 | 41 |
| Architecture and planning | 6 | 34 |
| Drama | 5 | 47 |
| Music | 5 | 41 |
| Education | 5 | 38 |
| Psychology | 4 | 44 |
| Hotel management, food sciences | 4 | 42 |
| Geography | 4 | 41 |
| Surveying | 4 | 41 |
| Economics | 4 | 35 |
| Law | 4 | 34 |
| Social studies | 3 | 37 |
| Business studies | 3 | 36 |
| Combined arts | 3 | 36 |
| Government and public administration | 2 | 38 |
| Accountancy | 2 | 30 |

*Source*: CNAA Transbinary Database. Based on a reorganization of two tables in Warren Piper (1994: 190).

The report also notes that the positive and negative scores achieved by students can be aggregated to produce a single score for an institution, course or department thus providing a basis for comparison with other similar units.

The approach has been criticized because, although avoiding arbitrary weighting of the inputs, it assumes an interval scale for outcomes – the difference in value between a first and upper second is the same as the difference in value between an unclassified degree and a fail (Gallagher, 1991). This does not preclude the possibility of a suitable weighting of outcomes, or, alternatively that aggregates could not be defined in terms of the ratio of 'better than expected' to 'worse than expected' results.

A second criticism is that it assumes that degree classifications between sectors and between institutions are comparable and there has been some question concerning the validity of that assumption (CVCP, 1986; CNAA/DES, 1989; Cave *et al.*, 1991; Alexander and Morgan, 1992) (see also Table 4.2).

A more fundamental criticism of the value-added approach developed in the United Kingdom concerns the narrow interpretation of what counts as value. What is the value that the degree classification represents? What does degree classification measure? An approach developed in the USA attempts to address these issues. McClain, Krueger and Taylor (1986) describe the Northeast-Missouri State University Value-Added Assessment Program. In this system, the value added to the student is evaluated along three different dimensions: performance in the liberal arts and science component of the programme (usually first two years); performance in affective learning which considers cultural awareness, interpersonal skills, self-esteem, problem-solving and functioning in the larger society; and evaluation of students' performance in the major field of study. Using this system, therefore, the breadth of the learning, transferable skills and specialist subject knowledge are all separately assessed using a range of tests. Similar approaches have been used in other institutions and as part of other research programmes designed to explore value added in the United States (Jacobi, Astin and Ayala, 1987; Pike *et al.*, 1991).

This concurrent approach to value added (Cave *et al.*, 1991), where each student's achievements are assessed at different points in their university careers has been criticized on the grounds that, first, the tests are not of benefit to the students and that they have no incentive to do well. Second, it is questionable whether the tests accurately and validly assess the concepts that they are intended to measure. Third, the system is extremely time-consuming and costly. Fourth, it might encourage 'teaching to the test'. The use of the approach to make inter-institutional comparisons is also questioned as it might lead to a reduction in diversity. Value-added systems of this nature need to take account of the individual missions of institutions (Bauer, 1986; Cave *et al.*, 1991).

Despite the reservations and criticism of various methodologies for value-added, the approach provides one of the few attempts to measure the enhancement side of transformative quality. It is one of the few areas where quality policy comes close to the evaluation of student attributes. However, at the policy level, value added has not seriously been adopted as a system, or as a comparative performance indicator.

### Student evaluations

A significant amount of research into student evaluations of teaching has taken place in the USA where student-feedback questionnaires are widespread and have been in use since the 1930s. Academic staff often raise questions about the validity and reliability of student evaluations of teaching quality. Concerns are expressed that the views of students are influenced by variables unrelated to the quality of teaching, such as, class size, workload, degree of difficulty of the subject and prior student interest in the subject. The development of an instrument for Students' Evaluation of Educational Quality (SEEQ) casts doubt on these concerns, as it has demonstrated that nine evaluation factors (learning; enthusiasm; organization; group interaction; individual rapport; breadth of coverage; examination grading; assessment of students; and workload) are to be found across different academic disciplines and different academic years (Marsh, 1982).

Arguments concerning validity focus on issues such as whether or not there is a correlation between effective student learning and high student evaluations of teaching quality. It has been suggested that students may not be best placed to evaluate teaching quality at the time of study and that they may be able to take a more objective view after they have had the opportunity to apply what they have learned in later study or after graduation. However, research has demonstrated that student evaluations are quite reliable when based on responses of ten students or more and suspected sources of bias in student ratings have little impact. Retrospective ratings by former students agree remarkably well with the evaluations that they made at the end of a course. Similarly, student evaluations correlate moderately well with student learning, as measured by standardized examination, and with affective course consequences, such as application of the subject matter and plans to pursue the subject further. In addition, staff self-evaluations of their own teaching show agreement with student ratings (Murray, 1984). Student evaluations are frequently used as a feedback mechanism to staff in the United States to help them improve their teaching and there is some evidence that they are effective in this (Marsh, 1982).

Although student evaluations can be valuable within institutions it is more debatable whether they can be used to make comparisons between institutions (Cave *et al.*, 1991). Student characteristics are an important potential moderator of the comparative validity of student feedback (Dowell and Neal, 1982). Even where an instrument is developed and provides a useful tool for local policy decisions, the particulars of the student characteristics may render it unsuitable for inter-institutional comparative purposes.

A major problem with typical student evaluations of taught units or even whole programmes is that they tend to be limited to fairly narrow concerns with teaching rather than a wider consideration of the student learning experience.

Research on the use of student evaluations as a performance indicator for comparison between institutions and subject areas has been prompted by the AVCC/ACDP working party on performance indicators in Australia, which advocated that student evaluations of teaching quality should be used as a performance indicator. Paul Ramsden (1991) has attempted to develop a technique for using a student-evaluation questionnaire to provide valid data at the departmental and institutional level. On the basis of his previous research on teaching quality and effective learning, Ramsden argues that there are four characteristics of teaching quality at the departmental level which correlate highly with effective learning by students. The key characteristics are good teaching (clarity of explanation, level at which material is pitched, enthusiasm and help with study problems), freedom in learning, clear goals and standards, and appropriate workload. The Course Experience Questionnaire (CEQ) was designed to measure differences between educational units (departments and faculties) on these factors. Ramsden recognizes that there might be other factors which contribute to teaching quality, such as course design and relevance of content.

Following a national trial, a short form of the CEQ (25 items) is being used as part of a national annual survey of all graduates organized by the Graduate Careers Council of Australia (GCCA). The results of the trial suggest that the instrument is capable of showing the existence of medium to very large differences in perceived teaching quality within the fields of study represented in the trial. However, significant differences were found in average ratings between fields of study on a national basis which 'argues for making any comparisons among institutions within fields and disciplines, rather than across them'. Recurring differences were also found between disciplines within a field of study and the author suggests that caution should be exercised in interpreting differences among institutions across broad fields of study.

From 1995, results of the annual survey were aggregated by field of study and made publicly available. This will enable prospective students to find out how the courses they are thinking of applying for are rated by graduates. There is a commercial *Good Universities Guide* that gives the ratings alongside other information like entry requirements, as well as a universities-sponsored code of practice for interpreting the results.

Despite some initial reluctance, universities are beginning to see the value of the results as evidence of their strengths and for purposes of internal quality assurance and improvement. There is as yet no other satisfactory indicator of university teaching performance available in Australia. 'The evidence from our own studies is that satisfaction with the university experience as a whole is much more strongly related to the CEQ results than to perceptions of facilities and resources' (Ramsden, 1995: 1).

Ramsden indicates some difficulties in using CEQ as a performance indicator for reporting to funding bodies. He points out that performance on different scales could be combined to produce a single average score thus making inter-institutional comparisons easier, but questions the validity of so doing when the interrelations among the scales are small. He also questions the appropriateness of using CEQ mean scores to rank units as the data would be norm-referenced and therefore say nothing about whether a unit is good or bad but only whether or not it is better or worse than another unit. He therefore recommends the use of absolute data as well as norm-referenced data.

The student evaluations so far reported concentrate mainly on the quality of teaching in terms of the lecturer's interaction with the students. The Student Satisfaction Approach at the University of Central England (UCE) in Birmingham, introduced in Chapter 2, takes a broader view, linking satisfaction to the student learning experience and basing the research instrument on the expressed views of students during focus-group discussions. All areas that impact on student learning are included, ranging from teaching, through the provision of learning resources, to accommodation, cafeterias and financial circumstances.

The aim of the research is to produce indicators that will help the institution measure, and thereby improve, the quality of the student experience. Indeed, the survey is embedded in a top-down accountability process that identifies responsibility for action to address student concerns. Nonetheless, despite its very important role in quality assurance within the institution it is doubtful whether it could be the basis of inter-institutional comparisons. The very nature of the process inhibits such comparability (Green, 1990; Harvey *et al.*, 1995). Each year students identify the key elements of their learning experience and the research instrument changes and evolves over time. The main concerns in one institution are not necessarily the same as in another. There are, it is true, a core of items that change little over time and between institutions, but simply to adopt these as the basis for inter-institutional comparisons would probably result in the omission of major areas of impact on the student learning experience at the local level.

Crucially, the issue is not one of identifying statistical indicators that measure performance, but of providing insights into student perceptions that are used to initiate specific institutional, faculty or programme-level initiatives to improve on provision. Student Satisfaction at UCE is a process that is locked into attempting to enhance the transformative learning experience.

The benefits of using student evaluations as a performance indicator is that they are a direct measure of teaching quality, and, in some cases, of student learning. The validity and reliability of student evaluations have been shown to be quite high. There are difficulties, however, in adopting them as performance indicators for inter-institutional comparisons because they are rarely universal, that is to say that they vary depending on the character of the subject being studied, the character of the institution and so on. Although some countries, such as Australia, are pressing ahead with identifying performance indicators that can be linked to funding, quantitative indicators do not figure prominently in Britain. In 1990, a comparison of Britain and Netherlands, suggested that, after 1985, Dutch higher education emphasized peer judgements while performance indicators appeared to dominate British quality assurance (Goedegebuure, Maassen, and Westerheijden, 1990). The situation no longer applies, although the image seems hard to shake off on the international stage (Murphy, 1994). The critical determinant of British funding allocations is performance against contract. In England, money is allocated on the basis of type of student, mode of study and subject area, modified by historical circumstances, efficiency gains, and so on. Higher education institutions contract to deliver student numbers in various categories and failure results in a clawback of funds by HEFCE. Performance indicators are not used in this process, although they are used by the National Audit Office to monitor the financial health of each institution.

Indeed, in the development of quality monitoring in Britain, there has been a tendency to shift away from *performance indicators* and instead place far more emphasis on a process of audit and assessment in which a variety of statistical indicators is taken into account in more or less rigorous ways by peer review groups assessing research quality, teaching quality or the effectiveness of quality assurance mechanisms (see Chapter 5).

## Conclusion

Higher education policy since the mid-1980s has increasingly been concerned with accountability and value-for-money as the sector has expanded. The notion of 'quality' has been employed as a vehicle to legitimate a policy of steadily reducing unit of resource and increasing centralized control. Quality, as value-for-money or as fitness-for-purpose is rooted in a 'philosophy' that asserts that the economy cannot support the full cost of expansion in higher education, while at the same time arguing that higher education is a central element in the future competitiveness of the economy in the world market.

Although 'quality' crept on to the British political agenda for higher education in the middle of the 1980s, initial concerns about universities were dominated by issues of efficiency, effectiveness and the maintenance of standards. Slowly, a focus on outputs rather than inputs came to dominate policy. With the rapid increase in higher education the emphasis was placed firmly on accountability and value for money. A concern with outputs became ever more prominent with the search for sector and institutional performance indicators. However, little attempt was made to develop performance indicators of student learning, and those that might appear to relate to learning are tenuous. It was left to institutions to develop a transformative, improvement orientation to institutional, learning-related performance indicators, such as the Student Satisfaction approach at UCE.

In essence, in Britain, as in many other countries, the primary concern has been with accountability rather than improvement. At root, quality policy has not addressed transformative learning. It has been preoccupied with other notions of quality, such as value for money and fitness for purpose, which, as we suggested in Chapter 1, are insubstantial operationalizations of transformative quality.

We have concentrated in this chapter mainly on the impact of quality policy on the development of an educated work force. However, references to the impact of policy on research show a corresponding process. The Research Assessment Exercise and the growing centralized control of the research councils are indicative of the short-term, value-for-money, pragmatic approach to research funding dressed up as rewards for excellence. There is a dearth of evidence for any long-term support for research that could really underpin Britain's economic recovery.

There is little to suggest that current policy on research in higher education has much to do with developing a transformative research culture. While the Research Assessment Exercise has required clearer accountability there is little to suggest that it has palpably improved research output. Results of research into the impact of the Research Assessment Exercise are due as this book goes to press. Initial impressions and anecdotal evidence suggest that rather than a transformative research culture, government policy has encouraged a compliance culture that has produced an over-reporting of underdeveloped research, with little transformative potential. Furthermore, there is a suggestion that it has a negative impact on teaching and learning (Jenkins, 1995a). Similar concerns occupy UNESCO:

> Emphasis on short-term gains and the pressure of budgetary constraints can lead to serious long-term consequences for higher education institutions as the proper seats for the advancement of knowledge and the training of future scientists and industrial researchers. Research departments in higher education institutions, although costly, are a crucial source of skills and ideas in the context of the global economy based on knowledge and constant technological change. The best way to make the general public, government bodies and economic organization aware of the role of research in higher education is to demonstrate, through convincing results, the scholarly quality, economic value, humanistic perspective and cultural relevance of research and the related study programmes and teaching.
>
> (UNESCO, 1995: 29, para 81)

In Chapter 5 we explore the extent to which external quality monitoring, an increasingly worldwide phenomenon, has become the focal point for quality policy in the mid-1990s and the extent to which it has become a vehicle for linking quality and accountability to improvement of the student learning experience.

## Note

1. For example, value for money for research funding is often based on peer assessment of the 'worth' of the research. This is the case in Britain where expert panels assess the research output of all the universities receiving government research funding. Panels rate the research on a scale of excellence, which directly informs funding allocations. In this case, value for money is mediated by

an exceptional notion of quality. In the case of teaching and learning, 'excellence' often serve as the basis of accountability assessments as it does, for example, in Australia. In other countries, such as Britain, value-for-money accountability is mediated by mission-related fitness-for-purpose.

# 5

# External Quality Monitoring

External quality monitoring (EQM) has grown rapidly and has become a significant factor in higher education systems around the world. The International Network of Quality Assurance Agencies in Higher Education has members in over 40 countries, and the number continues to grow each year. EQM is a feature of all types of higher education systems, including: 'market systems' such as the USA and the Philippines; 'semi-market' systems such as Taiwan and Brazil; centralized systems such as China; newly-devolved systems such as those in Eastern Europe, the Baltic States and Scandinavia; the 'Continental model' of 'centralized autonomy' found in much of Western Europe including Italy, France and Austria; and the 'British model' of autonomy also found throughout much of the Commonwealth.

The organization, degree of government control, extent of devolved responsibility and funding of higher education systems vary considerably from one country to the next. However, the rapid changes taking place in higher education are tending to lead to a convergence towards a dominant model of delegated accountability. Central to this process is the emphasis placed on quality as a vehicle for delivering policy requirements within available resources. As we have seen in Chapters 3 and 4, this means making higher education more relevant to social and economic needs, widening access, expanding numbers and doing it, except in some Pacific Rim countries (e.g. Cheong, 1993), with a decreasing unit cost.

EQM plays a crucial role in the process as it provides both a vehicle for accountability and a means to reassure external stakeholders, such as employers, professional bodies and the general public. In short, EQM is the operational mechanism through which 'quality' is used to legitimate policy.

## The nature of EQM

EQM is an all-encompassing term that covers a variety of quality-related evaluations undertaken by bodies or individuals external to higher education institutions. It includes the following.

- External quality audit of internal quality assurance procedures, such as the academic audits of institutions undertaken by the Quality Audit

Division of the Higher Education Quality Council in Britain (HEQC DQA, 1993a). Institutional audit is a process designed to assess the extent, adequacy or effectiveness of quality assurance procedures within institutions. There is no attempt to assess the quality of the institution, just to ensure that the institution has clearly defined internal quality monitoring procedures that ensure effective action.

- External evaluation of institutional status, such as the assessment undertaken by the Consejo Nacional de Univeridades in Venezuala, which evaluates and grants licences to new, experimental higher education institutions and continues to evaluate them until they attain full autonomy (Ayarza, 1993).

- Accreditation of courses or institutions as used, for example, in North America. Accreditation in the USA is a self-regulatory process by which non-governmental voluntary associations recognize institutions or programmes that have been found to meet stated criteria of quality (Adelman and Silver, 1990). At least 14 accrediting bodies now operate simultaneously in the USA and Canada (Peace Lenn, 1995; Petersen, 1995), although in the USA discussion continues about the future of these accrediting bodies (NPB, 1994; PWGA, 1995).

- External assessment of institutional provision, such as that undertaken by the Comité National d'Évaluation (CNE), in France, which evaluates each institution holistically (Staropoli, 1991; Ribier, 1995), or by the Australian Committee for Quality Assurance in Higher Education (CQAHE) whose function is to examine quality assurance portfolios volunteered by universities and to make recommendations about additional incentive funding (Meade, 1993). Subsequent rounds of the Australian approach have focused on specific elements, such as teaching, research performance or community interaction.

- External evaluations of teaching and learning provision at a programme or subject level, such as the assessment of subject area provision undertaken by the Quality Assessment Division of the Higher Education Funding Council for England (HEFCE, 1994a) or the evaluations undertaken by the independent Centre for Quality Assurance and Evaluation of Higher Education in Denmark (Thune, 1993).

- Evaluation and appraisal of research, such as the Research Assessment Exercise conducted by the Funding Councils in Britain (HEFCE/SHEFC/ HEFCW, 1993), research evaluations undertaken by the Academy of Finland since the early 1980s (Luukkonen and Ståhle, 1990) and the recent Lithuanian evaluation of research performance (Mockiene and Vengris, 1995).

- Evaluations of community interaction and impact on the local economy, such as the element included in the third round of the Australian quality assessment programme.

- Accreditation and validation of programmes of study, such as those undertaken in some countries by professional and regulatory bodies, for example, the accreditation of medical education undertaken by the General Medical Council in Britain (Harvey and Mason, 1995) and the pilot departmental evaluations undertaken by professional associations in Taiwan (Su, 1995).

- External examination of students, such as the use of external examiners to monitor standards on British undergraduate degrees (Silver, 1993; Warren Piper, 1994). External examiners are also used in Denmark, Ireland and several Commonwealth counties including New Zealand, Malaysia, Brunei, India, Malawi, Hong Kong and in the technikons in South Africa. Several of these countries make considerable use of overseas examiners.

In the following section we explore the evolving, dominant approach to EQM. This approach, we suggest, is predominantly accountability-led and consigns quality improvement to a secondary role. We explore the extent to which the dominant approach to EQM addresses transformative learning.

## Dominant approach to EQM

International economic imperatives, including competitiveness, mobility of labour, rapidly changing technology and so on, have come to exercise a major influence on higher education systems (see Chapter 3). In many countries, higher education systems have been subjected to extensive and continuous reform and upheaval since the 1980s (Gungwu, 1992; Green and Harvey, 1993; Girdwood, 1995). As part of that process, systems of EQM have been introduced and these have been adapted and modified in response to:

- changing government policy;
- the cost of the system of EQM, both in terms of percentage of the higher education budget and of the burden placed on academic staff and institutional managers;
- the scope and focus of EQM – there is an ongoing debate between stakeholders about the merits of detailed examinations of programme provision and broader institutional overviews;
- shifts in ownership and control of EQM;
- a shift from quantitative indicators to qualitative evaluations, in part reflecting a growing awareness of the need for EQM to place higher priority on improvement.

The development of most EQM systems has been as a result of a pragmatic response to government mandates. They have often been rushed and usually concerned with short-term political imperatives. The result is thus a situation of flux as systems adapt and respond. It thus makes it difficult, and to some extent fruitless, to attempt to specify the detail of any one system, as it becomes outdated very rapidly. However, within this fluid situation, some common themes emerge, suggesting a convergence to a dominant accountability-led approach.

*Figure 5.1* Convergence to accountable autonomy

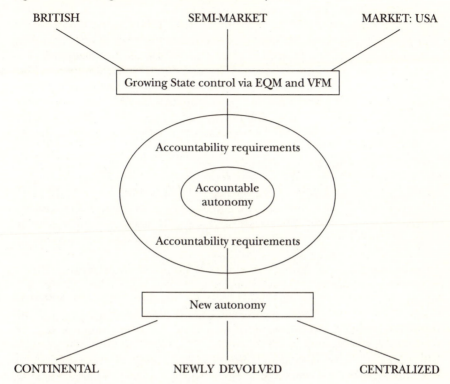

# EQM and academic autonomy

At the risk of oversimplification in the introduction to this chapter we identified six broad types of higher education system. This is a further breakdown of the 'traditional' tripartite model of 'American', 'British' and 'Continental' systems (Clark, 1983). Faced with rapid change, any such classification will become dated and, indeed, recent research has suggested that there is less differentiation in such things as institutional governance than the tripartite model implies (De Boer and Goedegebuure, 1995).

What appears to be happening is a convergence, from very different starting points, to a dominant form of accountable autonomy (Figure 5.1). The systems that have traditionally espoused a market approach (Gorospe, 1995) and those that have been influenced by the traditional British system of autonomous institutions supported by the State are finding their autonomy being eroded by government-backed requirements to demonstrate accountability and value for money (Bauer and Kogan, 1995).

In New Zealand, for example, with a tradition of strong university autonomy, there is now a requirement for higher education institutions to define objectives that are approved by the Ministry of Education (Ministry of Education, 1991). Similarly, in Australia, financial stringency has been used to legitimate the requirement placed on universities to develop quality assurance procedures to provide accountability for public funds (Commonwealth of Australia, 1991; Baldwin, 1992; NBEET HEC, 1992).

Where central control was, or continues to be, exerted over higher education, for example in Eastern Europe, South America and Scandinavia as well as China,[1] there is increasing delegated responsibility for quality, but at the price of being required to be accountable and open to scrutiny.

Austria is a prime example of the Continental model, in which a high level of legal control and regulation by the Ministry of Science and Research results in weak institutional autonomy with little opportunity for local governance. The resulting conformity of the system of higher education makes it unnecessary to evaluate outcomes at either the system or institutional level. However, since 1991, reform of the Austrian system has increased autonomy for institutions with the development of managerial bodies to make decisions. Yet, deregulation and diversification have required new types of quality assurance, especially assessment of outcomes, which are being encouraged by the Ministry with a heavy emphasis on self-evaluation (Pechar, 1993).

The same principle underpinned the introduction of quality monitoring in Netherlands, one of the first countries to develop a procedure for external quality monitoring (Ministry for Education and Science, 1985). Higher education institutions secured greater autonomy but committed themselves, in agreement with the Minister of Education, to take certain actions in order to assure the quality of education. 'The philosophy is that national policy aimed at increasing the autonomy of the institutes implies – of course – a duty to answer to society in general' (van Schaik and Köllen, 1995: 7). About the same time, Finnish universities were given more autonomy in return for increased accountability (CoSD, 1986).

In Romania, since the revolution, university autonomy has been the central principle in the governance of higher education institutions. However, the trade-off for academic autonomy is the acceptance of external evaluation mechanisms. The Accreditation and Recognition of Diplomas Act, which came into force in January 1994, specified the aims of accreditation and academic evaluation, including encouraging institutions to develop their own mission-based performance evaluation mechanisms, 'protecting the community from institutions that do not have the capacity to fulfill their public commitments' and providing the community with 'information on the capacity and performance' of various institutions. Although the intention is not to use the public financing of universities as an excuse for restricting the administrative autonomy of universities, financial autonomy requires overall public accountability.

> To protect the population and to assure it of quality educational services, as well as provide the Ministry of Education with criteria for the allocation of funds, a complex system of accreditation and academic evaluation needs to be set in motion.
>
> (Ifrim, 1995: 14)

A similar process can be observed in the Argentine. The Law for Higher Education, approved by the National Congress on 20 July 1995, guarantees university autonomy including freedom to decide about their own government, create undergraduate and graduate programmes and to set the profile and scope of their degrees. The corollary of this is the establishment of a process of internal and external quality monitoring to be overseen by the National Commission for University Assessment and Accreditation (NCUAA), a state organization, autonomous and independent from government.

## Methodology of the dominant model

The convergence to accountable autonomy is reflected in the commonality of EQM methodology. Although there are differences in the focus of evaluations and status of the EQM agencies the methodology incorporates various combinations of three basic elements (Green and Harvey, 1993; Frazer, 1995):

- a self-assessment;
- peer evaluation, normally in the shape of an institutional visit;
- statistical or performance indicators.

The emphasis is on the self-critical academic community rather than direct external inspection of provision. In those countries where a new accountable autonomy is being granted, self-assessment is seen as indicative of the shift to self-governance. In those countries where universities have traditionally been autonomous, self-evaluation is seen as not only politically pragmatic but a necessary vehicle to ensure the institution focuses its attention on quality issues.

A process of self-evaluation 'checked' by peer review in one way or another is the norm in countries as diverse as the USA, the Argentine, Brazil, Mexico, Britain, Netherlands, Norway, Portugal, Australia, South Africa and China. In most countries self-evaluation, while guided by an indicative framework, is mediated by reference to the 'mission' of the institution, to allow for diversity within the system. Peer review usually includes a 'visit' by a group of 'respected' academic peers to the institution being evaluated. Most countries outside the British Isles do not include direct observation of the teaching situation as part of peer evaluation.

Performance or statistical indicators play a role in quality monitoring methodologies, and some countries such as Australia are working on developing new indicators. In other countries, the advent of EQM has resulted in a de-emphasis of quantitative indicators. In England, for example, performance indicators were expected to play a significant role in the subject assessment methodology. As the methodology was piloted, and subsequently amended, the quantitative indicators were reduced in importance and became re-labelled as 'statistical indicators'. Although each published report is prefaced by a statement that 'the assessment derives from an analysis of the institution's self-assessment, informed by statistical indicators . . .' there is little reference to statistical indicators in the text. Those that are mentioned tend to relate to the increase in student numbers and the percentage of 'good degrees'. Typical is the following:

> The number of students joining the history programme has increased by 28 per cent between 1988 and 1992 . . . Mature student numbers have risen significantly to 27 per cent in 1992, fulfilling history's commitment to widening access . . . Degree results, notably in single-subject history, showed an increasing preponderance of First class and Upper Second class degrees, in line with similar institutions in the UK.
>
> (HEFCE, 1994b: 4–5)

In Wales too, assessment of overall quality is supposed to have regard to a number of indicators including experience and qualifications of students on entry, completion rates and qualifications achieved, use of resources and staff development. However, these quantitative indicators have only a support role as the Funding Council recognizes that 'their relevance is in the extent to which they impact, directly or indirectly, on the quality of the learning environment experienced by students' (HEFCW, 1994: para 33).

A similar shift to qualitative assessments based on peer reviews is also taking place in other countries. In Tennessee, for example, the first State to develop a process of accountability-based external monitoring, there has been a marked shift away from broad quantitative performance indicators to qualitative assessments. The Tennessee Higher Education Commission (THEC) has, since 1979, been prescriptive in using quantitative indicators, including numerical ratings of satisfaction, as a basis for allocating up to 5 per cent of institutional budgets. What is noticeable is that, with each of its four iterations of assessment criteria, crude quantitative indicators have gradually become replaced by qualitative, peer-review evaluations. Furthermore, the qualitative indicators are far more acceptable to academics than performance indicators or standardized tests of students (Banta, 1995).

## Openness and explicitness

There is also a growing openness and explicitness about quality and standards in higher education. This is evident in the increased transparency of provision within institutions on the one hand and in the openness of the evaluation procedures and outcomes on the other. EQM has been a major force in encouraging higher education to specify institutional 'missions' and programme aims and objectives (Mercaddo del Collado, 1993; Ifrim, 1995). Similarly, course content, student assignments and programme outcomes have been made explicit as a result of EQM, often for the first time. Likewise, EQM can lead to an increased sensitivity towards teaching and learning methods (Chan and Sensicle, 1995).

Most, if not all countries, have open EQM procedures: the methodology and criteria on which evaluations and assessments are based are available to those being evaluated. However, there is less consistency about the dissemination of outcomes. Publication of EQM outcomes varies from limited circulation 'confidential' papers to full, publicly available documents, as, for example, in France, Denmark and Britain. Sometimes publication is accompanied, as in Korea, by high-profile announcements in the mass media about the quality assessment outcomes. The focus of the publication also varies. Sometimes publications refer to single institutions, as in the case of the HEQC Quality Audit Reports, or even to single programmes or to subject areas or to research programmes within an institution, as with the Quality Assessment Reports in England. In other cases, composite documents are published which summarize cross-sector or cross-discipline outcomes of EQM.

Publication is assumed to be in the interests of accountability. Publication of evaluation reports supposedly ensures that the sense of accountability of higher education institutions towards society will increase (Ifrim, 1995). Publication also provides external stakeholders, such as professional bodies and employers, with information about programmes or institutions. For example, the Central Council for the Education and Training of Social Workers in Britain 'receives all external quality monitoring reports and requires its own staff to comment upon them' (Harvey and Mason, 1995: 44).

Publication also, supposedly, provides potential students (and their parents) with information on which to base choices. However, it is questionable whether potential students assiduously scrutinize quality monitoring reports. There is little evidence that applicants to courses read quality assessment reports in Britain, nor is there evidence that they read institutional quality audit reports. There are, realistically, only two ways that potential students encounter information from external quality monitoring reports. First, those parts selectively quoted in institutional prospectuses and other recruitment publicity, and second, those parts taken out of context and used to construct league tables, charts or 'good university guides'. While this repackaging of the information makes it generally more accessible, it is often fraught with dangers of interpretation and is usually devoid of 'health warnings'.

Publication of comparative data has been seen as a major plank of quality *improvement* within an accountability-led approach. Where the focus is on review of what is provided, rather than on building enabling processes into EQM, the only way to encourage any improvement or to disseminate good practice seems to be to make monitoring outcomes public. The consumerist argument is that prospective 'customers' have the right to comparative information on which to base their choices and customer demand will expedite change.

In Australia, for example, publication linked to league tables is seen as a major incentive to universities. 'When we started out, money was the big incentive. But after the first report, some institutions would have been happy to give the money up if they could have got into group one' (Wilson, in Maslen, 1995: 8). However, this process is not fundamentally about improvement but about status. The quality programme is perceived as relating to the prestige of institutions and has little if anything to do with the total learning experience of students.

> Suddenly, where a university was on the ladder counted for a great deal. And it was not just parochial prestige, either. International reputations were at stake, not to mention the prospect of overseas students taking their fees elsewhere.
>
> (Maslen, 1995: 8)

The view that publication provides a spur to quality improvement is resisted on the grounds that comparisons are neither meaningful nor likely to aid a process of continuous quality improvement. In Ontario, for example, the evaluation reports of graduate programmes have been kept confidential to encourage an improvement process and only the final summative judgements were published to inform funding decisions (Filteau, 1993). Institutions in Ontario expressly opposed rankings on the grounds that they drive institutions to conformity and homogeneity rather than promote improvement of quality in the context of diversity, a view shared by critics in Australia (Massaro, 1995). The principle in Ontario is that universities are autonomous institutions, that autonomy is necessary to their functioning and that confidentiality respects that autonomy.

Publication of reports, especially if linked to league tables, is seen to have an intimidating effect (van Vught, 1991; OCUA, 1992). The standard argument in favour of confidential proceedings is that self-evaluations will be more honest and critical. However, for some, openness is:

> a cardinal point in regard to the overall target of making evaluation the platform for qualified knowledge of the merits of various study programmes. The Danish Centre for Quality Assurance and Evaluation of Higher Education has therefore decided that procedures and methods must be known and all report findings published or made available.
>
> (Thune, 1995: 12)

## Linking EQM to funding

Linking quality assessment to funding has been an area that has caused considerable debate and one where there appears to be a rift in the dominant approach with some countries making a direct link between EQM and funding and others proposing, at most, an indirect relationship. Britain and Australia make some more or less direct link between EQM outcomes and funding as do several states in the USA, including Tennessee, Kentucky, South Carolina, Texas, Arkansas and New Mexico.

A funding link is seen as necessary if EQM is to have any direct impact on the quality of provision, since funding is the single motivating factor to which institutions will respond. On a negative note, the 'accountability-led' view of quality improvement is dependent on the effectiveness of a funding sanction.[2] Without a funding link, evaluations are seen to have no 'teeth'

(Filteau, 1993: 14). The link tends to reward excellence and in some cases withdraw funding from 'unsatisfactory' or 'poor' provision. No attempt is made to redirect resources to enhance inadequate provision.

In Australia, the injection by the government of a significant amount of money (Aus$70 million per year), contingent on EQM ratings, has supposedly generated considerable change. There is a view that the quality initiative has given the reformers in Australian institutions the support to undertake activities and initiate changes that the previous inertia had made it difficult to do (Baldwin, 1995; Maslen, 1995; Massaro, 1995).

The direct linking of funding to quality may have an impact on institutional management, particularly with increasing delegated responsibility. However, it is likely to have much less of an impact on academic staff, and subsequently on the quality and nature of teaching and research. The funding link would need to be substantial and highly correlated with quality ratings if there were to be any notable effects. The close link, in Britain, for example, between research ratings and funding has led to a major reappraisal by staff of their research practices and output. A quality premium of between 2 and 5 per cent for subject areas rated excellent in teaching is unlikely to have the same motivation. The impact of the funding carrot or stick is thus likely to be marginal in relation to teaching and learning at the point where it really matters – the staff–student interface.

However, even if the link is substantial, as in the case of some research funding methodologies, this does not mean that the *quality* of the research improves. On the contrary, what improves is matching of research to the criteria of assessment. More papers published, more funding attracted, and more postgraduate students completing do not mean better quality, or more useful output. The monitoring and funding methodology determines what is proposed as 'good quality research'. The shift to a research compliance culture in Britain has been rapid and marked. For example, in many engineering departments staff are expected to meet publication and income targets (such as three overseas journal papers and £40,000 per year) in preference to the 'rapid and timely exchange of scholarly output provided by the conference': an approach that is destined to 'encourage piecemeal research' and 'to discourage the theoretical researcher' who has modest income and research requirements (Fidler, 1993: 14).

Many countries have avoided linking quality monitoring directly to funding. There is no direct link, for example, between evaluation and the level of funding in Denmark, Sweden, Netherlands, Portugal or Brazil. In France quality assessment by the Comité National d'Evaluation (CNE) is only indirectly linked to funding (Staropoli, 1991). However, in some cases, the absence of a direct link can be misleading. In the Argentine, for example, there is no proposed direct link between quality monitoring and funding: indeed, it has been forcefully opposed (Lobo, 1993). However, a *de facto* link is being made by linking quality to funded development projects through the Fund for the Improvement of University Quality (FIUQ) a World Bank-backed initiative. Resources of the FIUQ will be allocated by taking into account academic quality, using such indicators as faculty qualifications and publications, internal efficiency and the outcome of peer review (Marquis, 1995).

The objection to a direct link is that it inhibits the external quality monitoring process. A direct link is seen as threatening and unlikely to result in a meaningful evaluation of provision (Engwall, 1995). For example, a threat of withdrawal of funds tends to lead to an excessive concern with the nature and justification of the monitoring methodology rather than to encourage a focus on improvement. Widespread objections about the academic and pedagogic arbitrariness of EQM occur. Furthermore, the methodology of EQM has to fit in with the funding allocation procedures: if there is no congruence between the funding methodology and the monitoring methodology the translation of monitoring results into funding allocations becomes mechanistically and administratively arbitrary. In addition, given that quality assessment 'has in most cases been better suited to a type of education which continues the traditional approach from the nineteenth century' (Debrock, 1995) linkage to funding would seem to be unfair and to disadvantage innovative institutions.

A direct link between funding and quality has also been resisted in most countries because it is likely to lead to the emergence of a 'compliance culture' (van Vucht, 1992; van Vucht and Westerheijden, 1992). This will be exacerbated if the burden placed on staff by external quality agencies is heavy. Far more time may be spent addressing how to deal with the external monitoring process than will be spent on quality improvement within the institution (Vroeijenstijn, 1995).

Arguably, compliance is exactly what is wanted, whether by autonomous or financially-coerced means. Nevertheless, the issue is not one of compliance but of the educational philosophy to which institutions are complying (Middlehurst and Woodhouse, 1995). The issue, then, is not whether quality should be linked to funding but whether funding can be used as an incentive to improve the student learning experience or whether the link acts merely to ensure that institutions conform to accountability requirements.

## The burden of quality assurance

A related issue to those of method and publication is the growing burden that increased accountability places on institutions and the staff who work in them. Britain, arguably, has the most burdensome approach to EQM with multiple layers of audit, assessment, accreditation and external examining (Harvey, 1994a) (Table 5.1). The burden imposed by just one of these agencies, the English funding council, became a focus of a debate in the House of Lords inaugurated by Lord Annan:

> My Lords, I beg leave to ask the Question standing in my name on the Order Paper because the Government have inflicted four bureaucratic burdens upon the universities during the past three years. The Higher Education Funding Council requires universities to create mechanisms for ensuring the quality of teaching. The Council next requires a quite

separate assessment by another quango of the quality of each subject taught. Thirdly, it requires the quality of research in each department to be assessed. Finally, it requires the costs of such research to be calculated in what one can only call a grotesquely complicated way . . . Why has this inquiry and the three others been forced on the universities? I am sure the Government will reply that since student numbers have risen so dramatically universities need to develop new techniques for teaching . . . But there is a larger and more tragic reason why the Government have imposed these new burdens. During the past five years the Government have shown that they do not trust the universities to teach or research.

(Annan, 1993)

Britain is not alone in placing enormous quality monitoring burdens on universities. A similar, but even less co-ordinated process is going on in Spain. In the academic year 1993–4, for example, the University of Zaragoza, was part of the self-evaluation programme of Spanish universities promoted by the National University Council, was involved in the evaluation project on the quality of management within the Programme of European Cohesion, was evaluated by an external consulting group ordered by the Social Council in relation to the development of a strategic plan for new studies, had its veterinary faculty inspected by a group of experts appointed by the European Community and undertook internal monitoring, including annual teaching evaluation by students, voluntary evaluation of teaching and research and evaluations done by deans and directors of centres (Escudero, 1995).

At a time of declining resources it is important to get the balance right between the demands on academic staff to respond to external quality monitoring (including being involved as peer reviewers) and the need to invest in continuous improvement of the quality of the student experience, through staff development, innovation in teaching and learning, research and scholarship. The problem becomes potentially greater as higher education becomes increasingly international in scope. One nightmare scenario involves universities being confronted with external scrutiny by teams not only from five or six domestic stakeholders, but also from their European and international counterparts (Green, 1993).

## Accountability, improvement and transformative learning

In Chapter 4 we showed that quality policy is dominated by accountability concerns. We argued that this accountability orientation overlooks the transformative process of learning. We have also suggested that there is a tension between accountability and continuous quality improvement (Vroeijenstijn and Acherman, 1990). This tension is clearly evident in external quality monitoring arrangements. Accountability is about value for money and fitness for purpose and sees quality in those terms. Continuous

Table 5.1 Quality monitoring and improvement mechanisms in Britain

| Level | Type | Responsibility | Focus |
|---|---|---|---|
| External | Teaching quality assessment | HEFCs QACs | Cognate subject area |
| | Research assessment exercise | HEFCs | Subject areas |
| | Professional accreditation | External professional body | Profession |
| | Quality audit of assurance systems | HEQC | Institution-wide (audit trails) |
| | External examiner system | HE Institution | Course/programme of study: assessment |
| | Judicial review | Legal system | Student assessment or complaint |
| Internal – institution/ faculty | Staff appraisal and/or development | Institution or faculties, Educational Development Unit | Individual, research, teaching, job-related |
| | Teaching evaluation | Institution (using peers or 'inspectors') | Assessment of teaching ability |
| | Institutional audits | Quality Assurance Unit | Library, examiners, placement assessment, etc. |
| | Complaints procedure | Senate subcommittee | Harassment, unfair treatment, etc. |
| | Appeals procedure | Senate subcommittee | Student assessment: procedures, medical grounds |
| | Student feedback/satisfaction | Student Satisfaction Unit/Quality Assurance Unit | Institution-wide student views |
| | Student representation | Student Union | Representatives on Senate etc. |
| Internal – course/ programme | Annual course review | Course director/lecturers | Overview/self-assessment of the course |
| | Formal student feedback | CD/lecturers/students | Questionnaires (course or unit); evaluation session |

| | | |
|---|---|---|
| Course audits | Quality Assurance Unit | Institutional monitoring of course quality |
| External examiner reports | External examiner | Course content, student performance, arrangements for examining |
| Student representation | Elected students | Representatives on Boards of Study, etc. |
| Course committees – Board of Studies, etc. | Staff (+ student reps) | Administration and overview of course |
| Course meetings | Student group | Overview of course |
| Informal feedback | Individual/group of students | Direct feedback on unit, in sessions or in private |
| Assessment appeals procedures | Individual student | Second/third opinion (informal, formal) |
| Personal tutor system | Tutor and student | First-line support and guidance system |
| Unofficial course guides | Students' Union | Alternative view to that in university prospectus, etc. |

improvement in teaching and learning is about enhancement of the student experience, empowering students as life-long learners.

The accountability-led view sees improvement as a secondary function of the monitoring process. Such an approach argues that a process of external monitoring of quality, ostensibly for purposes of accountability, is likely to lead to improvement as a side effect. Requiring accountability, it is assumed, will lead to a review of practices, which in turn will result in improvement. We suggest that this is a mistaken presupposition for three reasons.

First, it is likely that, faced with a monitoring system that demands accountability, academics will comply with requirements in such a way as to minimize disruption to their existing academic practices.

Second, where accountability requires the production of strategic plans, clear objectives, quality assurance systems, and so on, then there may be an initial impetus towards quality improvement. However, there is considerable doubt whether there will be any sustained momentum as a result of this initial push. Accountability systems, in short, are unlikely to lead to a process of *continuous* quality improvement.

Third, accountability approaches tend to demotivate staff who are already involved in innovation and quality initiatives. Not only do they face the added burden of responding to external scrutiny there is also a feeling of being manipulated, of not being trusted or valued, by managers and outside agencies (Harvey, 1994b).

In short, accountability approaches to EQM are indicative of managerialism. Collegialism is distrusted. EQM becomes a top-down control mechanism, which places responsibility for quality in the hands of institutional managers, rather than those at the student–staff interface who can deliver improvement.

In turn, academic staff distrust the EQM process, which they see as a managerialist ploy, either threatening their job or requiring increased productivity without increased resources (Amaral, 1995). The following view from South America could just have easily been voiced in any other part of the world:

> Higher academic authorities and high-level professors seem to be more convinced as to the need for and usefulness of establishing some sort of evaluatory process, than most university teachers. The latter generally view these processes as mechanisms for controlling people (at a risk to their academic careers or their tenure), rather than as elements contributing to a better understanding of an institution's shortcomings and strengths.
>
> (Ayarza, 1993)

The accountability-led approach to EQM implies that staff will only address quality issues if they are coerced into doing so. The bureaucratic top-down quality monitoring process is a response to the perceived cloisterism in higher education. The implicit argument is that external scrutiny forces institutional managers and teaching staff to review existing practices and procedures. Such a review will, it is presumed, focus attention on shortcomings, open debates about the nature of teaching and learning, encourage systematic and receptive assessment of views of students and employers, and so on. Indeed, proponents of the accountability-led approach argue that, without the pressure of an external monitoring process, it is unlikely that any substantial and rapid innovation will ever take place in higher education, given the conservatism embedded in academic autonomy.

Much of the evidence about the impact of EQM is anecdotal, which is not surprising given that it is a relatively new phenomenon and that 'impact', itself, is a 'deceitful concept' (Saarinen, 1995). In Spain, for example, 'evaluation fever' is seen as having 'developed too quickly, too anxiously, making sometimes too much noise, but showing less effectiveness than expected' (Escudero, 1995). In the United States, with a longer history of evaluation, informed commentators have suggested that the impact is only peripheral (Marchese, 1989).

The limited research evidence suggests that EQM has provided an initial impetus to change, but that it offers little by way of continuing momentum. In the Netherlands, for example, the Inspectorate are of the view that the institutes pay attention to the quality of education in a more systematic and structural way than they did before a systematic process of EQM was established (IHO, 1992). At the institutional level the procedures for gathering information are more formal and there are more systematic procedures for discussion and decision-making about programmes, organization, and so on. However, although quality is clearly on the agenda of institutions, it is difficult to find a linear relation between recommendations made by the visitation committees and measures taken by the institutes (Frederiks, Westerheijden and Weusthof, 1993; Ackerman, 1995). In a similar vein, the Inspectorate concludes that institutes, in general, still have problems with the formulation and realization of consistent, well-planned and managed responses to the reports of visitation committees: improvements are scattered and actions have a *short-term* character.

These conclusions appears to be borne out at the Hogeschool Holland, where EQM has helped to clarify the purpose and focus of internal quality assessment resulting in an improvement in self-evaluation and the development of a self-evaluation management culture (van Schaik and Köllen, 1995). The emphasis, however, has been on developing systems of quality assurance rather than on enabling effective, continuous improvement of the student learning experience.

Initial research into the impact of external quality monitoring in Norway (Karlsen and Stensaker, 1995) and Finland has suggested that, in a significant number of cases, 'the process of assessment alone is of intrinsic value', especially the self-evaluations, which 'create an arena for communication' and provide a 'legitimate way to openly discuss possible solutions to the present complicated problems' (Saarinen, 1995: 232) a point also made in a British context by John Rear (1994c) and reinforced at a recent OECD conference (Barblan, 1995; Bell, 1995; Rasmussen, 1995; Rovio-Johansson and Ling, 1995). Sometimes self-evaluations are also put to short-term uses within the institution, ranging from internal competition for resources to external marketing of the institution to potential students (Stensaker and Karlsen, 1994).

In the rather exceptional circumstances of a four-year process of evaluation of an institution attempting to achieve degree-awarding status in Hong Kong, the impact of EQM on the institution's development was considerable and included the development of a quality assurance culture among staff, the development of internal quality control and validation processes and more effective course and programme design (Chan and Sensicle, 1995).

The Appraisals Process in Ontario also appears to offer an example of the positive impact of EQM. Research suggests that there is sufficient evidence to show that the process, overseen by the Ontario Council on Graduate Studies (OCGS) has been effective in maintaining and improving the quality of graduate programmes. Improvement can be seen in terms of quantitative, summative indicators such as completion rates and time to completion, and in terms of improvements in peer evaluations over a seven-year cycle. Although involving both formative and summative assessments, the primary purpose of the OCGS evaluation is programme improvement. The confidentiality and consultative nature of the process has been claimed to be an important part of its effectiveness, which is due to the fact that 'it is co-operative, mandatory, is dynamic and evolving, has gained the "trust" of government, is collegial, and is based within the institutions themselves' (Filteau, 1993: 1).

It *may* be reasonable to argue that, because of considerable resistance in the higher education system, unused to any significant amount of external scrutiny, an approach designed to confront cloisterist prejudices and preconceptions is necessary. Indeed, it is arguable that an external focus on quality and accountability has aided the emergence of the new collegialism.

The question remains, though, can a process that is imbued with confrontational procedures, designed to engage cloisterism through checking, actually lead to *sustained* improvement? We have argued that accountability-led, funding-linked, quality monitoring will, at best, only have a short-term impact on quality and is much more likely to lead to a compliance culture in the long-term. Its main impact will be to awaken management and academic staff to possible financial gains and losses and alert them to a new set of rules and procedures that need to be played out. The impact on quality improvement will be rapidly dissipated. Accountability-led quality monitoring will thus have no long-term impact on a process of continuous quality improvement, a view endorsed by people close to the EQM improvement process in Britain and New Zealand:

> Improvement can only succeed through the individual and group efforts of providers of higher education; and external interests can only offer sanctions or rewards as incentives to assist the process. Unless providers are able to draw upon intrinsic motivation to achieve improvement, the best that can be hoped for is a level of compliance with external requirements. Compliance may pass for improvement in the short term, but as soon as the need to display 'improvement' has passed, old habits are likely to re-emerge.
>
> (Middlehurst and Woodhouse, 1995: 263)

Although it may be desirable to reduce the burden of EQM, is it feasible to combine accountability and quality improvement in a single external quality monitoring agency (INQAAHE, 1995; Vroeijenstijn, 1995)? Middlehurst and Woodhouse (1995: 263) argue that, whatever the logic in keeping accountability separate from improvement, accountability-oriented agencies already tend to be advisory and thus the two functions are combined in practice. They are then thrown back again on to the issue of whether improvement as a side-effect of accountability would be adequate or, indeed, cost-effective. They suggest that 'fully external quality assurance arrangements are likely to be a costly and inefficient means of achieving lasting improvement'. In essence, they argue that quality involves judgements of value and these differ at the levels of accountability and improvement, thus the two are, and must remain, conceptually and practically distinct.

We have argued that, at root, accountability-led EQM is underpinned by an ideology of financial stringency while improvement-led EQM is preoccupied with the empowerment of the learner. The only way to overcome the tension is, as we shall argue in Chapter 6, to consign accountability to a back seat. The way forward is to prioritize and engage the transformative process, an approach singularly lacking in existing EQM approaches.

## Attempts to engage student experience in EQM

There are very few EQM models that seriously attempt to engage with the student experience of learning. Wales provides an unusual example that goes close to engaging transformative learning directly. The Higher Education Funding Council for Wales (HEFCW, 1994: paras 28–30) places great emphasis on the 'total learning environment which students encounter in pursuing a designated programme of studies', key components of which include:

- the quality of student achievement relative to previous experience and attainment;
- the quality of the teaching and learning activities (instruction, lectures, demonstrations, practicals, field studies, seminars, tutorials) in relation to course objectives;
- the quality of assessment and feedback of and about teaching and learning;
- the quality of the overall course or programme design and curriculum coherence, and fitness for the stated purpose.

The Welsh approach is very much improvement-oriented, with an emphasis on quality judgements that encourage and support improvements in the learning environment for students. Such judgements describe perceived strengths and weaknesses and recommendations highlight priorities for action. However, the approach is still predicated upon a mission-determined, fitness-for-purpose notion of quality and institutions are invited to identify additional features or elements of performance against which they would wish to be assessed.

HEFCW is also constrained by accountability requirements that cut across its innovative, student-focused approach and these undermine the potential for transformative improvement. Accountability for quality requires an institution to have rigorous systems and procedures for internal reviews which allow it to assure itself and demonstrate to others that it is meeting its own and Funding Council expectations. These include an assurance that the aims and objectives of institutions and departments, as expressed in mission statements, are appropriate.

In the last resort, the Council is answerable to the Secretary of State, and is required to ensure that an effective process of external accountability monitoring is in place such that all those who have an interest in the quality of provision in the higher education sector can feel confident in the outcomes. Although emphasizing quality enhancement, HEFCW is required to have a method that is 'able to identify, unequivocally, those programmes in which the quality of learning fails to achieve a threshold of acceptability' (HEFCW, 1994: para 37).

Sweden provides a rare example of improvement-led model. Although the evolution of the process is stalling under the weight of new political imperatives, the initial dismantling of the highly centralized system focused on the development of an improvement model driven from the bottom-up. The 1993 higher education reform, under the slogan 'Liberty for Quality', devolved authority from the government to the universities and colleges, whilst simultaneously raising obligations for quality assurance and accountability by institutions (Bauer and Franke-Wikberg, 1993). While this has a familiar ring about it, the difference is that the obligation on each institution to set-up effective quality assurance systems was not driven by external accountability requirements, rather:

> it is improvement-oriented, is centred on local responsibility, seeks to employ the smallest amount of necessary information in reporting systems, and puts the emphasis on practical results and operational feedback . . . These characteristics describe a highly decentralized self-regulation scheme with the goals of employing only enough regular mutual or collaborative effort as is required to ensure that quality assurance and control are achieved.
>
> (Kells, 1992: 141)

The Swedish model aims to 'build the quality assurance from the bottom-up rather than top-down'. It does not rely on top-down strategies, either operated by the universities' own association, such as the VSNU in the Netherlands, or a state national committee such as CNE in France. Unlike the British system, where accountability is to the level above, the Swedish system is not hierarchical: instead, the emphasis is on stimulating a horizontal approach to evaluation, whilst encouraging co-operation at different levels. It encourages initiatives to be taken at any level by any individual rather than await managerial prescriptions. Furthermore, the Swedish system also encourages a variety of methods and mechanisms of quality assurance rather than imposing a comprehensive, homogeneous model on all institutions, disciplines or programmes. In short, the quality assurance system in Sweden is 'intended to become a *quality-driving instrument,* not an administrative obligation' (Bauer and Franke-Wikberg, 1993: 4–6).

Unfortunately, the lack of clarity about some responsibilities embodied in the 1993 Higher Education Act has been compounded by policy backtracking. Rather than leave institutions to assimilate the changes in funding and governance, the government imposed an expansion in student numbers on the universities, without a directly comparable increase in funding, and moved the initial reforms towards 'a supervisory model of governmental steering'. The result is that the Swedish model is faced with the same tension that confronts most other countries, albeit having come to it from a different direction. The new National Agency for Higher Education (Högskoleverket) now faces a contradiction. On the one hand it has an accountability and controlling rôle, for which it is responsible to the government, and on the other it has a quality-development rôle working with institutions. 'Put in another way, the University Chancellor has to be trusted from the top and from the bottom' (Askling, Almén and Karlsson, 1995: 12). Somewhat more cynically, one might suggest that the improvement potential has been usurped by the accountability requirement although the work of the Högskoleverket is intended to minimize government pursuit of accountability requirements.

Picking up the notion of transformation, Judith Sachs (1994: 24) argues that in some Australian universities 'a transformative and developmental approach is evident'. Although failing to cite any cases, she asserts that the approach relies on peer review and has, at its core, a commitment that the experiences of all participants must be enhanced. It 'bars any outside voices dominating the activities as they relate to quality within a university, and empowers the participants by giving them the opportunity to influence their own transformation'. She goes on to assert that this quality improvement framework is 'future directed with its goals being the transformation of current practice'. Furthermore, improvement is seen to be in the best interests of staff and is driven by the organization's desire for improvement. All staff are involved in devolved decision-making for improvement. The quality improvement process, she argues, not only serves the needs of internal stakeholders but can also respond to the demands of external stakeholders as it 'is driven by the shared goals and needs of employers'. Perhaps Sachs was thinking of Griffith University, her own institution, in constructing this ideal, a view that in part is endorsed in the Quality Review Report undertaken on behalf of the Committee for Quality Assurance in Higher Education. In its conclusion it notes:

> The long-held commitment to review and to self-assessment [at Griffith] has been reaffirmed through the processes to develop and to implement the Quality Management Plan . . . The process has involved extensive consultation with staff and students, ensuring strong support for change across the University. Students are supportive of the teaching philosophy of the University.
>
> (CQAHE, 1994: 10)

Although a long way from Sach's ideal, the pressure of externally imposed obligations has resulted in a significant development in teaching and learning at the University of Adelaide, a research university with traditionally conservative approaches to teaching. The external requirements provided the leverage by which highly motivated and well-organized innovators were able to obtain university-wide support for, among other things, mandatory professional development in the teaching role for new staff and mandatory and regular student evaluation of teaching (Cannon, 1994).

Despite a growing interest in teaching and learning and a responsiveness to external stakeholders indicative of a new collegialism, this openness is still far from widespread even in the improvement-oriented context of Sweden (Bauer, 1995), or in the USA with its considerable experience of evaluation (Dill, 1995). There are many factors that inhibit the development of an explicit professionalism directed towards enabling transformative learning. Not all of them can be laid at the door of accountability-oriented EQM – certainly disproportionate rewards for research over teaching do not contribute to collegialism. However, EQM has both failed to encourage a new, responsive professionalism and to tie this in with innovation in teaching and learning. Despite EQM, some institutions are taking teaching seriously in promotion to professorship but those that require explicit, high-level teaching competence are rare. One such is the University of Otago (1995), where the promotion criteria for applicants for professorship are that candidates should demonstrate at least high level competence, and preferably outstanding leadership in teaching, assessment and curriculum development.

Existing models of EQM around the world have had some impact in shaking-up cloisterist attitudes within the academy, but it is now time to abandon the accountability-led approach for one that encourages continuous quality improvement. What this might look like we explore in Chapter 6.

# Notes

1. Nationwide evaluation is becoming difficult to sustain and several provincial ministries have delegated responsibility for evaluation of Master's degrees programmes, including Shanghai (Wei and Gui, 1995), Jiangsu, Sichuan, Hubei and Shaanxi (Wang and Li, 1993).
2. Although financial sanctions are the 'bottom-line' they may not always be direct. Publication of assessment outcomes may act as a major sanction (or carrot). The assumption is that publicity will encourage mobile students to seek out the better-rated institutions. This will lead to more money going to these institutions on the assumption that money follows students, although what happens to quality is another issue. It is possible, however, that publicity will act as a sanction/carrot in another sense. High-rated courses will, it is assumed, attract more applicants and thus will be better able to recruit the better students – assuming that there is such a thing as a better recruit to higher education and that the recruiting procedures are able to identify who these are.

# 6

# Quality as Transformation

## Reprise

With this chapter we move from the way that quality has been promoted in recent years, both in Britain and elsewhere, and orient ourselves to ways of developing quality learning. As we suggested in Chapter 1, we set an ambitious goal: it is desirable, but not sufficient that learners should have a good grasp of the concepts, procedures and knowledge that pertain to their subject of study; it is desirable, but not enough, for them to master a series of what might be called general, transferable skills in so doing; the goal we set is that they should go beyond both of these, that they should be, in a sense, transformed. The product of such a transformation was sketched in Table 1.2 (page 11). It should be someone who is able to deploy a variety of frameworks and to stand outside them; to have a commitment to continued learning and reflection; to be able to do this with a high degree of autonomy; and who has integrated this with a set of developed values relating to the self as a learner and as a doer.

However, we have argued that a variety of actions and circumstances have conspired to impede learning, even at the lower, desirable levels that we identified. In part, the growth in the number of students, notably in the UK but globally too, has not been accompanied by a growth in the unit of resource. Everywhere, government spending is seen to be in danger of being out of control and a common response is to try and roll back the welfare provisions made in easier times. Whether education is truly welfare provision or not is beside the point: across the world, governments are looking to make savings in the cost of education provision. Worse, from higher education's point of view, is the belief that it is cheaper to invest in pre-school education and the view that the benefits of doing so are enormous (see, for example, Woodhead, 1989). It is hardly surprising, then, if politicians ask questions about the value to the state of higher education, especially as higher education in many countries can be depicted as principally benefiting the middle classes, whereas cheaper pre-school education is seen to benefit all and to offer some alleviation of the gross social problems that characterize some Western states. In such circumstances, higher education has been hard pressed to cope with the resources at its disposal and, despite the common view that higher education is vital to a nation's economic well-being, it faces increasing competition for funds.

Perhaps it is unremarkable, then, that efforts to improve the quality of higher education have focused on bureaucratic accountability. We do not wish to deny that such accountability *can* lead to reform of teaching, learning and the curriculum. What we have tried to argue is that it is not a direct influence on the quality of learning nor that it is likely to have a sustained impact (Chapter 4). Indeed, there is the spectre that such accountability may damage learning by diverting academic staff's attention away from the improvement of learning, to compliance with the bureaucratic imperative and to attempts to improve performance on indicators that are, at the very best, only proxies for learning quality (Chapter 5). Although systems of accountability and for quality improvement vary from country to country, there is a tendency to judge quality by reference to indicators that are of doubtful value (Johnes and Taylor, 1990).

We have noted that there is room for the suspicion that in such circumstances the imperative has been to make higher education more cost-efficient, not to improve the quality of learning.

However, stakeholders in higher education, whether they be internal stakeholders (Chapter 2) or employers (Chapter 3), have a definite view that quality is related to the learning process. That is not to say that they are unmindful of funding considerations, but rather to observe that for them the test of quality lies in the experiences of learning. This is particularly marked when looking at the views of academic staff and students (Chapter 2), where data mainly drawn from the UK show that what matters to them is the process of learning.

Employers take a somewhat different line, although one that is consistent with the views of internal stakeholders. They want to see graduates who have certain desirable attributes (Chapter 3). We suggested that this posed no threat to the academic integrity of degree courses, nor to academic freedom. The qualities that employers seek are ones that can be advanced by using certain ways of working within degree programmes and by ensuring that a good range of learning activities is provided. Where this is done, then the attributes valued by employers are likely to be fostered, allowing universities to couch their claims to develop graduates in whatever terms they wish: in terms of competences, of attributes, or of general, transferable skills (of which more in the next chapter). Employers' views do not prescribe content but suggest a pedagogy. In fact, one of the more striking findings reported in Chapter 3 is that employers are relatively indifferent to the principles and concepts mastered in degree programmes, giving academics a free hand to teach more or less what they wish.

Given the importance that stakeholders attach to the quality of learning, it is incumbent upon us to suggest ways in which this priority might be reflected in mechanisms for quality improvement, as well as to indicate, in some detail, how learning quality might be enhanced at departmental, course and module levels. This latter concern shapes the following four chapters, which analyse learning in order to offer suggestions for the improvement of assessment procedures and teaching. Necessarily, this leads us to consider issues of personal and professional development, which occupy Chapter 10. However, it is first necessary for us to offer a view of how quality assurance systems might be developed that support such teaching, learning and assessment processes.

## An alternative approach to EQM

On the basis of our argument so far, an appropriate system of external quality monitoring (EQM) must clearly focus on learning. It must embrace a transformative notion of quality and ultimately examine ways in which students are being empowered as life-long learners. Such a model should:

- see EQM as facilitating and ensuring a process of *continuous quality improvement* rather than bureaucratic accountability;
- facilitate *bottom-up* empowerment of those people who can effect improvement;
- enable *top-down audit* of the continuous quality improvement process;
- be *efficient*, non-burdensome, rational and effective.

The proposal is distinct from external assessment controlled from outside the institution and from audit of quality assurance procedures. The model emphasizes internally-driven quality improvement. External monitoring would assess the legitimacy of the improvement claims, while simultaneously reviewing standards. In short, the external monitoring would audit the claims about quality and standards that are annually codified in examiners' reports, course reports and so on.

## Continuous quality improvement

The focus on continuous quality improvement (CQI) is a deliberate attempt to move EQM into a second, and more effective stage. The process to date can be likened to launching a spacecraft on a voyage of discovery. Accountability-driven EQM provides the initial thrust to get the launch rocket off the ground. In some cases this is sufficient to ensure the spacecraft successfully goes into orbit. In others, the initial impetus is insufficient and the rocket crashes back to ground before the spacecraft gets into orbit. The best that accountability-led EQM can do is to get the spacecraft in orbit, but eventually the orbit will decay and the craft get burned-up on re-entry. To set off on a voyage of discovery requires more than initial momentum: it requires a process that encourages and facilitates the desire and motivation for change. In the second-phase of EQM, it is vital that the emphasis shifts from accountability to improvement and that, in the case of teaching and learning, the process is one of continuously improving the student experience.

External monitoring could change its focus and emphasis to improvement but it would only be effective were there unambiguous support for continuous quality improvement from strategic managers in institutions. Such commitment also requires them to accept a facilitating role.

In a CQI process institutional management does not direct or manage quality but provides a context to facilitate quality improvement, in particular, the dissemination of good practice and the delegation of responsibility for quality. Management has seven strategic functions in respect of continuous quality improvement:

• setting the parameters within which the quality improvement process takes place;
• establishing a non-exploitative, suspicion-free context in which a culture of quality improvement can flourish;
• establishing and ensuring a process of internal quality monitoring;
• enabling the consistent gathering of relevant evidence to inform analysis and reflection;
• disseminating good practice through an effective and open system of communication;
• encouraging and facilitating teamworking amongst academic and academic-related colleagues;
• delegating responsibility for quality improvement to the units that are going to deliver continuous improvement at the staff–student interface.

These functions may not suit managers (and employees) immersed in the confrontational management style of the 1980s. CQI is not congruent with managerialism but reflects a considered view of academic management, compatible with new collegialism, that emphasizes the importance of trust, ownership, personal commitment and independence in the management of change (Middlehurst, 1993; Middlehurst and Gordon, 1995).

## Bottom-up empowerment

If the emphasis is to be on improvement, then EQM must empower those who can effect the improvement – the student, the teacher, the researcher. This is an issue of ownership and control of the improvement process. EQM in most countries, as we saw in Chapter 5, is owned and controlled by external agencies and institutional managers. Disputes relate to issues of accountability: whether the external agencies are government-owned and controlled; whether they are independent or directed collectively by the higher education institutions; and the appropriate balance between internal autonomy and external control of quality monitoring.

Adopting a CQI approach recasts the issue of ownership and control. The emphasis shifts from concern about ownership and control of quality monitoring agencies to the ownership and control of the quality improvement process. Reviewing a recent evaluation procedure established at the University of Bergen, Sigurd Trageton and Edmund Utne (1995: 13) conclude:

> The be-all and end-all of a successful venture to safeguard and improve quality in research and teaching is that the chosen model for an

evaluation is accepted by the academic environments. This is difficult to achieve if those to be assessed are not given a reasonable opportunity of exerting influence on the scheme and its implementation.

Although continuous quality improvement needs to be driven from the bottom-up it must be based on a responsive, outward looking review and appraisal of what is provided. In short, the process will only work at the 'new collegiate' rather than 'cloisterist' end of the collegialism spectrum. The quality-improvement agenda must take into account a range of concerns and different stakeholder perspectives in an open, self-critical manner. It is of no use as a quality improvement tool if it simply looks inwards and is written as a self-congratulatory document.

### The 'new collegiate' team

A bottom-up approach to quality improvement requires identifiable teams of academics working together to identify quality targets, setting agendas for action and reporting clearly on intentions and outcomes.

The nature and constitution of such teams will vary depending on the type of institution. However, effective functioning for quality improvement will require that the teams consist of people with a common focus and responsibilities. These might be based on administrative units (such as departments or schools) programmes of study (teachers and administrators servicing a particular course), or subject discipline groupings. It is important that the teams ultimately self-select as they need to be coherent working groups. In any event, the teams must relate to recognized areas of activity and be able to act as coherent working groups. Team decisions should involve everyone. It is imperative that the team operates as a unit and that decisions are team decisions and not imposed by a team leader or by an external senior manager.

Team-building is very important (Acherman, 1995) but getting such teams together is not always easy, especially among academic staff, given the individualism of much teaching and a reluctance to spend time on pedagogic issues when a much higher return for effort appears to be achievable from research activity (see Chapter 10). There is no immediate prospect of fundamental change, on an international scale, in the reward and recognition procedures in higher education. Thus 'local' tactics are required to encourage the development of 'new collegiate' teams, including:

- placing a requirement on identified teams to document their agenda for improvement;
- ensuring that students are members of all such teams;
- making it clear that teams can make whatever decisions they think appropriate and have clear ownership of the improvement agenda;
- providing a clear focus, in the first instance, on a limited range of issues.

A suggested focus for initial team deliberation is the assessment of student work (see Chapter 8). The team might consider what is being assessed, why and how. It might identify the assessment profile of a typical student undertaking a programme of study and examine the range of assessment tasks, and the variety of elements being assessed. In particular, it might consider whether transformative learning is being encouraged through the assessment system. If a complex modular system is in operation, teams dealing with different clusters that might be taken by a student should exchange information about assessment processes. Assessment acts as a Trojan Horse, because an exploration of the rationale and practice of student assessment leads to questions about the coherence, transparency and integration of the learning experience (Harvey, 1993b; Brown and Knight, 1994; Knight, 1995).

The corollary of this is that the team must accept responsibility for continuous quality improvement within its domain. This involves a number of specific team responsibilities including:

- identification of its *area of operation* and the specific aspects of quality that the team will monitor: these may relate to teaching and learning, curriculum content, research, external employer-relations, and so on;
- specification of appropriate mechanisms for *assessing and maintaining standards* and procedures for action in the case of inappropriate standards;
- identification and implementation of *procedures for monitoring quality*, such as obtaining student feedback about their learning experience. All such procedures must be made explicit and transparent;
- identification of *procedures for improving quality*, such as review and updating of curriculum content and design, staff development and training, staff–student seminars, and so on. In many circumstances, procedures will already exist that can be adopted or easily adapted to fit the proposed approach;
- ensuring that its procedures and improvements are set in the context of a *local, self-critical review and strategic plan*. Such a plan will be constrained by the parameters of institutional strategic planning but, within that, should identify longer term goals and, more importantly, one-year, attainable, quality improvements (Harvey, 1994b).

This fifth responsibility is central to an effective process of continuous quality improvement as it provides the mechanism for ensuring transparency, closing the quality loop, and ensuring appropriate action.

*Use of annual report to set agenda*
A useful mechanism for doing this is an annual report. Many institutions currently expect academics working on a programme of study to provide an annual review. While this is laudable, these reports predominantly tend to be retrospective and are often produced by a programme director rather than by a co-operating team. The type of review envisaged in the new-collegiate approach would be one that is predominantly prospective, setting a clear agenda for action. It would also clearly identify how the previous quality-improvement agenda had been fulfilled. It should be succinct, cross-refer to policy documents and to reports of student feedback, examiners' reports, and append details of recent publications, staff development workshops and research funding.

A suggested structure for the content of the report might include the following:

- setting out *long-term goals* (and indicate how these have changed from previous reports);
- identifying *areas of action* for the forthcoming year;
- *reviewing* the previous year's plan of action;
- *evaluating changes* that have been introduced;
- reporting on the *quality* of what is provided by the team;
- commenting on *student evaluations* and those of other relevant stakeholders;
- indicating what will be *done* to address stakeholder views;
- identifying actual and proposed *changes to procedures* for monitoring and improving quality;
- *assessing* the suitability of the *research profile* (where appropriate) and the way teaching relates to research;
- *assessing* the *teaching and learning process*;
- *assessing* the level and range of *student attainment* (Harvey, 1994b).

The whole team must be involved in the production of the report (even if one person, on a rotating basis, edits the final version) because it provides a focus for exploring quality issues and is an important element in the culture of quality improvement. Most importantly, working as a self-critical team sharing experiences encourages dialogue, transparency and integration, three key elements in the development of transformative learning, identified in Chapter 2.

It goes without saying that the report must address the realities of the situation, be honest and reflective if it is to serve the purpose that is required. It is of no use at all if it is just a self-serving eulogy.

How can a realistic quality report be achieved? In part it can be achieved through an appeal to professionalism embedded in the process of delegated responsibility and team control of the quality process. Such an appeal should not be underrated – although many governments and their agencies are increasingly revealing a fundamental lack of trust in such professionalism (Annan, 1993; Mulgan, 1995).

A second way to ensure that the report is meaningful is for it to be subject to review and discussion by those to whom the report directly refers. While it is necessary that the team produces the report as an operating unit, it is also important that it takes account of the people to whom it is responsible and of those who have responsibility to it. For example, a report by a course team should be open to commentary by students and by faculty managers. A report by a faculty management group should be scrutinized by teaching staff and by senior managers, and so on. Extending this to a full 360-degree appraisal (Jacobs and Floyd, 1995; Ward, 1995) of the quality report by having parallel teams commenting on each other's reports would help disseminate good practice, encourage dialogues between different subject areas and provide another level of critical scrutiny.

A third approach is to adopt a process of external monitoring and checks through an audit system. This would involve top-down monitoring of the setting and achievement of the quality agenda. Despite the direct monitoring of reports through a system of review and commentary by those to whom it refers (the customer–supplier chain in Total Quality Management (TQM)-speak), there are also four reasons why reports should be more formally audited. First, it would be naïve to presume that a quality culture will be so pervasive that an appeal to professionalism and delegated responsibility will suffice to ensure the adequacy of the system. In short, some people will be less inclined to take up the challenge of team-based self-regulation than others. Second, there is a need for an institutional overview in order to inform strategic decisions. Third, there may be very different conceptions of what constitutes a quality higher education provision, especially in the early years of such a system. Fourth, it will thus be imperative that the audit process also involves dissemination of good practice and operates within a remit of substantial staff development.

## Top-down audit

Although quality improvement is driven from the bottom-up, it must be based on a responsive, outward-looking review and appraisal of what is provided. The quality-improvement agenda must take into account a range of concerns and different stakeholder perspectives in an open, self-critical manner. It is of no use as a quality improvement tool if it simply looks inwards and is written as a self-congratulatory document.

Top-down auditing should operate at two levels: internal audit conducted within the institution on a frequent, comprehensive basis and an external audit on a periodic or irregular basis conducted by a national or regional agency.

The top-down monitoring would operate, in principle, in a way similar to the audit of the financial accounts. Instead of statements of account, the institution would need to provide a set of layered accounts of quality and standards, along with supporting evidence.

### Internal audit

Each quality report produced by a team should be audited internally by the institution on an annual basis. This may involve simply receiving and reading the documentation or it may require some investigation of elements of the claims being made.

To ensure confidence in the process, internal audits should be undertaken by relatively independent unit reporting directly to the (pro-) vice-chancellor or to senate. Reporting at the most senior level gives clear signals of the importance of the process and gives a high profile to improvement activity.

If the report is to be a keystone in the process of continuous quality improvement, then it is essential that the conclusions are not linked in any direct way to internal funding allocations. If funding is linked, there will be little likelihood of self-critical analysis. The central function of the report is to identify action for future improvement.

To verify the report's conclusions, the internal auditors would probably:

• require clarification of claims made in the report;
• require evidence of unsupported claims;
• undertake an audit trail of the way the quality assurance process operates;
• observe teaching;
• examine output from scholarship and research activities;
• talk to students and other stakeholders.

An important aspect of the process of audit is that it should lead to effective action. The direction of action is set by the bottom-up process of team-defined, improvement agenda-setting. However, the audit process must ensure that the agenda is pursued assiduously. Feedback must be given to those who provide assessment information and effective action for improvement must be seen to take place. This requires that clear lines of responsibility and of reporting are established. In collegiate institutions (such as the older British universities and many European universities), this may be more difficult to establish than in institutions with more hierarchical management structures (such as the ex-polytechnics in Britain).

*External audit*

The internal audit should also result in an institutional quality report. The single-volume institutional report should be a compilation of the team quality reports, including improvement agendas, complemented by the institutions' own self-critical, analytic overview of quality improvement and standards issues. The full institutional report should be published, or at least lodged with an external independent body, on an annual basis. This report should be subject to external audit on a periodic basis.

The aim of the external audit will be to assess the quality of provision and the adequacy of quality procedures and relate them to the self-critical appraisals. In essence, this top-down, bottom-up framework, would:

• assess whether institutions are doing the job they set out to do (fulfilling mission);
• explore how this might be done better (disseminating good practice);
• possibly suggest modifications to the mission in the light of changed national circumstances or local requirements.

External audit would need to restrict itself to auditing the documentation produced on a regular basis by the institution rather than expect special documents to be produced to order. The external auditors could comment on the institutional quality report and undertake a more detailed audit on a periodic basis to authenticate the claims. The detailed audit, probably using peer review, would assess the validity of selected team reports and the effectiveness of the internal audit process. This might involve direct observation of the teaching and learning process, examination of available resources, assessment criteria, and so on.

The independent audit should result in a public report (with an executive summary and brief reply paper) that focuses on the effectiveness of the improvement process. A public report would not only help satisfy accountability expectations but would provide additional impetus to the process of continuous quality improvement.

This improvement-led approach, despite an external audit, differs from an accountability-led approach in several ways:

- it is driven by a bottom-up process of continuous quality improvement;
- it evinces trust in the work force and delegates responsibility for quality to them;
- external audit responds to internal initiatives rather than directly sets the agenda;
- improvement-led external audit is able to develop a strategic perspective rather than spend time on the detail of internal quality assessment procedures;
- audit processes at all stages are linked to staff development;
- it identifies the ways in which the ultimate responsibility of institutions for quality can be put into practice;
- it would be a relatively cheap approach, far less expensive, for example, than current accountability checks in Britain.

## Efficient and effective

A single external auditing agency would be required to fulfil this audit function. This agency should also take account of employer interests and professional body accreditation where appropriate (Harvey and Mason, 1995). There would be very little need for any ongoing audit of institution-wide quality mechanisms alongside the detailed course/subject-area audits, since the latter should clearly indicate audit trails and effective action based on student, staff and external stakeholder views.

The advantage of an improvement-led approach is that accountability naturally follows continuous improvement (Yorke, 1995a: 6). Accountability-led approaches do not lead inevitably to any, let alone sustained, improvement, as we have argued, which is why quality enhancement agencies are needed alongside accountability agencies (Middlehurst and Woodhouse, 1995).

Not only will accountability be a spin-off from a process of continuous quality improvement, it will be achieved at reduced cost, reduce the burden on the institution and reduce aggravation and hostility, there should be a pay-off in terms of quality improvement greater than any that can come from a compliance culture located in the hostile, conflict-ridden and suspicion-laden environment that results from accountability-led approaches.[1]

Thus the cost of an improvement-led approach would not only be less in absolute terms, but in terms of opportunity cost it would be far cheaper. Only needing a single external monitoring organization and a single set of visiting peers, it would substantially cut the cost to the institutions and the taxpayer. The cost to institutions would be less, as the external audit would be solely of internal quality-monitoring processes and would require no special documentation (however brief). Furthermore, the opportunity cost would be far smaller because effort expended would be directly linked to quality improvement. In short, institutions would be investing in internal continuous improvement rather than wasting money on a cumbersome quality bureaucracy. The taxpayer would be paying for a streamlined quality auditing body.

The team-based quality report, which might appear an extra burden, would, in many cases, replace (or at the very least inform) annual course reports, which are now widespread in higher education. Furthermore, in the long run, the annual team report can be used to directly feed into external quality assessment or audit processes and thus minimize or eliminate the need for additional documentation in the event of an audit or assessment visit.

Producing a quality report may have an unintended detrimental effect if teams see it as an unnecessary extra pressure. The quality-improvement agenda may become overly bureaucratized and possibly fossilize an informal and dynamic process. This could possibly occur if institutional managers and external auditors require a set format for team reports and agenda. Despite such misgivings, it is more likely that a quality report will help to clarify the informal process of improvement, which is frequently less complete, explicit and transparent than it might be. The whole approach is also compatible with the outcomes of the recent trial audits undertaken on behalf of the Standing Conference of Rectors, Presidents and Vice-Chancellors of the European Universities (for example, CRE, 1995).

## Contingent features of the proposed approach

The approach suggested is contingent upon five elements. First, that quality is seen, essentially, as a transformative process. For teaching and learning, that places the emphasis squarely on the enhancement and empowerment of the student. Improvement should thus focus on the student experience of learning, with a view to continually improving the process of enhancement and empowerment. Second, that continuous improvement is driven bottom-up. This requires placing trust in the professionalism of academics. Third, this trust can only be earned in the future if the collegiate group adopts a responsive, open and empowering approach. Fourth, there must be a quality-improvement process in place that results in effective action. The loop between genuine quality concerns raised by stakeholders and action to effect changes must be closed. It must also include a process of feedback, to relevant stakeholders, of action that has been taken in relation to their concerns. Fifth, external monitoring must be sensitive to internal quality improvement procedures. Accountability will result as a consequence of a planned and transparent quality improvement process. Placing a primacy on accountability and hoping that quality improvement will result is likely to inhibit, rather than encourage, a process of continuous quality improvement.

## Conclusion

An effective model is one that develops a quality culture of continuous improvement. Such a model shifts the primary emphasis on quality from external scrutiny to internal effective action. In terms of teaching and learning, for example, this means devising a quality system that drives improvement from the staff–student interface. However, accountability is ensured through external quality monitoring, which audits the quality activities of effective teams, in much the same way that the financial accounts are audited.

Continuous quality improvement must, then, be driven from two directions: bottom-up and top-down. The key is to encourage and ensure the former, whilst developing a sensitive but effective external monitoring process.

In the end, the approach proposes the development of a quality-improvement culture that is contingent upon trusting the professionalism of the workforce. This is not a mystifying professionalism wrapped up in a cloak of isolationist academic autonomy, but an academic professionalism that embraces openness, dialogue and transparency (see Chapter 2).

Despite some superficial similarities to TQM, the suggested approach is not directly compatible with TQM philosophy. There are elements in the approach that reflect concerns of some TQM exponents, such as the emphasis on teamwork, delegated responsibility for quality, commitment of senior management to facilitating quality improvement and developing a quality culture. TQM is concerned with fitness-for-purpose. The suggested approach to EQM endorses a transformative notion of quality.

> At root, TQM is fixated on a product or service supplied to a customer (or client). Higher education is a participative process. There is no simple, discernible end-product of higher education, it is an ongoing transformative process that continues to make an impact long after any formal programme of study has been completed. In essence, TQM addresses a partial 'pragmatic' notion of quality that is of marginal use in the context of higher learning and knowledge development.
>
> (Harvey, 1995b: 141)

## Note

1. The only flies in this ointment, at least in Britain, are the interrelated ideological ones of hard managerialism and consumerism. Hard managerialism, as has already been suggested, is about direct control of higher education, which is dressed up in the cloak of customer choice. The resulting invidious rankings and league tables, often as counterproductive as they are beguiling, are anathema to the suggested improvement-led approach. These trappings of accountability are not

just a legitimation for differential distribution of resources but reflect a fundamental shift towards more central government control of higher education. While this persists, and accountability rides roughshod over real quality improvement one can only expect an external-control approach to quality assessment and assurance.

# 7

# A View of Learning

## The complexity of learning

Learning is complicated. Psychology is rich with:

- theories about the development of learning as we develop from infancy to adulthood;
- evidence of the quirks of learning;
- theories of perception that attempt to describe how information ever comes to our attention, which is, of course, necessary if it is to be learnt;
- models of memory, short-term and long-term, those based on information processing and those based upon scripts and schemata;
- models that attempt to map the structure of the ways in which we store information;
- accounts of the ways in which we retrieve information that attempt to explain why we remember, why we forget and why we do not always manage to bring to the fore that crucial information that is lurking somewhere in our brains;
- stories about the ways in which we use what we have stored and retrieved; with competing notions of the interplay between the conscious and the unconscious mind;
- claims about the importance of our feelings with respect to learning, feelings that dispose us to learn some things but which, for example, make us quiver at the thought of learning calculus.

Many of these theories, claims and positions recognize that individual differences are important, so that neat generalizations about human learning have limited power.

Any account of learning is going to be complicated but incomplete and to be open to dispute by those who believe that some theories have been unreasonably neglected, whereas others have been promoted without good cause.

Yet, hopeless though the task may seem, teachers need a view of learning, even if that view has no more power than that of a heuristic. In fact, a stronger claim can be made, teachers *do* have theories about human learning.

The problem is that often these views are 'naïve theories', the product of personal experience, of unchallenged common sense and, often, of expediency. So, the claim at the beginning of this paragraph needs to be modified. Teachers have theories of learning that may owe much to experience, common sense and expediency. They need theories that have also been informed by systematic and principled reflection on the nature of human learning. Such theories guide the professional task of teaching into channels that are believed to be better than those that many of us have dug on the basis of our experience, common sense and need to cope with our work. They can suggest ways of organizing learning so that it can become transformative rather than replicative.

To appreciate the meanings of transformative learning it is helpful to begin by considering how we deal with new information. Frequently we do not notice it. The plant on my (PK's) desk is flowering. I noticed that today but not yesterday when it must also have been flowering. I'm sure that last week it wasn't. The new information has been available for some days, I suppose, but I did not notice it.

A second response is to assimilate the new information into existing mental structures. Suppose your view of essay writing is that the more work you have done, the more books you have read, the better the essay. Suppose you get feedback that says: 'You've worked hard for this and read widely. However, you could have said more about the deprofessionalization thesis. The structure of your essay would also bear attention: your argument does not come across clearly enough.' Assimilating the comment would mean that you conclude that you need to read more widely (about the deprofessionalization thesis) and that you give little importance to the point about essay structure. This example shows that sometimes assimilation proceeds by glossing over discordant data and focusing on the data that fit existing mental structures. Assimilation enhances what is there. It can hardly be described as transformation, since it is essentially additive. In fact, it can be a substantial bar to transformative learning. Just as medieval scholars had the data that implied that the sun did not go around the earth, so people often unconsciously ignore information that cannot be assimilated.

The third strategy involves a quantum leap, where we change our base ideas or structure, accommodating them to the new information. Kuhn's provocative account (1970) of the structure of scientific revolutions showed how rarely societies go through periods of accommodation, when new ways of knowing emerge to accommodate information that does not fit into conventional structures. Likewise, learners who come to see that an essay is not a collection of information but an argument have accommodated their mental structures to take account of information and feedback that have not supported the 'collection' view. Accommodation is hard. Assimilation and overlooking are our default strategies, not least because, for much of the time they are appropriate strategies. However, it is hard to recognize when they are not the appropriate default strategies and harder still to make the phase-change from assimilation to accommodation. Yet empowerment relies on accommodation.

# Transformation and learning

## Preview

What follows is a discussion of three areas in which there may be transformation: in the discipline, in general achievements, and in meta-critique and values. It is implied that if such transformations are to be sought, then higher education institutions will also need to be transformed. This theme is teased out over the three chapters that follow this one.

The first view is that transformation comes about as learners come to new understandings of the subject matter or domain, which is to say that the quality of scientific, sociological or architectural understanding at the end of the course is markedly different from that at the beginning. The learner moves from being a novice in an academic culture towards expertise in it.

A second view is that while the first is desirable, it is not a sufficient return on three years of study. Academic knowledge is all well and good but it is fatally limited in at least two ways. One is that knowledge dates and nothing is more certain than that today's knowledge will be of limited value in five or ten years time. The second objection comes from asking what it is that graduates are to do once they leave higher education. By and large, they will not be academics. They will move into occupations, even school teaching, in which command of their subject might be necessary but is certainly not sufficient for success. What graduates need, says this view, is mastery of some generic skills that allow them to function in new environments with a degree of independence.

The third view, which was sketched at the end of the last section, is that neither of these is sufficient. Here the goal is for the graduate to become a critical, life-long learner.

## Transformation of understanding in a domain

Learning is both individual and communal. Individuals with their own histories, mental structures and concepts, and modes of perception and of thinking, form understandings of the world that are simultaneously special and common. The 'specialness' of the understanding comes from those elements of me that are distinctive of me. However, if learning were dominated by this solipsistic bent, we would all be imprisoned in autism. Strong forces, notably language, society and cultures give feedback on our understandings and encourage the formation of shared understandings. Indeed, so strong are these forces that it is easy to assume that people all form the same understandings and that learning problems are the result of some failure of processing power that stops some learners from handling particularly complex information.

Constructivist approaches to learning provide a complementary interpretation. Some learning problems come because learners, who have a variety of mental structures and understanding, do not see the same material in the same ways. Different students experience the same lecture in quite different ways, and that this is associated with quite different sorts of understanding. Likewise, varying the standard lecture format by incorporating activities for the students within lectures has much to commend it, but where students have lecture 'scripts' (preconceptions about lectures) that neither include nor recognize the relevance of such activities, then 'their experiences of the lecture do not relate to these activities but to the presentation aspects of the lectures' (Prosser, 1993: 27).

Constructivist views suggest that learning problems can arise because people have different expectations and understandings and therefore, to some degree, learn different things from the same stimuli. To compound the problem, people who have built up understandings that are alternatives to the intended ones may not realize it, and they may use the official language without giving signs that it has alternative meanings for them. The result is that one solution, which is to provide feedback that alerts students to the fact that they have formed alternative understandings, is far from straightforward, not least because it is not always evident which learners have formed these alternative understandings.

It follows that it is not sufficient just to encourage learners to transform their understandings through new accommodations but that some accommodations are to be preferred to others. If that is to happen, it is necessary to give feedback to the learner about these new understandings.

*Structure*

There are many barriers to this transformation but within the context of learning a subject a major barrier is misapprehension of the nature and structure of the subject. The learner who understands history as the acquisition of fact into a collection, or who sees nursing as the mastery of a recipe-like craft will be severely limited unless a better conception is developed. Unfortunately, there is a body of evidence that many learners do have such naïve conceptions of the subjects that they study (Hounsell, 1984). These naïve concepts affect their perception, guide assimilation and limit accommodation. Transformation depends upon discarding naïve views of the subject of study, for without a transformed view of what is being studied and why, thinking will be fatally limited.

This might be extended into a general principle. If accommodation is to be encouraged, learners need to have sight of the goals and to understand the structure of the material that they are working upon. So, the learner who sees history as a collection of information is likely to understand history material very differently from the learner who sees it as the construction of arguments. So, the learner who sees academic excellence to lie in producing a neutral narrative of events is likely to see material very differently from one who sees that the Frondes of seventeenth-century France can be seen as a test of the view that French society remained essentially feudal.

This echoes the work of Jerome Bruner who argued, amongst other things, that learners ought to engage with the structure of a subject, not just with relevant information. In some domains, particularly the natural sciences, 'structure' might refer to the organizing concepts of a subject but it would also refer more generally to the key concerns, to the nature of truth and to the mode of discourse typical of a subject. In some form, even the novice learner could and should have a sense of what was distinctive about science, art or history. Bruner proposed that curriculum might then be seen as a spiral, with information being organized around this spindle-like structure. As information was added and reorganized and as the learner became more expert, so the notions of structure would become more extensive and more sophisticated: accommodation is implicit in upwards movement around the spiral. Although this model has been most commonly applied to school learning, it is no less applicable to higher education, pointing as it does to the importance of the learner understanding what sort of study they are undertaking, thereby supplying something that is vital if we wish them to transform information and their understandings within the boundaries set by communities of discourse. It follows that tutors also have such clarity of vision and strive to make it available to learners.

The work of Lev Vygotsky also pointed to the importance of structure, arguing that new learning might be encouraged where learners engaged in tasks that were slightly too hard for them, in what has been called 'the zone of proximal development' (ZPD). This implies that teachers have a view of what lies beyond learners' current achievements, that they have some notion of progression within a subject or domain. He argued that learners ought to be helped to move into the ZPD through scaffolding, which might take the form of carefully structured work provided by the teacher or through the process of working collaboratively. Although there are disputes as to how collaboration might advance understanding, there is general goodwill to the claim that a group of three learners, for example, may together be able to work at levels just beyond those within the reach of any of them individually (Ratcliff and associates, 1995). This social scaffolding would help learners to develop fledgling understandings, which would be consolidated by further activities and, according to the model of complex learning proposed by Norman (1978), by considerable practice of the new understandings, concepts or skills.

So, the notions that domains or subjects have structures and that a progression of understanding may be described, give rise to ideas about the ways in which the accommodations that constitute this progression might be fostered: through attention to the structure of the domains; through learning experiences intended to access the ZPD; through collaboration; and then through application and practice to tune and consolidate the new accommodations. In this way the novice might become an expert, although it does have to be emphasized that expertise comes through plentiful experience. That point is made because it is not clear that university programmes that allow considerable student choice lead to the coherence and integrity of learning that are necessary conditions for the development of expertise: in the words of Ratcliff and associates (1995: iv) 'students learn more from a coherent and developmental sequence of courses'.

*Approaches to learning in a domain*

This process of growth within a domain might be described as active learning, although that raises the interesting question of whether any learning can be truly passive. A more common way of describing it is to say that deep processing characterizes this learning: information is acquired and stored purposefully and can be retrieved along with concepts and other information that have been associated with it. Learners who do this may be said to have taken a deep approach to learning. This term has become common currency in discussion of higher education and it is widely accepted that a goal of university education is to support deep approaches. Characteristic of deep approaches is the intention to transform ideas or information by understanding them for yourself. This involves relating ideas to previous knowledge and experience; looking for patterns and meanings; appraising evidence and the conclusions associated with it, in the process subjecting arguments to critical scrutiny; and, in short, *working on* the material (Entwistle, 1994). It can be seen that deep approaches can be understood as a re-expression of the learning process that has been described above. However, some aspects of that process can also be represented by a pathology of the deep approach that is known as a surface approach. This might be described as a coping strategy, where learners concentrate on routine memorization, with the aim of becoming able to reproduce the information as faithfully as possible (Entwistle, 1994). This might be seen as a form of assimilation but it is a stunted form, since the lack of mental engagement and the lack of effort to appraise the information mean that the information is likely to be lodged in a separate file, hardly linked with related sets of concepts and meanings. There is a view that this is likely to make the information harder to store in long-term memory and harder to retrieve: certainly, the new information has hardly been transformed; nor, for that matter has the learner. What is crucially absent is the possibility of accommodation and growth.

It is important to appreciate that this is a discussion of learning approaches, not of learning styles. 'Learning styles' is a seductive construct which suggests that people have preferred styles of learning, or approaches that they tend to use regardless of the task. However, studies of Kolb's Learning Style Inventory (Kolb, 1984) have cast doubt on the validity and reliability of the instrument, hence on the underpinning constructs (Sims, 1986; Newstead, 1992). Moreover, the research tradition that led to the notion of 'deep' approaches has also led to an awareness of the degree to which performance is task- and context-specific (Trigwell and Prosser, 1991). If we follow the idea of learning styles, we will say that some people will consistently take *this* approach to any task rather than *that*. However, this dreadful determinism hides evidence that tasks and other factors in the context *as perceived by the learner* can encourage people to take a deep approach or to adopt a more coping approach. It follows, then, that if learners are adopting 'surface' approaches, it may be the fault of the learning environment, of which task demands are one aspect. The converse is that the learning environment is, in principle, within human control.

Trigwell and Prosser (1991) conclude their report of studies of the interaction between the learning environment and student learning by suggesting that deep approaches to learning should be positively encouraged, which implies that:

- feedback is helpful and adequate;
- there are clear course objectives, assessment criteria and expectations;
- the course is both relevant and interesting;
- there are opportunities for student questions and for consultations with tutors;
- the quality of tutor explanations is high;
- tutors understand student learning difficulties;
- students have a say in what they learn and how they learn it.

They, and others since, suggested that universities that wished to promote deep approaches would be well advised to attend to the total quality of the learning environment, rather than try and adjust isolated features (Biggs, 1993; Knight, 1994; Springer *et al.*, 1994).

Just as learning environments can foster deep approaches, so too with surface approaches. Increasingly, 'surface' approaches are being seen as a pathology, the result of educational environmental pollution. The pollutants may be excessive workloads, low academic motivation, personal history (so that high-school success, for example, could be won by memory, drill and speed-writing), inappropriate assessment requirements, authoritarian relationships between tutors and learners and, in specific cases, gender, class and other cultural assumptions.

The conclusion is relatively simple. Scrub the pollutants from the atmosphere. Trigwell and Prosser's suggestions provide one list of suitable actions. However, just as removing pollution from our air is not entirely within human agency and tends to be expensive, so too with cleaning up the learning environment.

Several general suggestions about effective learning result from this section, where the aim is transformation through the development of domain-specific mastery. That is just one of three senses in which learning might transform the learner. An environment favourable to deep approaches should support a learning cycle that involves both assimilation (or enrichment) and accommodation (or empowerment). There are other views of the learning transformation that ought to occur in the undergraduate experience. It is to the second of these that we now turn.

## Transformation and general, transferable achievements

A major objection to domain-specific learning is that, at worst, learners master a body of knowledge that will soon date, while the most likely alternative is that they will gain knowledge and understanding, but have little to offer except as engineers, sociologists, theologians or midwives. These achievements may be more or less valued, according to the fluctuations of the labour market. Yet, what employers need, goes the argument, is people who have skills that transcend the disciplinary or vocational heartland, achievements that are general and transferable. Nor is this just an English phenomenon, for in the USA federal aims for higher education are based on the premise that whatever the programme, learners should master general abilities as well as domain-specific ones.

The idea that education should promote general, transferable skills has a strong common-sense appeal. However, a recent review of studies of the transfer of learning argued that 'skills learned in one domain usually transfer only within that domain' (Garnham and Oakhill, 1994: 277). Where general thinking skills have been taught, the impact has been on people starting from a low level and there are questions about how long lived the effects are. This does not mean that it is worthless trying to promote general, transferable skills but it does mean that we ought to be careful about making too grand claims about what is likely to be achieved.

### General, transferable skills

One approach to identifying the skills that might be fostered in higher education has been to ask employers what they look for in a new graduate and to try and respond appropriately. The Employer Satisfaction survey (Harvey with Green, 1994, see Chapter 3) revealed that knowledge of an academic subject came low (52nd of 60) on their list of *desiderata*, while transferable skills were prized. However, these employers, as Table 3.3 has indicated, were not always satisfied that universities made a good job of fostering them.

Few would disagree that it is better to be skilled in such areas than not. However, there are a number of reasons why it is not simple for universities to make the development of these areas central to their work. In the first place, there is uncertainty about what it is that makes these skills appropriate to *higher* education (Atkins, 1995). Some should be evident in infant classrooms (Edwards and Knight, 1994), and in each case there are problems with explaining what sorts of performance would be appropriate to new graduates.

The difficulty of identifying which general transferable skills are appropriate to higher education is a problem faced in England by the National Council for Vocational Qualifications. At the time of writing, General National Vocational Qualifications (GNVQs) have been developed to level 3, which is university entrance level. GNVQ students should be adept at the core skills of the application of number, information technology and communication. There are doubts whether this trio will be suitable if GNVQs are developed for higher education. Perhaps more academic core skills will need to be developed, for example, argumentation?[1]

The MENO thinking skills service operated by the Cambridge Syndicate for Local Examinations offers a model of these core academic skills, believing them to be: critical thinking, problem-solving, communication, understanding argument, numerical and spatial operations, and literacy (Hamilton, 1995). A tension is evident between the MENO list and employers' preferences, as seen in Table 3.2. The problem is that there is no shortage of desirable, apparently general skills that might be developed. Yet, long lists are sterile, since curriculum developers and tutors cannot handle too many demands.

Moreover, there is a problem of authority. If prudence suggests that any selection of core skills might be parsimonious, some principles of selection are needed. Not only is it hard to see what they might be, but, as we said in Chapter 3, it is equally difficult to cut the knot by saying that one stakeholder's views, such as employers' views, ought to be preferred over others. Underlying this is a major philosophical and psychological issue, namely the nature of human capability (Tomlinson and Saunders, 1995). The specification of core skills implies an account, albeit an incomplete one, of what it means to be capable. There is, however, no consensus on what would constitute an adequate account.

However, we have no wish to abandon the idea that higher education may transform more than just undergraduates' views of their subjects or areas. We suggest two other ways of approaching this issue.

*Research skills*
An alternative to the search for general transferable skills is to equip learners with 'research skills'. This takes place within a disciplinary context and has the goal of making it possible for learners to work on problems and issues with increasing degrees of independence. This independence may be the independence of working alone or it may take the form of learners working in teams on problems and issues. For example, Independent Studies (in some guises) permits learners to choose the problems or issues to be investigated (Percy and Ramsden, 1980).

Such an account of Independent Studies has attractions, not the least of which is that a deep approach seems to be almost requisite for success and the chances of it being manifest are enhanced by learner choice and autonomy. It also seems to promise some savings of academic time, on the basis that self-directed learning is sometimes expected to need less from the tutor, more from the student. Finally, in any discipline, there is substantial agreement about the main research paradigms and techniques, although there tend to be tiresome, time-expired battles about whether qualitative research methods are intrinsically better than quantitative methods. Even so, it means that there is an identifiable body of procedural knowledge that can be taught and justified with more confidence than any selection of 'transferable skills'.

However, before independence comes dependence. In order to be able to work on history, engineering or psychology problems, learners need to have a view of the domain and to know something about the issue in question – or know how to get that knowledge. Additionally, they need to know appropriate research skills and to be skilled in self-directed learning. Research skills can be taught, and learning how to learn needs to be learned. It cannot be presumed that learners know how to work independently, even as late as the final year of their degree programme.

So, independent learning ought not be characterized as an absence of structure. The opposite is contended. A structure is needed to guide learn-ers to the point where they are ready to undertake work, alone or in groups, that is akin to academic research. It follows that academic staff who value independence need to have a view of learning and a view of how people get to be effective autonomous learners. This is not straightforward, since there are competing accounts of how learning takes place and of ways in which learner autonomy might be fostered (Robbins, 1988).

This position does not suit all proponents of independent learning. A highly-valued feature of Independent Studies at Lancaster University is stu-dent freedom to choose the topics for study (Knight, 1996). This is not merely a freedom to choose a problem from the major discipline of study but a complete freedom to choose any topic for study that can be super-vised within the university, in any ways that can be sold to supervising tutors. The tenor of the argument so far has emphasized the necessity of structure which is in some degree of tension with the Lancaster approach. One resolution is to say that the structure should be seen as permissive, which is to say that students would be invited to work within it but allowed the option of doing their own thing.

*Metacognition*
The notion of metacognition cuts across the two approaches to general transformation that have been discussed. Considerable interest has been shown in metacognition, that is in thinking about our thinking,

> Metacognition refers to *knowledge, awareness,* and *control* of one's own learning. It subsumes various aspects of intellectual competence and performance, such as conceptions of the nature of teaching and learn-ing (metacognitive knowledge), perceptions of the nature, purpose, and progress of current learning (awareness), and the decisions made and behaviours exhibited during learning (control).
>
> (Baird, 1988: 145)

However, the concept, as it stands, is rather too broad to be useful. Flavell, Miller and Miller (1993) distinguish between three aspects of metacognition, identifying metacognition about persons, about tasks and about strategies.

Metacognition concerning persons embraces our thinking about 'what human beings are like as cognitive processors' (Flavell, Miller and Miller, 1993: 150), that is knowledge and beliefs about the nature of mind and human cognition. It is widely documented that adult knowledge and beliefs in this area is commonly deficient (Ross, 1981). For example, it is often found that we believe that our actions are constrained by circumstances whereas others' actions are driven by their personalities: we are blameless because of the situation in which we find ourselves, whereas others act badly through personal defects. While this aspect of metacognition is of direct interest to teachers of humanities and the social sciences, it is less important for present purposes than the other two aspects.

Knowledge of tasks includes knowledge of how easy different types of task are as well as knowledge of the extent to which the quality of information available is related to the quality of conclusions that may be drawn, to the quality of solutions that may be offered. The importance of learners being able to reflect upon task demands and upon the nature of the information needed to meet those demands is striking. Learners who have faulty understandings of the nature of the tasks they are set – as well as of those they set themselves – are limited as learners. This theme, that transformation can be advanced where learners have a metacognitive awareness of tasks will be developed further in the next chapter.

The third category, metacognitive knowledge of strategies, includes what 'you might have learned about what means or strategies are likely to succeed in achieving what cognitive goals' (Flavell, Miller and Miller, 1993: 151). Ideally, we are looking for a situation where the learning environment is conducive to deep learning, where learners' task knowledge recognizes this and where they have the metacognitive awareness of the strategies necessary to deploy a deep approach to those 'deep' tasks. The implication is that higher education should be fostering an awareness in learners of the nature of tasks and of the nature of effective strategies for engaging with them. Such metacognitive awareness would seem to be important and something generalizable and transferable.

The appeal is twofold:

- meaningful learning requires active cognitive processing of information;
- efficient learning requires metacognitive regulation (Ferguson-Hessler, 1993: 175).

In other words, learners learn better when they think about their own learning strategies and when they consciously try to adapt them to tasks in hand and to improve them. There is considerable research to support this first claim about metacognition, namely that learners who show greater metacognitive awareness score higher on tests of performance in a domain, and that it is productive to coach them in *learning* in a domain (Folds *et al.*, 1990; Volet, 1991; Flavell, Miller and Miller, 1993). However, the evidence is not unmixed: for example, students who have greater awareness of their strategies for memorizing are not always found to perform better on memory tests.

The second claim is that metacognitive achievements are in some degree transferable. Learners who consciously regulate their thinking transform themselves to the extent that they, on this view, develop a general power of thought that may be transferred to a variety of disciplines. What distinguishes this claim from other accounts, such as Piaget's, of the development of human thought, is that it holds that *conscious* reflection on the process of thought is both beneficial and necessary. However, it has to be recognized that '*how* we think is to some extent tied to *that* which we are thinking about and the *context* within which all of this occurs' (Gavelek and Raphael, 1985 *cit.* Bråten, 1992: 16; Ferguson-Hessler, 1993). Consequently, 'data pertaining to the transsituational character of metacognition are still sparse' (Perkins and Salomon, 1989; Bråten, 1992: 17). In other words, the hope that in metacognition we have found something that offers the key to the development of better, general and transferable achievements in students may be over-optimistic. Here the fate of general thinking skills programmes is of interest. Such programmes, often marketed as 'pop' paperbacks, claim to improve one's IQ, creativity or thinking power. On their own terms they appear to be successful, but it is disputable whether they make much difference to performance in everyday life, let alone in the higher levels of academic work.

However, interesting work done on secondary school science learning has suggested that where learners were taught science in a thoughtful way, thinking not simply about the science concepts but about ways of working and learning in science, then not only did their science scores improve against those of a control group, but so too did their maths and English scores, even though the programme had been confined to science learning alone (Adey and Shayer, 1994). It is possible (although more research is needed) that long-term programmes to make learners more aware of their thinking in a domain may help to make them more thoughtful in general. Or, as Flavell, Miller and Miller (1993: 151) observed:

> if you are a metacognitively 'intelligent novice' . . . , you know you do not have the background knowledge needed in some domain about which you are reading, such as twelfth-century Japanese poetry, but you know how to go about getting that knowledge . . . Such activities are not necessary in your area of expertise.

So far metacognition has been considered only in respect of the cognitive pay-offs. There is another, intriguing line to be explored. Attribution theory explores the way people account for their performances and the relationship these accounts have to their motivation. Attributions may be categorized on two dimensions. One dimension concerns the nature of the factors influencing performance: are they stable, hence largely uninfluenceable, or labile and influenceable? In other words, is it believed that the impact of these factors can be changed or not? The other dimension relates to the cause of success or failure: is it in us, or are external circumstances to blame? Where a student believes that fixed factors have led to poor performance, whether they take the form of their own low, perceived ability or of a hostile university learning environment, there is little incentive to try and motivation is predicted to suffer. Where the factors are seen as labile, so that performance is related to the learner's own efforts, strategies or to the level of help available from peers, then motivation is not damaged and may even be enhanced. Perry (1991: 37) offers a good review of thinking in this area, arguing that 'college students who experience temporary loss of control are unable to benefit from effective instruction, performing no better than if they had received ineffective instruction'.

The link with metacognition is that when metacognitive awareness is promoted, learners are encouraged to see that difficulties may be the result of inadequate metacognitive knowledge about tasks and strategies – the product of an inadequate sense of the game (Flavell, Miller and Miller, 1993). This is an area in which they might exert control, where it is possible to attribute difficulties to something alterable (metacognitive knowledge) rather than to something stable (their own perceived lack of ability). Moreover, where learners have good metacognitive knowledge, they are more aware of possibilities and may have a greater sense of control.

It may be that metacognition promises rather greater transfer of learning than will actually be experienced. However, the development of metacognitive awareness may have important potential for transforming some learners' sense of control in their learning, with important implications for their motivation.

We have tried to avoid making some of the bolder claims about higher education's power to transform learners in general, non-discipline-specific ways, while also recognizing that it is possible to foster approaches and habits of mind that have a great deal of potential. Again, we wish to draw attention to structural features of universities that fragment the learning experience at the expense of sustained and coherent programmes that encourage the development of these approaches and habits.

## Transformation, values and life-long learning

Transformation need not be seen as a cognitive change alone: indeed, we argue that the most extensive transformation will have involved disciplinary and general accommodations but that these are stunted without a changed sense of self. A commitment to life-long learning, to critical reflection and to riding the continuous flow of change are all characteristic of our view of transformation. There is an acceptance of the idea that learning is provisional and never ending; that today's certainties will be tomorrow's myths *and* that this is the path of personal and professional growth, the dialectic between here and now on the one hand, and then and there on the other.

Barnett (1994: 153) argued that learning in higher education was limited were it to be confined to learning general skills or to expertise in a domain. Drawing on critical theory in particular, he contended that a goal should be the development of wisdom, defined as 'a form of deep reflection, collective exchange, and a recognition and even a critique of inner values'. Central to this is the idea that learners who have such wisdom will be able to transcend both disciplinary and skill-based paradigms of higher education and, being initiated into life-long learning, will be able to develop a sense of self that uses but is not bounded by the insights of these two approaches.

This might be clarified by examining what is known as the learning paradox (Smith, 1993). How is it that starting with limited understandings and achievements we are able to create something greater than them? The paradox is that inferior mental tools produce superior ones: something inadequate produces something better than itself. Barnett appears to be arguing that domain-specific and skill-based approaches to higher education are inadequate. Yet, as with the learning paradox, from them can be created a higher form of learning, characterized by intelligent self-actualization, where meta-critique enables learners to develop an intelligent conception of themselves with a moral stance towards the world of human life. The key point is that human *being* is best realized when we deploy our learning to help us to reach a position about life, not just about skills and subjects. Necessarily, this involves the scrutiny of values, the development of a reasoned beliefs system, an attitude of continued learning (and not just learning within a profession or job, but also learning *for* life) and the motivation to do so. Therefore, higher education is about transforming the person, not (simply!) about transforming their skills or domain understanding.[2]

This is a timely reminder that much that is learned at universities is neither to do with subjects, nor with the skills that were considered in the last section. Eighteen-year-old students develop a sense of independent identity, often at the cost of personal pain, while mature students often find that higher education is intimately connected with a redefinition of self and a changing sense of personal identity, as counselling service personnel will confirm. For many students, the legacy of higher education is strongest in terms of personal identity: an identity that has been formed while studying but which is produced as much by being a student as by what is taught during it. In other words, transformation frequently takes place not so much through the deliberate actions of the university but through the exigencies of the experience of taking on the student role. Work at the National Center on Postsecondary Teaching, Learning and Assessment and within the *QHE* project emphasized the importance of looking at the complete student experience, not just at the cognitive and scheduled elements of it. Interestingly, some of the factors that make for greater self-understanding do not necessarily make for greater academic achievement, which raises some important questions about the purpose of higher education: is it about academic achievement at the expense of self-awareness? (Springer *et al.*, 1994; Ratcliff and associates, 1995).

Arguably, the bigger problem is not one of having the wrong sort of influence but is rather being able to act to have *any* influence in this resilient area of beliefs and values. We can say that universities are not uninterested in this area. The rise of 'health-promoting' higher education institutions is evidence of some concern for learners as people, not just as academic units, and the provision of counselling services is stronger evidence of such a concern. Yet both are basically separated from the academic exercise, suggesting that being and learning are two different things. There is also a variety of tutorial or pastoral systems but while they may have a closer link with learners' academic life, they are rarely devised to integrate the academic and the human sides of the learning experience through, for example, a system of records of achievement and regular review of the undergraduate experience as a whole. Besides, even where this does take place, a transformative purpose seems to be lacking: the goal of encouraging people to go beyond the givens of subjects and skills does not seem to be present.

Individual academics might have such a goal but in the fragmented, post-modern world of modularization and choice, their impact can only be muted. Departments might have more scope and university-wide policies would be the most powerful. Yet, it is well known how difficult it is to implement university-wide policies, and where the goal is as subtle as that suggested here, there is likely to be considerable difficulty in developing understandings of its meanings amongst academic staff. This can be illustrated here by reference to the church colleges in the United Kingdom. These are higher education institutions sponsored by a church and with a Christian mission. They are one representation of the idea that higher education should be about more than domains and skills, embodying a belief that the spiritual development of all members of the college is important. The problem is, as Goodlad (1995) observes, that only a minority of students have committed themselves to this particular vision of human being and questions have arisen as to whether these colleges are actually able to do what they were intended to do – to develop the whole person, notably through a concern for the spiritual aspects of the undergraduate experience. Gedge and Louden (1994) show how difficult it has been to discharge this mission in the first 25 years of one church college, noting that the change from being a small and, by implication, select community to a larger site for mass higher education caused considerable problems. If it is accepted that higher education should be helping students to learn something about themselves as people in the world, then there are hard questions about how this transformation is to be promoted. This is not just a matter of institutional structures, although that is a hard enough problem, but also one of pedagogy.

In Chapters 8 and 9 we return to the first two senses of transformation. Having views of the transformations that institutions might encourage, we approach the issue of how that is to be done. Many factors need attention here but Chapter 8 explores the larger question through consideration of just one, the means whereby student learning is assessed. It is arguably the most significant of those factors.

# Notes

1. We owe this point to conversations with Dr C. Boys of NCVQ.
2. The dialectic underpinning our notion of transformation is a materialist one grounded in praxis (reflection on practical activity) within a specific structural and historical milieu. It is based upon a view of critical social research (Harvey, 1990) that is at variance with approaches that espouse a critical methodology based on a reworking of critical theory of Habermas and other members of the Frankfurt School, which is grounded in an idealist Marxism (Larrain, 1979).

# 8

# Assessment for Learning

## Introduction

> The single, strongest influence on learning is surely the assessment procedures ... even the form of the examination questions or essay topics set can affect how students study.
>
> (Entwistle, 1994: 10)

Why should assessment be given such prominence at this point, especially when the emphasis in earlier chapters has been put on learning and given that there is a history of assessment being seen as antipathetic to understanding and 'deep' approaches to learning? An answer uses a metaphor developed by Patricia Cross (1995). Imagine, she says, learning archery in a dark room. You have all the best equipment and expert coaching but you shoot in the dark and get no feedback about your performance. The current situation with student learning and assessment is like that, except that the lights are turned on after the trainee archer has left, scores are recorded and sent to the archer's sponsor. It might be, she says, that there is a case for having even a dim light on while the archer is firing: imagine what a difference that might make.

In other words, assessment ought to provide students with feedback to help them to improve their learning. As it is, students are often shooting in the dark until the course or programme is over. In this view, assessment is something done by the tutor to shape learning and the learner. Unfortunately, the way it is often done arouses negative emotions in learners (Race, 1995), emotions exacerbated by the way assessments are communicated, in terms that Boud (1995a), following Rorty, has called 'final vocabulary'. Moreover, unless assessment tasks are well conceived, they may encourage learners to adopt surface approaches to their work, to ignore the ostensible and commendable messages of the planned curriculum for the prosaic demands of the assessment tasks.

We have seen that employers, academic staff and students think that the quality of the assessment of student learning is related to the perceived quality of programmes within higher education (Chapters 2 and 3). Assessment data can, and ought to, support learning and assessment tasks have the power to reinforce the goals of transformation or to subvert them completely. Transformed higher education needs transformed and transforming assessment.

To illustrate this, we offer two brief case studies of North American institutions that have sought to transform learning by transforming assessment. The North American focus reflects the importance that has been placed upon the assessment of student learning in the USA since about the mid-1980s. In some cases, State legislatures required higher education institutions to assess things of questionable educational worth using instruments of dubious validity. Where higher education does not have in place good quality evidence of student learning, institutions are vulnerable to politicians who impose their own, common-sense measures with unwelcome effects. In other cases, as with the two described here, institutions saw the political (as well as the educational) need for sound programmes for the assessment of student learning. In those cases, not only has it been possible to defend academic freedom, it has also been possible to argue that the quality of student learning has been improved through well-conceived assessment practices.

As a preliminary, we note that in the USA, 'assessment' may refer to the assessment of student learning or it may refer to the evaluation of programmes. It will often be understood as testing, that is as a reliable procedure for collecting summative data, but it can also refer to the making of inferences based upon student performance on 'authentic' learning activities, whether the inferences are for summative or formative purposes. This chapter is not about testing alone, since that is only one form of assessment, nor is it only about programme evaluation. It is about making inferences about learners on the basis of data that can be depicted as fit for the purpose, which may be a summative or a formative purpose.

## Alverno College: a case study of assessment-as-learning

Alverno College in Milwaukee (USA) began its work on assessment in the early 1970s, which means there is a well-developed programme in place, grounded in plentiful reflection upon experience and buttressed by copious data.

Two key principles may be identified. The first is that assessment is a powerful point of leverage in the curriculum: thinking about assessment demands thought about teaching, learning and curriculum. The second principle is that assessment should further the college's mission statement through the promotion of generic competences, or outcomes, embedded in disciplinary contexts. There are eight general abilities that should be developed through the Alverno experience, as well as six performance characteristics, which are not directly assessed. Domain-specific programmes embody a selection of these abilities. Assessment is designed to document learners' growing command of the relevant abilities and should help learners, their peers and academic staff to identify points for remediation or development. Rather than being contrasted with learning, as is sometimes the case with testing, at Alverno they speak of assessment-as-learning. The reasoning is that Alverno assessment activities are educationally valuable in their own right, as well as providing feedback to learners and tutors that supports further learning.

The eight abilities are: communication; analysis; problem-solving; valuing ('recognize different value systems while holding strongly to your own ethic'); social interaction ('know how things get done in committees, task forces, team projects and other group efforts'); global perspectives; effective citizenship; and aesthetic response (Alverno College Faculty, 1995: 1). Since these abilities are repeatedly and variedly assessed, then they effectively define the curriculum: a typical assessment in English will involve the integration of analytic ability with understanding of a given literary work or works, of literary concepts and principles and of historical times and their impact. In other words, these eight generic abilities underlie the learning outcomes specific to each of the subject departments in the college.

This systematic articulation of assessment, curriculum, teaching and learning is striking and has grown directly out of the institution's mission statement. Naturally, in the USA as elsewhere, institutions with different missions will identify different outcomes. For example, the core competences identified at Blue Ridge Community College, Virginia, are: communication, learning, critical thinking, wellness, culture and society, science and technology, human relations, and computation and computers. There is, then, room for debate about what would constitute the set of outcomes that best expresses a mission at a point in time. More significant is the Alverno position that the programme needs to be continually researched in order to keep it dynamically improving.

At the time of writing, skill with information technology was subsumed at Alverno under 'communication'. Whether this was the best way of conceptualizing it was being examined: should information technology be defined as a separate ability or as a component of every ability? How would the provision of more advanced equipment be used to *improve* learning? So there is a commitment to what might be called 'continuous quality improvement' based upon analysis and evidence.

The interconnectedness of assessment and the curriculum can be seen in course-planning documents. The college mission statement and the set of general outcomes head the documentation, and are followed by a set of outcomes for the student majoring in the given field and a set of specific course or module outcomes derived from them. These, in turn, lead to details of the arrangements for assessing these outcomes and to specific assessment criteria. The criteria are designed to be informative to students, not just convincing to validators. Attention is also paid to how feedback is to be given to students.

Clarity of outcomes facilitates programme review and continuous quality improvement. This is taken seriously at Alverno, where ten academic and support staff undertake continuous research and evaluation work. Three per cent of the college budget is taken up with this continuous quality improvement work, which pervades the institution. Moreover, it is possible to produce some impressive 'before and after' evidence of the learning that takes place in those years. This is a better way of expressing the 'added value' of the college years than the rather convoluted approaches discussed in the United Kingdom (CNAA, 1990a) or North American approaches that lack validity.

The clear specification of learning outcomes in the form of statements of assessment criteria, allows learning to be individualized in a purposeful manner. Academic staff are able to give feedback to learners that is directly related to the assessment criteria and which can look forward to criteria that are yet to be encountered, as well as offering diagnostic comments on present performance. There is here the potential to offer more useful and focused feedback than is usually the case where goals and criteria are tacit. Furthermore, the developmental sequence of criteria can have a motivating force through showing learners what they need to do and where they are headed, through target setting. Moreover, with explicit criteria, it not only becomes possible to encourage self-assessment, it is arguably necessary to do so, and Alverno students are required to appraise their own and others' achievements. It is not just at Alverno that self-assessment has been identified as something of value in its own, as an important part of becoming more autonomous as a student, and as a prerequisite for becoming a life-long learner (Boud, 1992). Such self-awareness is an important outcome of the Alverno process, and constitutes one of the six performance characteristics. Furthermore, this approach makes it possible for learners to progress at their own rate and provides a basis for the accreditation of prior experience and learning – learners need to demonstrate that their previous experience and learning have led to mastery of criteria related to a selection of the eight core abilities.

Another distinctive feature is that assessment activities are designed as learning activities. In a sense, of course, all assessment activities have the power to be learning activities, but at Alverno assessment activities are also normal, natural learning activities: producing a written report, performing, giving a presentation, discussing aspects of literary texts, and so on. While this emphasis on authentic assessments in multiple modes and contexts may seem unremarkable to some United Kingdom readers, it is less familiar to North Americans who often see assessment as testing, and as multiple-choice testing at that. Alverno procedures emphasize the *validity* of the assessment tasks: instead of being distinctly different from normal learning activities, normal learning activities are designed to offer opportunities to assess learners against the key criteria. No grades are given: assessment involves judgements of performance related to the criteria derived from the learning outcomes. The goal of all assessments is to document achievement and to use that evidence to plan both for further practice and for future development, an overwhelmingly formative approach that encourages learners to understand their learning rather than to be 'grade hunters'.

In context, it is hard to criticize the Alverno system. Students graduate with transcripts describing the ways in which they have demonstrated a command of a selection of the eight abilities integrated with the content of the profession or discipline in ways that delineate their chosen field of study, and not with a grade point average or classified degree. This frees the college from some measurement problems that might otherwise interfere with the educational integrity of its assessment arrangements. Since so much of the assessment is formative, the pressure that assessment be 'reliable' is also reduced on the grounds that the on-going nature of assessment (as a continuous process, not as an occasion) and the element of learner–tutor and learner–learner negotiation allow for different interpretations of performance to be heard and for nuances that might be lost in more 'reliable' assessments to be appreciated. To put it another way, assessment at Alverno is not an act of measurement but is a process of judgement in which both meaning and learning are valued above the shibboleths of (inappropriate) psychometrics.

Yet, it would not be fair to say that Alverno ignores the reliability issue, for students face multiple assessments of the same ability over their four years and faculty have developed a degree of shared understanding of the criteria. This shared understanding has neither been quickly nor cheaply achieved. This is not a research university, although faculty do exemplify Boyer's (1990) 'scholarship of teaching' by publishing reports of their innovative work. Additionally, academic staff are expected to work together in teams to plan and develop their courses. And, this is a development that has been under way for about a quarter of a century and the academic staff recruitment policy has been used to recruit faculty whose disposition is consistent with this emphasis on teaching-as-learning. So, formal, psychometric-style consideration of reliability does not have the priority at Alverno as it does in other United States universities and the small size of the college (116 full- and 94 part-time faculty) is conducive to the generation of shared understandings. There is an interesting parallel here with developments within the UK system of vocational qualifications in which reliability is increasingly understood in terms of the degree to which evidence of performance can be associated with performance criteria (Boys, 1995).

In Chapter 7, three senses aspects of transformation were considered: within a domain; in terms of general, transferable skills; and as a meta-awareness. The first two have been considered here in the context of the Alverno approach. As to the third, faculty at Alverno say that their assessment and learning systems should combine to help students to be more adept at transferring their learning from context to context. This is supported by 'external assessments', which might be better understood as assessments that are not linked to any one course but which require learners to synthesize and, perhaps, to apply, their grasp of several competences and their learning from several courses. However, we have argued that developing such metacognition is not an easy matter: has Alverno found an answer? Their programme in some ways resembles the CASE project described in

Chapter 7, through which learners within the domain of science were helped to be reflective and planful in their work strategies, just as they are at Alverno. Evaluation of that project concluded that those exposed to this process did better in science and in English and mathematics too. Not only does this parallel suggest that transferability might be achieved at Alverno, but the Alverno emphasis on self-assessment and self-awareness has a metacognitive resonance. Further evidence is contained in a paper published in the mid-1980s that reported a study of changes in 750 students as they progressed through Alverno and that documented the perspectives of 60 recent Alverno graduates (Mentkowski and Doherty, 1984). The findings indicated that the students became self-sustaining learners, came to value liberal learning, and developed generic abilities and moral sophistication. Recent graduates valued the interpersonal skills they developed at Alverno, felt competent and continued as self-sustaining learners. Longitudinal research continues, with recent reports confirming and extending the 1984 findings (Alverno College, 1993). It is possible to claim that an integrated approach to learning, goals, teaching and assessment has brought about a learning community in which there is transformation. The institution has been transformed over many years and transformational learning now characterizes its work.

In the sense that it provides some confirmation that the vision outlined in the previous chapter is not a mirage, this is helpful. The high international reputation that the college enjoys indicates that many academic staff share that opinion. However, a little caution is needed. Although something has been done, it does not mean that it can be reproduced anywhere under any circumstances. As Alverno faculty observe,

> Looking back, we can see that our formal and informal traditions gave us three important resources: a habit of dedicating time to faculty discussion and work sessions, an unusually strong emphasis on initiating the student into the higher education process, and a mission to serve women.
>
> (Alverno College Faculty, 1992: 3)

The Alverno experience affirms that transformation is possible but it also alerts us to the difficulty of the enterprise, a theme that will be revisited in later chapters. The most striking feature of that system is the horizontal integration of learning, curriculum, assessment and teaching. This integration pervades the validation procedures and course documentation, as well as being evident in practice. There is also a vertical integration, in the sense that what students do this year is conceptually and practically connected with what they will do next. The difficulties of achieving that in other institutions cannot be ignored and will be revisited in Chapter 10. Current trends, in the United Kingdam in particular, to increase student choice and to disaggregate the curriculum into modules can only exacerbate those difficulties. For the present, the point is more modest. Had the assessment system not been the subject of 'permanent revolution', then the goals and hopes for learning and teaching would have come to nothing.

# James Madison University: a case study of assessment and continuous quality improvement

In the mid-1980s James Madison University ( JMU), Harrisonburg, Virginia (USA) recognized that universities needed to be able to demonstrate their effectiveness to state legislatures if funding was to be preserved. A Director of Student Assessment was appointed to run a five-year programme to improve the methods of assessing undergraduate learning and thence to improve the quality of learning itself. Although the approach was based on testing, which is common in North America, there was a concern to ensure that the tests were not only reliable (again, a common preoccupation in the USA) but also that they were valid, that is they measured student learning in terms of the curriculum that they worked with. A major criticism of some North American approaches to assessment is that what students are assessed upon, even in a common subject such as chemistry, might not be closely related to their curriculum, with the result that the assessment procedure would lack validity.

The intention at JMU was that improved assessment procedures should:

- make measures of learning more rigorous;
- provide students with formative feedback;
- provide better quality summative information for students;
- facilitate the evaluation of courses;
- enhance the learning processes;
- provide hard evidence which could be used in support of requests for additional resources;
- recognize the growth in public accountability through mandated assessment and forestalling any State moves to impose assessment procedures on the University.

The Director of Student Assessment has university-wide responsibility for developing approaches to the assessment of student learning in co-operation with departments. This includes responsibility: for the development of assessment instruments appropriate to the considerable range of learning outcomes valued by departments; for analysing and commenting on the data, particularly with regard to the implications for university policies and developments; and for spurring developments in pedagogy and in assessment. This might be described as assessment for continuous quality improvement (CQI). By 1995, he was supported by a team of three other professionals, by secretarial colleagues and had assistance from graduate students from time to time.

To begin with, departments nominated a member of academic staff to work with the Office of Student Assessment (OSA) on the development of an assessment programme for that department. A key feature of this early work was the identification of what exactly the department did or wished to do. Given the degree to which teaching and programmes are often based on tacit assumptions and sometimes on semi-private practices, this was sometimes felt to be a threatening process.

This departmental mission was to be cast in the form of learning goals, or outcomes as they were known. Outcomes could relate to specific knowledge but could also refer to skills, processes or procedures to be mastered. Whatever their focus, the form of the outcomes had to be:

- specific and discipline-related;
- expressed in terms that are easily understandable (for instance to parents, students and potential funding bodies);
- as far as possible, measurable, which means that outcomes expressed in terms such as 'students will appreciate', 'understand', 'be familiar with' are not acceptable (OSA responds to such fuzzy outcome statements by asking faculty 'How will you know?', 'What will that look like?', pushing faculty towards formulations that embrace specific assessment criteria).

With the needs of assessment having led departments to identify their learning goals, the OSA worked with them to identify suitable assessment tools. In principle, the assessment instruments should have been characterized by:

- reliability (establishing this is not a simple, nor a common-sense process. The OSA team has the expertise and resources to help faculty here, since few academics could, unaided, establish the reliability of their instruments);
- validity, which implies that the assessment instruments match the programme's proclaimed learning outcomes, both across the range and at the level of individual questions;
- discrimination – the level of difficulty of each test item is calculated, so that the overall level of the assessment instrument can be set appropriately.

It was not unusual for a department to begin by buying into a commercial package for the first year or two but it was frequently found that 'off-the-shelf' instruments were not sufficiently sensitive to the individual department's goals and curriculum. The result was that departments would then turn to the OSA in order to modify the assessment package or to replace it with a home-grown alternative. Interestingly, JMU was concerned to establish the psychometric reliability of its assessments, in line with common North American practice.

A wide range of assessment methods is now in use in the university. Certification examinations, patterned after postgraduate professional examinations, have been constructed in accounting, dietetics, fashion merchandising, finance, interior design and management. Other assessment methods have included: personal artistic performance histories in art, music and theatre; review of student research and position papers in history, English, philosophy and religion, social work and psychology; portfolio reviews in art and interior design; performance critiques in art, dance, theatre and kinesiology; external supervisor ratings of internships and student teaching in social work, middle-school education, early childhood education and secondary education; employer surveys in accounting, early childhood education and secondary education; clinical preceptor evaluations in nursing and health science; ratings of affective development in speech pathology and audiology, and social work; and external advisory councils in hotel and restaurant management, school psychology and counselling psychology.

In many traditional assessment systems data are collected but not used. At JMU, as at Alverno, there is a sense that a giant action-research project is underway, with assessment data being used to guide reflection and development. On the assumption that the data come from valid and reliable assessments, and care has been taken to get the best possible levels of reliability and validity, it is now possible to use assessment to measure the effects of teaching. For example, one way in which the impact of teaching has been estimated is by applying the same summative tests to groups of students who have not had the benefit of the formal learning experience, as well as to those who have participated. In some cases it was found that the course did not appear to be associated with student mastery of the course objectives: in other words, some students who had not done the course performed as well as or better than some who had. One analysis seemed to identify a course that had a negative effect on student performance. This then leads to questions about the source of those achievements that have not been fostered by the taught programme, and gives rise to thought about the degree to which out-of-class activities, such as learning from employment, counselling or service in the community, might be the source of displays of competence. This has the potential to open up programmes by making it possible for learners to gain credit, in human communication, for example, on the basis of performance on these criteria-related tests, rather than on the traditional basis of attendance at scheduled classes.

However, the OSA does not tell departments what to do with the data. It is seen to be important to give faculty the responsibility for acting on the information gathered, thereby confirming their power, ownership and responsibility and recognizing that they are the experts in their domain. So, departments are expected to use this information in their decision-making processes, supplementing, or perhaps supplanting, the usual forces of politics, tradition, logic and intuition.

The sorts of questions departments are invited to consider include the following.

- Does our teaching achieve what we said that it sets out to achieve?
- What do we do when the evidence is that it does not? Options include reforming teaching procedures, focusing on learning rather than teaching or making a case for rewriting the assessment measures.
- How do we respond to evidence that student success in meeting learning criteria may come from other sources such as informal or work-based learning, or from community service or from paid work?

This is very time consuming. Moreover, there is a danger of academic staff going into compliance mode, and going through the motions of responding to the data, or of adopting 'change without change'. For example, where assessment shows that some students have competence at a higher level than that required or taught, departments are generally reluctant to consider 'fast-tracking' these students.

Apart from the departmental level of response, there are also powerful institutional considerations. In the USA, as in the UK, the visible quality of higher education is becoming increasingly important as higher education competes for funds against other programmes (such as building of prisons in Virginia) or against other forms of education provision (such as nursery education in Britain).

This is the final stage in the assessment process, using well-founded data, based on measurable performance outcomes to make bids for state funding and to forestall state interventions that are predicated on the belief that higher education is unwilling to give a serious account of itself. Where institutions do not forestall state intervention, as JMU has done, then they risk either failing to secure funds or being locked into state-mandated assessment patterns that threaten their academic freedom. So, at JMU, there has been state funding for information technology resources because the OSA has been able to provide evidence showing that it leads to greater efficiency.

That is not to say that academics are necessarily happy that something so complex and precious as learning is being judged in the political processes of accountability and of competition for resources. They tend not to react well to being told how to work, an attitude that may have been encouraged by traditions of job security. Universities' claims that this accountability can protect academic staff from unfriendly outside attention is not necessarily accepted at face value. Sometimes, this is because the level of threat to higher education has not been fully appreciated. So, questions like 'What is it that your department does?', 'What are the desired outcomes?', 'What do you expect students to *get* from studying with you?' mostly at majoring level, are challenging to established academic cultures in at least two ways. First, many academics have not traditionally considered these questions and are genuinely perplexed by them. Secondly, there is a fear that the accountability that this process implies will be used against academic staff interests.

The JMU system shows how a system for the assessment of student learning has been used to drive continuous quality improvement. This form of accountability has, in turn, allowed the university to defend its position in difficult times. It has also allowed the university to do so on its own terms, rather than having to accede to bureaucratic modes of accountability and quality control that could have reduced academic freedom while doing little, if anything, to enhance the quality of learning.

## Assessment-for-learning: conclusions

We have argued, both here and in earlier chapters, that assessment can both support and shape learning. If the assessment system sends one set of messages and the curriculum another, then the curriculum is jeopardized, the thinking being that unless all parts of the academic system send the same messages, then learners may react to the confusion of messages by attending to the most salient, which may not be the messages intended by programme designers.

On this basis, we suggest that a quality programme in higher education should be characterized by an assessment system that has the following features:

- the intended curriculum aims should be clearly defined;
- the expectations attached to each learning aim need to be clearly expressed, or transparent, which is to say that both staff and students need to understand the assessment criteria that will be applied;
- a range of learning outcomes, both subject-specific and generic, should be assessed, which is to say that assessment should be integrated;
- assessment methods should be fit for the purpose, that is they should be valid measures of the intended learning outcomes;
- multiple programme aims demand multiple assessment methods;
- there should be evidence that students get useful feedback on their work through interaction with teaching staff and, perhaps, their peers – in other words, assessment procedures should give rise to dialogue;
- consideration should be given to making learning programmes, aims, criteria and outcomes public;
- assessment data give an indication of students' learning and, as such, should inform the processes of continuous quality improvement;
- it follows from the foregoing points that the collection and use issues require that summative assessment data be centrally stored in a form that is readily accessible to authorized staff and which can be readily analysed using standard statistical packages;
- similarly, universities should consider establishing Offices for Student Assessment.

We have suggested that social, economic and political pressures have led to higher education being subjected to increasing State attention. This has taken two main forms: State interest in the curriculum and demands that higher education give an account of itself. Together, they represent a threat to traditional concepts of the academic professions but the response that this makes them illegitimate ignores the stark fact that higher education has little choice but to respond helpfully, unless it wishes to see funds that have hitherto supported it being diverted to crime control, care for the aged or nursery education. We have shown how two North American institutions have used systemic approaches to the assessment of student learning to preserve their own initiative and, to a large degree, their own academic freedom. At the same time, they have been seen to be accountable to State governments and have been able to make well-based cases for funding. For example, funding for new teaching technology.

This leads us to two new tasks. First, we need to summarize the implications for teaching of our arguments in this and in the previous chapter. Secondly, we need to examine ways of transforming higher education so as to make university teaching something that is biased towards the business of transformative learning. These are the themes of Chapter 9.

# 9

# Teaching

> You know that I don't believe that anyone ever taught anything to anyone. I question the efficacy of teaching. The only thing that I know is that anyone who wants to learn will learn.
>
> (Carl Rogers, quoted in Buscaglia, 1982: 7)

## Introduction

Teaching and learning are frequently connected but the theme of Chapter 7 was that learning is complex, individual (within a cultural framework and a shared language), and somewhat unpredictable. We cannot say, then, that teaching causes learning: it may or it may not. A definition of teaching needs to recognize this, so we suggest that teaching be defined as planned efforts to bring about learning in others. The definition leaves open the question of the form of teaching, and certainly does not imply that teaching has to be didactic. It also emphasizes the importance of planning, which would include programme and course design, the design of assessment procedures and of other environmental features, as well as planning at the level of the individual learning unit, whether that be a seminar, lecture, workshop, part of a distance-learning package, work placement, examination, CD-ROM sequence, or whatever.

The purpose of this chapter is to review the previous two chapters in order to identify some principles associated with good teaching. Given the nature of the material reviewed in those chapters, it will be evident that these principles cannot be prescriptive. However, the position can be taken that the closer teaching approaches to those principles, the more likely it is, in general, that transformative learning will take place.

## Good teaching: personal or social responsibility?

It is increasingly accepted that teaching is an aspect of academic work that needs to be taken as seriously as research. Boyer's *Scholarship Reconsidered* argued that the 'professoriate' should recognize four types of scholarship:

discovery, integration, application and teaching. Teaching, at its best, he said, 'means not only transmitting knowledge but *transforming* and *extending* it as well'. Following Aristotle, he averred that 'teaching is the highest form of understanding' (Boyer, 1990: 23–4).

But in considering the elements of good teaching, teaching that brings learners to transformation, it is important to add two further qualifications. First, if the link between teaching and learning is, to some extent, unpredictable, it follows that attempts to define good or effective teaching are limited. Of course, if it could be shown that students taking a class with Professor X made more progress than those taking a class with Professor Y, it would be fair to conclude that there was something about the way in which X facilitated learning (taught, if you wish), that was better than Y's methods. However, the assessment of learning in higher education is so problematic that it is unlikely that such claims can be made with confidence.

An alternative to this is to examine the extent to which academic staff appear to measure up to criteria that have been agreed to characterize effective teaching. Some such criteria make up the body of this chapter. The problems with this approach are that the selection of criteria is itself problematic, which means that there arises the issue of whose criteria these are: bias is inbuilt in all social theory and a set of criteria such as this is no more than a social theory of teaching. A third and common approach is to observe academic staff at work. While it would be foolish to claim that this has no value, it is obvious that it is open to the same objections as the last suggestion, while the enormous problems of conducting reliable and valid observations compound the difficulties (Knight, 1993). Lastly, student acclaim should not be neglected, but always in the spirit that feeling good may be important to learning but does not guarantee it.

Besides, good teaching is not simply an individual responsibility. Prescriptions for teaching might well be read to say that if only individual academics took teaching more seriously and followed these suggestions, then all would be well. That is not the intention. Good teaching, like good learning, is a response to the individual's perception of the environment. It would seem to be obvious that teaching is affected by the environment at a time when academic staff work with larger classes, when there is pressure on library and other information services and when academic workloads are steadily growing. It does not directly follow that these changes have led to a worsening of teaching: not only has the proportion of good degrees awarded continued to rise, but it can also be suggested that these pressures have forced academics to abandon traditional but bankrupt 'information-conveying' approaches to teaching and to think hard about promoting learning through greater student independence (Gibbs, 1995a). Notwithstanding the issue of whether environmental changes have led to better or to worse approaches to learning (*via* teaching), the point is that the quality of teaching is not just a matter of individual responsibility.

This may be suggested by referring to a survey of 'how key instructional development people at universities and colleges in several countries perceive the potential impact of various teaching improvement practices'

(Wright and O'Neil, 1995: 2). Of nine categories of response, comprising 36 items, the most important referred to leadership by deans and department heads; the second to employment policies and practices; and the third to development opportunities and grants. In other words, for teaching practices to improve, structural factors need attention.

The reason for insisting that any assessment of teaching quality is a social construction of an important variable in the processes of student learning is to distance ourselves from a 'bean counting' mentality where someone in authority takes a set of criteria, such as those that follow, and tallies another's worth against it. There are many ways of helping learners to learn and good teaching is not, therefore, a matter of doing *this* rather than *that*. In some cases, doing *that* (lecturing, for example) may be preferable to doing *this* (asking students to grasp the elements of Louis XIV's foreign policy through independent library work). However, good teaching ought not to be reduced to neat formulae.

## Teaching, good learning and the undergraduate experience

One of the main findings of a substantial study of factors associated with student learning outcomes in the USA is that 'students learn more when their in- and out-of-class experiences are mutually supportive and reinforcing', which is to say that out-of-class experiences play a significant role in students' learning (Ratcliff and associates, 1995). Pascarella *et al.* (1994: 14) concurred, saying that:

> out-of-class experiences were somewhat more important to development of critical thinking than in-class experiences . . . We further suggest that these results argue for rethinking the current structural and functional relationships between academic and student affairs divisions in our colleges and universities.

Elsewhere in the USA, university authorities are doing systematic studies of the relationship between certain out-of-class activities and the quality of student learning outcomes (Erwin and Knight, 1995). The implication of this is that there will be many factors associated with learning that lie outside the control of the individual academic or department. For example, 'the main factor determining student learning . . . is individual studying by students outside the classroom' (Murray, 1991: 137). On this view, good teaching would be about supporting this engagement and motivating students to work hard and purposefully on worthwhile tasks.

The development in the UK of greater emphasis on student autonomy, for example, means that the quality of library and information services has become a very important factor in respect of the quality of undergraduate learning. Carey and Magennis (1995) report that on one campus, problems with library resources constituted the greatest set of difficulties that students had in pursuing their studies. There, 'good teaching' was being inhibited not through the qualities of any member of the academic staff but through an institutional failing.

To take another example, the structure of programmes may inhibit deep approaches to learning. In the UK a modularized programme organized in semesters can lead to students finding that there is little assessed work at the beginning of the semester and a deluge at the end; that all the work takes similar forms because semesters are too short to allow for a greater range of more time-consuming approaches to teaching and assessment; and to disconnectedness, so that the extension of student choice has ruptured any possibility of anyone helping the student to put all the pieces that are the module together in the jigsaw that is the programme. This latter point is interesting since one of Ratcliff's conclusions is that effective climates for undergraduate education create 'synthesizing experiences' (Ratcliff, 1995). In the previous chapter it was noted that Alverno College has developed a horizontally and vertically integrated curriculum and that impressive results are claimed to come from it. Previously we have argued that transformative learning needs integration, that is to say learning that draws from and is more than the collection of modules (Harvey, 1994b). At the very least, we suggest that the third, metaform of transformative learning that was discussed in Chapter 7 is less likely to happen in a fission-style modular system than in a fusion-style one. Again, the quality of individuals' teaching has little power in the face of this structural constraint.

Much the same could be said of the force of expectations. Students are more likely to adopt deep approaches to learning where they have some freedom, where they are not overloaded with work and where the work can be invested with some relevance. Programme expectations can discourage deep approaches and can, in turn, inhibit good teaching, where that is defined as teaching to enhance understanding.

Some environmental obstacles to good teaching can be lessened by planning. In an institution, it may be expected that lectures will dominate teaching but there are many things that can be done to make lectures effective as ways of developing learners' understanding (Angelo and Cross, 1993). Library resources may be under pressure, but coursework that required learners to search through the journal literature, rather than relying on standard textbooks, would ease the pressure and work against surface approaches to learning. Seminars may have become too big for the whole group to discuss anything with the tutor, but there are techniques for preserving both the discussion aspect of seminar work and a sense that the tutor is contributing to the quality of discussion (Gibbs, 1992). The Alverno approach to integration has been noticed as another example of the way that environmental factors can support effective learning.

Our first major point about good teaching is *responsibility*: that institutions bear responsibility for the environment that supports or discourages it; that individuals bear responsibility for the creativity that they bring to making good learning happen in less-than-perfect environments; and that, as a consequence, teaching quality is nobody's fault and everybody's.

# Teaching quality and the assessment of learning

A clear message from Chapter 8 was that the quality of learning is affected by the ways in which that learning is assessed, which leads to some claims about good teaching.

- Given the importance of feedback to learning, it follows that good teaching involves giving feedback that is useful (Brown and Knight, 1994) and that does not use the 'final vocabulary' that can demean and discourage (Boud, 1995a). This lies close to the dialogue model of learning proposed by Laurillard (1993).
- The criteria embodied in this feedback, hence the goals of the piece of work and of the module and programme, must be explicit and learners should frequently consider what they mean.
- One way of understanding the meaning of criteria is to use them. For this reason, even if for no other, self- and peer-assessment should be used. However, the development of judgement, especially of the ability to judge oneself, is important in its own right.
- A range of learning goals needs a range of assessment methods. Moreover, transformative learning involves choosing to use an insight or ability in a range of circumstances, which also implies that it is desirable to assess in a variety of ways. This has not always been recognized. In Chapter 2, for example, the use of a range of assessment procedures was not seen as an important criterion of quality, which suggests that expectations may need to be modified.

It is fair to expect a response to each of those points to be evident in any one tutor's own course or module. However, it was said in Chapter 8 that good assessment involves seeing it as a departmental and institutional issue, not just as a matter of personal responsibility. It is proposed that good teaching is characterized by contexts where:

- attention is given to making the assessment of learning reliable and valid, according to the uses to which the assessment data are to be put. However, the inherent limitations of the data are recognized: they are not performance indicators but a source of information to be used in the process of continuous quality improvement;
- hence, assessment is for learning, rather than learning being for assessment, accountability and administration;
- some assessment activities encourage learners to integrate or synthesize their understandings from different modules.

In terms of teaching quality there is an aspect of assessment, known as classroom assessment, that has not yet been considered. This is the term given by Angelo and Cross (1993: 4–5) to a set of activities 'to help teachers find out what students are learning in the classroom and how well they are learning it . . . the teacher is not obliged to share the results of Classroom Assessment with anyone outside the classroom . . . Classroom Assessments

... are almost never graded and are almost always anonymous'. What Angelo and Cross offer is a lively set of 50, often 'quick and dirty' techniques for getting a feel of what learners are understanding, what they are not understanding and where problems might lie. The aim is to help teachers to tune their teaching (and that may or may not be didactic teaching) to respond to this feedback from students. Uncontentiously, they associate this with good teaching practice: 'to improve their effectiveness, teachers need first to make their goals and objectives explicit and then to get specific, comprehensible feedback on the extent to which they are achieving those goals' (Angelo and Cross, 1993: 8); 'systematic inquiry and intellectual challenge are powerful sources of motivation, growth and renewal for college teachers and Classroom Assessment can provide such a challenge' (Angelo and Cross, 1993: 10).

The claim that classroom assessment is a criterion of good teaching may be defended also on the basis of the authors' analyses of the effects upon students:

> Academic staff often report the following four observable, interrelated, positive effects of Classroom Assessment on their students: more active involvement and participation; greater interest in learning, self-awareness as learners and metacognitive skill; higher levels of cooperation within the classroom 'learning community'; and greater student satisfaction.
>
> (Angelo and Cross, 1993: 372)

Whether it increases student learning is subject to debate, although given that it means that there is less time in class for tutor-controlled content coverage, the absence of evidence that student learning suffers under a classroom assessment regime is significant in itself.

That the *quality of assessment* is indicative of the quality of teaching is thus our second main claim about teaching.

## Teaching as mastery of technique

The quality of teaching is also related to the approaches used. One sense of this is that the quality of technique is important. Pascarella and colleagues (1994: 8) concluded that 'first-year students who perceived their instructors to be organized and prepared ... tended to demonstrate greater cognitive gains than their peers who experienced less organized and prepared instruction'. The teacher is to be preferred who, when appropriate, is audible, writes legibly and uses technology; who is knowledgeable, well-prepared and who alerts learners to the structure of the teaching session; who uses varied techniques; who is up to date in the field; who provides supporting material when necessary, and who does likewise with bibliographic advice; who is punctual and reliable; and who is clear. Who could deny the virtue of such qualities? Yet such a list, just as with the easy-to-observe schedules used to assess the quality of school teachers' performance, is severely limited, especially with the gestation of the electronic 'virtual university'. On the one hand, one could have learned to do all of these things and yet do little to help learners to understand – this could all be in the service of the pathology of surface approaches to learning. Secondly, the absence of some of these elements may be desirable (should students need bibliographic advice towards the end of the undergraduate experience?) and it may not matter (I lecture badly, so I replace lectures with other ways of teaching and, as an unexpected bonus, students seem to learn better). A further point is that it is possible to have these abilities, to want to promote deep approaches and still not to be seen as a good teacher.

So, if teaching technique and teaching quality go together (and it would be odd to say otherwise), it might be better to think about techniques for encouraging the esteemed deep approaches to learning, rather than techniques for doing a good lecture. Some relevant points have been mentioned: the purposes, focus and methods of assessment are crucial and the environment, as learners perceive it, is also important. The following can be done to promote deep approaches to learning within individual courses.

• Prefer depth over breadth: in effect, allow more time on any given task, since the adoption of coping strategies comes from asking learners to do too many tasks in the time they believe to be reasonable. Content coverage could be reduced since a study has shown that 'six weeks after taking an exam, students retained only about 40 per cent of the material' (Boyatzis *et al.*, 1995: 243).
• Keep questions, concepts, procedures and principles to the fore: information is valuable only in relation to them.
• Hence, emphasize mental activity: examine, for example, what is involved in laboratory work and why. 'The good stories [about laboratory work] came from students undertaking projects of an investigative nature ... Projects represented a real challenge, students felt fully involved and often experienced a sense of responsibility, independence and achievement' (Hazel, 1995: 157).
• Use a variety of teaching-and-learning techniques and tasks. In particular, consider the value of cooperative learning (Bothams, 1995; Millis, 1995).
• Some student choice is valued by learners and is associated with deep approaches. It is also consistent with the 'breadth-over-depth' principle. Maximize choice as far as is consistent with the development of principles, procedures, concepts and questions in this content area.
• Finally, to labour the points made about assessment, feedback from tutor to students and from students to tutor is necessary.

Our third claim about good quality teaching is that it uses *techniques* that are likely to support deep approaches to learning. It is also likely to show technical skill of another kind, which we might naïvely call 'teaching skill'. However, 'teaching skill' may be wrongly identified as performance skill and no more. That is a treacherous error.

# Teaching and personal qualities

Research reports frequently say that a series of dispositional qualities are important to good quality teaching. Hazel (1995: 174–5), writing about good practice in laboratory teaching, talks of 'sharing enthusiasm and making laboratory work an enjoyable experience for students'; 'respecting students'; 'supporting students warmly . . . showing encouragement and empathy'. Other studies have noted the importance of concern for students, stimulation of interest, availability and enthusiasm (Feldman, 1976; Murray, 1991).

However, our fourth point about good teaching is that *we need to be wary of attempts to link good teaching with the personal qualities of the teacher*. In part this is because personalizing the quality of the teaching in this way is sociologically naïve, amounting to a negation of micro- and macro-social influences, including the university environment. In part, it is because it is not clear whether teachers who have these qualities are good teachers as a consequence, or whether they are believed to have these qualities *because* they are seen as good teachers. In part, it is because there is no evidence that these qualities are anything like sufficient for good teaching: one might be enthusiastic, caring and the like but fail to give explanations that meshed with learners' understandings. And, above all, this personalization of good teaching has been repeatedly refuted by studies of school teaching. Not only has it been found that the qualities that are regularly cited are too bland and vague to be useful in teacher education but, worse, 'there is very little evidence that characteristics and qualities of teachers identified in prior research are linked in any way with the excellence or effectiveness of teachers' (Anderson and Burns, 1989: 6).

# Teaching and a sense of the game

We now return to the theme of the first three points made above, to what good teachers in higher education do. It is that good teaching involves having a sense of how the part (the module) fits with the whole (the programme). Naturally, that is not easy in days of fissile modularization. Yet, many universities lay claims to develop core competencies across the curriculum and most academics would see themselves as having a commitment to developing learners' expertise in a subject or area. A precise sense of the part-whole relationship may not be possible, but since good learning is partly dependent on learners having a conception of what it is they are supposed to be learning, on having a conception of the structure of the subject or area, it follows that good teaching involves locating the module within a vision of the whole. Dall'alba (1993) has shown how science tutors with different views of the subject take up different stances on science teaching. Since such views are, unfortunately, not normally made explicit to learners, the consequence is that they do not get a developing grasp of the nature of the subject or area but a series of accounts of parts of it, based on differing epistemologies. Some learners may arrive at their own resolutions but in many cases teaching, so far from helping learners to understand the nature of the subject or area, has actually contributed to misunderstandings. It is hard to see how good learning takes place in such a situation and it may usefully be recalled that Flavell, Miller and Miller (1993) identified metacognition with learners getting 'a sense of the game'. Good teachers have and share a view of the subject area and help learners to connect what they are doing in a module to that structure, to get a sense of the game. In Chapter 7 it was argued that learners benefit from a structured programme to help them to become skilled within a School of Independent Studies (Knight, 1996) and that the coherence of the undergraduate learning experience is important (Ratcliff and associates, 1995) and that Alverno College offers an example of how this might be worked out in practice.

If the individual module contains no sense of connection, then there is no acknowledgment by the tutor of the importance of relating the part to the whole and of laying this relationship before learners. If that is not done, transformative learning may still take place but it will be despite the tutor.

Therefore, our fifth point about good teaching is how we, as teachers, fit into the scheme of things – *how the part fits the whole.*

## The quality of teachers' goals

This all connects easily with our last claim about good teaching at the level of the individual academic. It is about bringing about conceptual change. Repeatedly, students say that good teachers give clear explanations. This does not have to be understood to mean giving clear oral explanations, let alone to give clear explanations in lectures, although it is possible that students weaned on such teaching approaches may have meant that. This raises the issue of what would count as a clear explanation. Presumably, clear explanations lead to understanding. But, the aim is to help learners to arrive at new understandings, which involves making a connection between learners' present understanding and some notion of what it might become transformed into. If this is to happen, then good teaching requires:

• a belief by academic staff that their job is to support this type of transformative learning, as well as lesser forms of learning. However, Trigwell (1995) has shown that academics in science departments may not volunteer such a conception of teaching, with the result that their teaching is characterized by activities that lack transformative power. That is not to deny that in their classes learners assimilate more information, nor to deny that learners may not, in some specific senses, accommodate their old concepts to new information. What will be lacking is a transformation of learners' understanding of the subject and of themselves as learners of the subject and in general. Lacking too will be insight into what it might mean to be a mentally active learner, choosing and wanting to seek for understanding through dialogue with self, experience and

others. Academic staff's teaching and their conceptions of learning are bound up with what they make it easy for learners to do;
- goals or visions: a sense of what might emerge from the module or programme. Needless to say, the learning and the assessment arrangements are designed to advance that vision at least;
- that these goals are shared with learners. This is the 'sense of the game' point in another guise;
- an understanding of what learners tend to believe and of the difficulties they tend to have. Materials or teaching will be sensitive to these problems, based on the axiom 'find out what learners know and teach them accordingly' (Ausubel, 1985: 82).

Finally, therefore, our last point about good teaching is that *it depends upon academic staff seeing their rôle as facilitators of transformational learning, not as merely purveyors of data.*

## Conclusion

Good teachers exploit their professional autonomy to do many things that encourage learners to stand with confidence as people who can get information, form concepts, and master and apply procedures. In Chapter 7 it was argued that learners should also be able to integrate their understandings from different sources and thereby to gain a sense of when to apply what they know, understand and can do. A desirable goal is for them to be able to bring all of this into harmony with a sense of themselves and to see that all knowledge and understanding can be seen through different lenses, some which magnify, others which distort. Good teaching, then, is anything that the tutor intends that promotes such transformation.

In summary, good teaching is encouraged by:

- the quality of the institutional environment;
- well-conceived assessment systems;
- knowledge of teaching techniques;
- seeing the parts in the context of the whole;
- academic staff's beliefs about their role as teachers.

It is not dependent upon the personal characteristics of the teacher.

The points outlined in this chapter are substantial. Yet academics are not powerless. Even in hostile environments, teaching may be better or worse. In pointing to what good teachers might do, and in denying that their personal qualities are related to teaching quality, this chapter has implied that teaching for learning is something that might be learned. It is the implications of the idea that teaching quality is something that is malleable, not an accident of personality, that occupy the next chapter.

# 10

## Professional Development for Transformative Learning

The average faculty salary ranged from a low of $34,307 for those who spent more than 70 per cent of their time on teaching to a high of $56,181 for faculty who spent less than 35 per cent of their time on teaching.

(Ratcliff and associates, 1995: iv)

Look at training as *the* research-and-development expenditure . . . fund it with at least 4 per cent of gross revenues. (That goes for burger flippers as well as multi-media geeks.)

(Peters, 1994: 297)

### Developing and being developed

If students are to be transformed during their undergraduate careers, then universities need first to transform themselves, moving from the rituals of teaching to the mysteries of learning.

Academic freedom is a central feature of Western universities and, even if its meaning may be contested, it seems to be in tension with any attempts by a university as a body to strive for homogeneity of any sort. Now, were it the case that teaching (or facilitating learning) were a marginal activity, then attempts to change it in certain, across-the-board ways might not be seen as much of a threat to academic freedom, since these would be changes at the margins. However, if Boyer's argument (1990) is accepted, that teaching is one aspect of a fourfold unity of academic identity, then teaching cannot be seen as a peripheral, low-status activity. So if universities move to take teaching more seriously as an aspect of scholarship, then it would hardly be surprising if subsequent attempts to change the ways in which people teach (or promote learning) were to be seen as attempts to impose change on their professional identities.

In schools, it has long been understood that all curriculum change is about changing people. Curriculum change refers not just to changes in content but also, and more problematically, to changes in teaching and learning methods. While a change in the content of the curriculum does cause problems for school teachers, the hardest changes to accept are changes in pedagogy, in ways of working with children. Despite folk beliefs that English primary schools are alive with 'modern' teaching methods, research has repeatedly shown the strength of tradition: changing the content of the curriculum is easier than changing teaching and learning styles. So when academics are enjoined to learn about learning and to rethink what that means for teaching, they are being asked to do something that research into school curriculum development tells us will be difficult.

In this chapter, professional development is going to be understood as professional development in relation to the scholarship of teaching or, as Boyatzis *et al.* (1995) have it, the scholarship of learning. We recognize that it is important for academic staff to develop in their areas of academic expertise too and that many universities spend a great deal of money on this, especially through sabbatical and study leave. The implication is that academic staff may need to be convinced that they should expect development in other areas too. Three further issues need attention at this point.

First, there is an ethical dimension to professional development. Who develops whom, in what ways and on what authority? The term 'staff development' is often used here, carrying with it implications that academics are employees to be developed, presumably in ways suitable to institutional management. Development can be seen, quite plausibly in some institutions, as a management device for re-educating the workforce so as to enable the institution the better to achieve some targets. Where it becomes associated with prescriptive views of good teaching, it is no big step to characterize staff development as a top-down control device, a university contribution to a Foucaudian panopticon.

Secondly, we recognize a problem of our own creation. We have not offered a prescriptive model of good teaching. We have insisted that the quality of learning is what is at stake; that teaching can be understood to cover a range of activities; that teaching is associated with learning in a variety of sometimes not well-understood ways; and that different 'teaching' approaches will be appropriate to different learners with different material in different circumstances. We have not produced a bureaucrat's checklist for measuring teaching quality. The points made about teaching in Chapter 9 constitute, we suggest, an agenda for professional discussion about the fitness of any particular practices for the learning purposes to which they relate. It follows that professional development for transformative learning cannot be a matter of seeing progress in the widespread adoption of, say, open learning methods; nor should despair necessarily be the response to the longevity of the lecture method.

Thirdly, in Chapter 7 we argued that transformative learning is most likely to take place where certain conditions are met, amongst them being where learners have some autonomy; where they are motivated and interested; and where they are not overloaded with work. The principles that we applied in Chapter 7 to undergraduates apply no less to academic staff, a consideration to which we shall return later in this chapter. Here, we are discussing how academic staff might transform their understanding of teaching and learning: we are discussing transformative learning by academic staff. Against that needs to be set the claim that universities are in the business of helping students to learn and, in general, to learn through changing their ways of thinking. It is quite reasonable to expect academics to be proficient in this key function of a university and, where they are not, both to support and, in many cases, to require change.

Our argument, developed below, is that a coupling of a university commitment to transformative learning with academic staff's freedom has the potential to reconcile universities' needs to direct with academics' rights. Should the line be that academics are employees like any others and have no compelling rights in this area, it is still possible to defend this loose–tight coupling on the grounds that it is probably more effective and efficient than any alternative power-coercive bureaucratic prescriptions.

The model of a loose–tight coupling between central direction on some issues and local freedom on implementation has important implications for the processes of educational development in universities. Before considering them we consider the learners in these processes, who in this case are the academic staff.

## The academic profession

Research reported by Fulton (1995) offers a picture of the academic profession in one country, England, in the early 1990s. At the time of the survey, some 80,000 people comprised the profession in Britain with almost two-fifths born between 1941 and 1950. About three-quarters were men. Academic staff had spent a median of ten years in their present institution. In the older (pre-1992) universities, promotion was discerned to be a reward for achievement, particularly research achievement, while in the newest universities it seems to have been associated with managerial responsibility. Overall, there are grounds for concern that promotion policies have not given women equal opportunities.

Teaching loads were high in comparison with those in other comparable countries studied at the same time and have increased since. In 1992 some 60 per cent of academics working outside the older, pre-1992 universities taught for more than 21 term-time hours per week. About one-third of academics in the older universities carried such loads. Virtually no one in those older universities said their primary interest lay in teaching and only a quarter of those working elsewhere identified it as their main interest. The figures are almost exactly reversed with regard to research, which implies that most academics see their job as research and teaching, although academics in the pre-1992 universities put more weight on the research element and their colleagues elsewhere gave more weight to teaching. Academics in this latter group were more likely to feel well prepared to teach but there was a strong feeling among staff in the pre-1992 universities that they were inadequately prepared as teachers.

While few academics regretted their choice of career, reports of personal strain were common and it was felt that the profession's status was declining. There was general discontentment with promotion prospects. In some areas of higher education institutional management styles were a cause of dissatisfaction and there were more general worries about the competence of institutional leadership, with concern about the quality of communication and some quite strong accusations of autocratic behaviour, even in the older universities, where more collegial norms might have been expected to prevail. In term time, research, which not all academics thought themselves sufficiently well trained to undertake, was overshadowed by administration and teaching.

While it is important to notice these pressures, it is equally important to identify the sources of identity and satisfaction. Most academics cited their discipline as their most important reference point, enjoyed the courses that they teach, valued the opportunity to pursue their own ideas and rated highly their relationships with colleagues.

Plausible implications for professional development work include the following.

- It would not be helpful for it to be seen as an arm of institutional management.
- There is a case for using strategies that work through disciplines in a collegial manner, encouraging the development of ideas arising from academic staff.
- Many academics may not have been trained as teachers but they are old enough to have well-grooved teaching practices and attendant beliefs. Change will not be easy.
- High teaching loads combined with a widespread interest in research mean that professional development will struggle for attention. Current evidence is that the extrinsic reward of promotion is not available (Ratcliff and associates, 1995). Unless professional development can be shown to reduce the burden of teaching, it will have to appeal to academic staff in terms of intrinsic motivation, notably to their enjoyment of teaching their courses.
- In the coming decade the baby boomers will retire, allowing universities to recruit staff with proven skill at promoting learning, if they so choose. However, Jenkins (1995b) concluded that the research assessment exercise in Britain had led geography departments to give priority to research over teaching. Furthermore, the national assessments of teaching quality had, made little or no impact at the time that his research was done (1993).

## Reflection and professional development: a bottom-up approach

A fashionable solution to such problems of professional development has been to invoke the concept of the reflective practitioner. This is the practitioner who consciously engages in a dialogue between the thinking that attaches to actions and the thinking that deals in more abstracted propositional knowledge. While it is too crude to speak of an interplay between theory and practice, because all practice is theory-driven and theory-forming, the crude phrase captures something important about the reflective practitioner. This practitioner is regularly thoughtful and continually learning from the interplay between procedural and propositional knowledge. It follows that if professionals could learn to make action and the thoughts surrounding it, and thinking and the actions surrounding it the subjects of continuing appraisal as a part of life-long learning, then professional development would have been guaranteed. This solution is politically attractive because it places power with the individual practitioner, taking away none of the autonomy that is seen as characteristic of a professional. Furthermore, it is a solution that acknowledges the complex and contexted nature of professional work, a solution that eschews panaceas and prescriptions and that values artistry and judgement and that is popular with the professional bodies studied by Harvey and Mason (1995).

There is no need to deny the attraction of this stance. However, being a reflective practitioner – hence helping staff to become such practitioners – is more than a matter of copious injunctions to reflect on teaching and learning. For example, reflection can easily be self-confirming.

Experience does not necessarily equal learning, observed Boyatzis and colleagues (1995: 76). If research into human social perception were not sufficient, then studies of schoolteachers' thinking would show that what we learn is considerably constrained by what we believe. There is a tendency for thought to confirm thought, so that when we think about an experience, we easily do so in terms of existing categories, scripts and beliefs, thereby confirming them. As the discussion of learning in Chapter 7 indicated, it is one thing to add information to existing ideas but very much another to use experience to change those ideas. In short, the danger of reflection is that it can tend to be self-confirming, which is why the notion of critical transformation, discussed in Chapter 1, is so important to our view of universities' work.

Research into schoolteacher thinking further illustrates the issue (Clark and Peterson, 1986). A distinction needs to be made between teachers' on-the-fly thinking, the often-subconscious agency behind the host of decisions that teachers make while working with children, and out-of-class reflection and planning. The latter category is of the greatest interest in the context of this book, although it is worth remarking that there is enormous scope for learning about academics-as-teachers by examining their thinking when they are working with students. When it comes to planning, teachers tend to concentrate upon organizing the content. Largely absent is consideration of learning outcomes. The focus is upon how content is to be *taught*, not upon how understandings are to be formed through a process of learning. It cannot be said that these teachers are not reflective: plainly, that is what they are doing in their planning. The problem is that the framework of reflection is, in a sense, egocentric, delineating how the teacher will handle concerns that are urgent in terms of delivering smooth-running lessons that cover the necessary content.

It may be that academic staff think differently, that their lack of teacher training fits them better to plan in terms of learning. That is an empirical question. The answer cannot invalidate the general point, namely that there is reason to be cautious of generalized injunctions to reflect if there is no accompanying recognition that reflection may follow comfortable grooves.

Eraut (1994) has drawn attention to another difficulty with the quality of the reflection. In certain professions, there are fairly obvious indications of when a professional is thinking well as opposed to badly. In teaching, this is less evident and the model of teaching and learning we have developed precludes any simple judgements about the quality of thought. However, it does not preclude informed appreciation of the thinking behind such practices and it does provide a series of principles against which accounts of such thinking may be judged. What is needed is evidence of *good* reflection, not of reflection, pure and simple. This might take the form of a requirement that evidence be adduced to support practice – especially to support practices such as examinations, lectures, grading, progress dependent on attendance, that are based on custom.

We are driving towards two complementary positions.

One is that 'reflection' is a good intention frequently found to be fallen on hard times. There is nothing to distinguish it from 'thinking', which is a quintessential human activity. What is important is the quality of thought. Is the focus on teaching (what I do) or upon learning (what they might gain)? Are claims to be put to some test, or is it the case that all reflections are equal? If that is so, surely the notion of the reflective practitioner is an illusionist's charter?

The second position is that professional development ought to contain the possibility of transformative learning for academics. In many cases it would be a transformation for colleagues' thinking to move from teaching to learning. This is illustrated through a summary of recent work by Trigwell (1995) and Boyatzis *et al.* (1995).

Trigwell was interested not so much in academics' thinking about teaching science at the level of tips for teaching but in their very conceptions of science teaching itself. His position is that the range of teaching strategies that academic staff are prepared to use is conditioned by their underlying conceptions of teaching, so that 'faculty who do think of teaching from teacher-focused perspectives will be unlikely or unable to accept strategies based on student-focused ideas' (Trigwell, 1995: 77). Building on earlier work, he identified six conceptions of learning, the highest two of which were 'an interpretative process aimed at understanding reality' and 'learning as changing a person' (Trigwell, 1995: 79). He proposed that just as these conceptions of learning tended to be associated with deep or surface approaches to learning, so too different conceptions of teaching would affect teaching. On the basis of interviews with twenty-four teachers in two natural science departments in each of two universities, he derived six conceptions of teaching: two cast the teacher as a transmitter of information;

two involve the teacher in trying to help students to understand the concepts and relations between them; and two relate to helping students to elaborate, extend and change their own conceptions or world views.

While one might disagree with the analytical framework he employed, there is no reason to doubt Trigwell's claim that 'teaching strategies are used and interpreted differently from the perspectives of different conceptions of teaching and learning' (Trigwell, 1995: 88). In other words, persuading academic staff to use any set of strategies will itself be difficult where they hold views of their jobs of teachers that do not allow them to see the point of those strategies. But, even if convinced of the value of a strategy, it will be applied quite differently by tutors with different conceptions of teaching, hence of the purpose of using the strategy. In other words, reflection is of limited value unless it involves attention to tutors' core notions of teaching and unless there is some attempt to move them from transmittive to what we are calling transformative conceptions.

This can be complemented by the experience of Boyatzis *et al.* (1995: 129), concerned to develop a new Master of Business Administration (MBA) programme, who show that 'student improvement is seen in areas where faculty intent [to develop a skill] is high . . . in areas where faculty intent is low, little change occurs in students'. This may be unremarkable but it allows the corollary that if academic staff do not intend for transformation to be a possible outcome of their teaching, then there is little reason to expect it to happen. Given that 'training and socialization into the professional, academic culture creates strong commitments to pedagogical methods that sustain the expert-teacher model of teacher behaviour' (Boyatzis *et al.*, 1995: 221) then for the new MBA programme to work, staff had to move from a view of themselves as researchers to one of teachers. Moreover, their view of themselves as teachers had to move from a transmittive view to one of teachers as people with expertise working within a *learning*-centred institution, focusing upon the whole person of the learner, not just upon the transmission of knowledge to her or him.

Reflection that had been confined to technical questions about teaching better would have missed the crucial significance of the need to shift from teaching to learning that characterized this MBA programme.

Clearly, it would be folly to deny the potential that reflection has in terms of driving professional development. Our claim is that reflection needs to be extensive, to involve examining lurking assumptions about what we do and why we do it. This is well captured in a position developed by Winter (1995) that arose out of work that began with the professional learning of social workers. Competence, he said, includes:

- a commitment to professional values;
- continuous professional learning;
- affective awareness, that is awareness of the emotional complexity of situations;
- effective communication;
- effectiveness in acting;

- effective grasp of a wide range of professional knowledge;
- intellectual flexibility.

Amongst the strengths of this account, we wish to highlight two things. One is the way that professional development is not seen as something done to the individual but, as with transformative learning, a process that depends very much upon the individual's own self-awareness. Secondly, questions about values are brought into a relationship with the practitioner's perceptions of the environment in which he or she works, which is in turn related to the practitioner's knowledge, understanding and development. It offers a systemic view of professional development: if reflection is confined to one element alone, the chances of change happening are limited.

# Policy and academic freedom: a top-down approach

Reflection may be depicted as 'bottom-up' change, where power lies with the person reflecting on practice. In many countries there has been a strong, modern preference for top-down, imposed change. For example, Trow (1993: 13) reports that one senior official in a British funding council saw the assessment of teaching quality to be a necessary procedure to discover whether the teacher ' "delivers the course the customer (i.e. the student) expected to get." In this conception of the academic's role, the teacher produces a product which the customer buys'. As he comments, 'this is a reasonably accurate (if partial) description of some parts of higher education: the straightforward transmission of skills and knowledge, where students and teachers share a notion of what is involved in the transaction' (Trow, 1993: 13).

What so easily happens with such top-down, policy-driven accountability approaches to educational development is that teaching becomes commodified. A number of problems can be seen with this approach to developing the academic profession through this commodification of teaching.

First, university teaching is diverse. Universities, like schools, recognize that different subject areas make different pedagogical demands and that learners with different achievements also make different pedagogical demands. Moreover, different departments teaching the same subjects may have different priorities. Angelo and Cross (1993) found differences in the importance attached to 15 teaching goals by nine different sets of subject specialists, although Harvey, Burrows and Green (1992c) did not find this difference in their work in Britain (see Chapter 2). Furthermore, orientations towards their teaching also change over time (Trow, 1993). In short, because goals and their explications differ, teaching will legitimately differ too. If teaching is seen as a commodity, then it is a very diverse commodity.

So, top-down attempts to specify the nature of good teaching founder on diversity. Yet, even where there is some agreement on features of good teaching, there is the further complication that there are intractable questions about how any tutor's skill at teaching and facilitating learning would be assessed fairly (Knight, 1993).

There are also grounds for doubting the desirability of top-down approaches to professional development. On one level, academic freedom would be much changed as a result. It might be argued that changes to the undergraduate curriculum would not affect tutors' rights to research and publish as they wished. To this there is the practical response that these changes would be so substantial as to risk discouraging research and publication in the interests of making time to become skilled at delivering the undergraduate product in the approved way. It is also likely that an academic profession that had been subjected to such an exercise of state power would feel cowed, whatever the proclaimed intentions of the state.

Perhaps the most worrying feature of top-down approaches is that if they are to have meaning, then it has to be possible to measure compliance with them. However, the performance criteria that would be implicated in such a development, would tend, for obvious reasons, to describe what is easily measured. There is a danger that attempts to improve teaching by commodifying it could end up defining both teaching and its products in terms of what is readily measurable – which might not be what it is most important to know, understand and do. There is also the danger that such criteria could freeze universities at a point in time, discouraging innovation in methods and content.

A further danger, which is that the external accountability that would be built into such a system could well lead to universities having to give priority to the bureaucratic processes of compliance. As Trow (1993: 20) points out, 'departments and individuals shape their activities to what "counts" in the assessments' so it would not be surprising if 'university activities begin to adapt to the simplifying tendencies of the quantification of outputs'. It is often said that academics have great scope for subverting attempts to control their work, but it is a delightful irony that they might best subvert the aim of improving teaching quality by complying diligently with such bureaucratic requirements. This does not lead to the conclusion that since teaching is a sophisticated activity of professional judgement (Chapter 9), and since efforts to assess the quality of teaching as a commodity are misconceived, then everything is in the individual's hands. Professional development, we suggest is about top-down *and* bottom-up change.

## Top-down and bottom-up: universities and departments

No university can abrogate responsibility for the quality of learning within it, nor for the quality of teaching activities. The question is about how quality is continuously to be developed. There are limits to what can presently be achieved at university level, since many of the objections to state attempts to define and police teaching quality can be applied to individual universities. However, there is some agreement amongst the gurus of organizational health that effective organizations recognize that there are limits to what can be achieved from the centre (Peters, 1992; Drucker, 1993; Semler, 1993; Handy, 1994). The centre is the seat of the organizational culture, the arbiter of a system for the identification, co-ordination and propagation of core values and key working principles. Thereafter, as far as possible, the ways of doing things should be decided by the people who actually will be doing them. In such organizations, there are not long chains of command; bureaucracy is minimized; and the centre does not lap up company incomes. Since a key element in these organizations is a commitment to continued learning, they have sometimes been referred to as 'learning organizations'.

Schein (1992) has offered a thirteenfold account of learning cultures and learning leaders in non-educational organizations. His claim is that learning organizations, amongst other things, are ones in which people believe that, in the face of change the organization is not helpless, but a contributor to its own destiny, not least through a commitment to active learning. An implication of this is that even the 'expert' has to listen and learn in order to work with others to venture ways of dealing with shifting circumstances: expertise ceases to be the routine application of wisdom and becomes identified with the adaptation of expert knowledge to situations that have to be treated as being, to some degree, novel. Implicit in this is a belief that:

> . . . control-oriented environments . . . are certain to fail as the environment becomes more turbulent and as technological and global trends cause problem solving to become more complex . . . a cynical attitude to human nature is bound to create bureaucratic rigidity at the minimum and counterorganizational subgroups at the maximum.
>
> (Schein, 1992: 367–8)

This does not map to simple assumptions about the organization of the work environment, for Schein recognizes that there is a case both for individualism and for what he calls 'groupism'. Inevitably, this entails 'the assumption that diversity is desirable', constituting a resource for the organization, rather than being a threat to it. Similarly, short-term perspectives may have their place, but a medium-term orientation is preferred, not least because any action takes place within a system (Biggs, 1993; Knight, 1994), and it is only by attending to the complexities and unpredictabilities of systems that organizational change can be contoured to be both beneficial and effective. Achieving such change takes time: quick fixes cause rather than solve problems.

There is room for some scepticism about the whole set of ideas. Culture is, for example, a slippery concept. How does one know when an organization has a culture? Why does it matter? Will any culture that involves trusting people to do their best suffice, or is this a skivers' charter? And how do such cultures get formed? Nor are these questions to be asked only of business enterprises, since similar ones have been raised about the claims that if schools learned from the research into school effectiveness, then the quality of education would be improved (MacNamara, 1988; Anderson, 1990). Just as in schools, the quality of leadership is often seen to be paramount. Unfortunately, it turns out that there are many different ways of being an effective leader, a finding that is further complicated by the insight that leaders can exist at all levels and the most important leader may not be the person who stands highest in the hierarchy.

However, there are attractions in a core idea in these writings that organizations are at their best when they exhibit simultaneous loose–tight coupling. This is a rather awkward phrase to describe a system in which the centre is an active system for setting and monitoring goals (not objectives), with regard to values (one of which is valuing and trusting the workforce), and in having a 'passion for excellence' (as Peters entitled one of his books). That is the 'tight' coupling' – all are expected to work within and represent this culture within the discipline of an orientation to continuous quality improvement. The studies of United States assessment systems in Chapter 8 illustrated this sort of tight coupling. Thereafter, the system is 'loose' coupled, meaning that responsibility for working out that passion for excellence is devolved to everyone and they are free to use all appropriate means to achieve it, a notion that we have explored in Chapter 6. Naturally, evidence of achievement has to be provided and this is more easily done within some economic enterprises, for example manufacturing industry, than it is within others, such as people-working service industries, of which social work would be an example.

In terms of the discussion of professional development, the implication is that the university has a responsibility for demanding that there be continuous quality improvement in learning; requiring departments or other units to undertake that as they see fit; expecting them to provide suitable evidence of the improvements; and encouraging them to act, like the university as a whole, as learning organizations. Evidence of this would be available for peer scrutiny and peers would clearly want to know why some ways of demonstrating quality improvement had been used in preference to others. The argument would hinge on force of reason, not upon force of authority or on compliance with specifications handed down from high places.

Departments, in practice, would be responsible for the professional development of academic staff that is necessary if transformative learning is to ensue. The bad news is that not only do departments not have the knowledge to do so, there is very little knowledge to call upon. Indeed, in earlier chapters we have reviewed a lot of material on the nature of good teaching and on what makes for good learning. However, a theme of this chapter is that professional development is about more than drawing attention to this knowledge. That may be necessary but in most cases it is unlikely to be sufficient. Ways are needed of helping faculty to engage with this knowledge, of helping them to open themselves to transformative learning about teaching and learning itself. So what techniques for professional or educational development are the most effective?

# Approaches to professional development

Five principal approaches to professional development were identified by Weimer and Lenze (1991), namely workshops, consultation, grants, resource materials, and colleagues helping colleagues. To this we would add action research and while the comments that now follow apply to it, we shall discuss the meaning of action research a little later, somewhat out of sequence so as to sustain a distinction we wish to make.

Weimer and Lenze's conclusions was that none of these approaches had been evaluated with the rigour that might have been expected and that there were few reports that allowed for any judgement to be made about the effectiveness of any approach. Moreover, these exceptional reports often had technical failings that should make readers wary of accepting the findings at face value. It has to be accepted that we do not know what are the best ways of bringing about professional development, let alone when in the career of academic staff is the best time to intervene.

The most recent empirical work on professional development is Wright and O'Neil's (1995) report on the beliefs of professional development personnel about what they saw as the most effective teaching improvement practices. About these data two points can be made. First, they show that there are differences in the rankings of Canadian, American, Australasian and British professional development personnel, leading to the conclusion that practices that are seen as effective in one setting may not be perceived to be effective in another. The quest for the best approach may be a very context-sensitive quest. Secondly, what we have is a report of beliefs, not evidence that these beliefs match reality. Interestingly, it is hard to discern in the practices that education-development professionals cited many that might be seen as things within their direct control. The two most highly ranked sets of practices relate to leadership by deans and heads of department and university employment policies and practices. An uncharitable reading would be that these professional development practitioners see themselves as having a marginal influence compared to that of senior staff and of university policies.

However, if it is not possible to say that certain practices are more effective than others, it may be possible to suggest that certain situations hold greater promise for professional development than do others. One word of caution is needed. Many of these situations are ones which will require teams and departments to react. In itself that is not necessarily bad but it can mean that people are forever having to respond to external demands at the expense of growing to be better at what they are already doing. As always, reactive professional development has an opportunity cost.

## *Development work*

The work of Boyatzis *et al.* (1995) provides a good example of the way that a development activity led to substantial professional learning, in terms of language and ideas and in terms of practice. So too are the examples of Alverno College and James Madison University in the USA, described in Chapter 8. At the University of Huddersfield in the UK, the adoption of a university-wide teaching and learning policy spurred all departments on to development work at some level, while in the University of Ulster, concern over the distribution of degree classifications led to a university-wide review of assessment practices and to departmental level development work (Moore, 1995). In many British universities, the change to modular degree schemes has forced a reappraisal of teaching and assessment, although one fears that the development work that this has occasioned has often taken the form of coping, not of improving. In this section the focus is mainly on development work at departmental or team level, whatever the stimulus for that.

The reasoning in Chapter 7 provides some principles for understanding why this might be so. The need for development itself challenges existing thinking and practices, although it has to be admitted that some staff and departments will react by domesticating the new circumstances to live with their old, well-grooved ways. The fact that something has to be done not only gives the development work some level of relevance but it also compels attention. Yet, where departments and teams act on some sort of collegial lines, as is often the case, the actual job of development is not unlike flexible or independent learning. In other words, the claim is that professional development in teaching and learning comes through doing and through reflecting upon that doing.

One question related to this stance is what might be the stimuli for development. After all, for years there was little development in many British universities because the only developmental needs that were recognized were the needs to be up to date in the subject and, perhaps, to publish. Nowadays, there may be internal stimuli for change and where a department or team can be described as a learning organization, then not only will this be a fruitful source of stimuli, it is also likely to be the most potent. However, in many cases it is external stimuli that will be the most common. These may come from the university, through its rôle in shaping systems and values and monitoring their migration to departments, teams and individuals, or from governments, often in the interests of accountability, cost-cutting or both. In modern times there is no shortage of stimuli for development work, with frequent demands for reviews of various aspects of policy and practice, which is a problem in itself. The overload encourages compliance culture and change without change.

A second problem takes up the earlier discussion of reflection. As we said in Chapter 7, new information may be ignored or assimilated. Accommodation is rare. Consequently reflection may not take place as calls for development are smothered by 'the games academics play' (Astin, 1991). Alternatively, development takes the form of a variation on existing concepts of teaching, learning, students, subject and tutors, which recalls Trigwell's (1995) point that better teaching techniques can be frustrated where staff use them in pursuit of unsatisfactory concepts of teaching.

Where individuals or teams of enthusiasts are working on a development, this problem does not arise. However, a major problem with curriculum and staff development is that too much of it is done by teams of enthusiasts or by individuals. One reason is because extraordinary people often tackle developments that are too ambitious for the average practitioner to emulate. Their work is not generalizable. What is frequently absent is department- or programme-wide development. Desirable though it is that enthusiasts enthuse, it is system-wide change (here taking the department or programme as a system) that has the power to make for transformation, which depends so much on consistent messages and orientation across the undergraduate programme. If departments are to be discouraged from assimilation as a response to calls for development, then it is obviously helpful if collegial practices emerge, so that reformist voices may be discordant with assimilationist voices. That cannot be sufficient, partly because assimilation will often carry the day and partly because even where departments have the will to change, they often lack knowledge of what is possible as well as knowledge of how to get there.

A common solution to these problems is to say that departments need external consultants who have substantive expertise as well as procedural expertise in the management of change. Usually, these people will be professional development experts, or in some cases, experts in the assessment of student learning (Tait and Knight, 1995). Obvious difficulties are that this is expensive, using a large amount of educational developers' time on just one out of dozens of departments in a university; the education development professional occupies a difficult rôle as an outsider, and doubly so as an outsider unlikely to have knowledge of, let alone prestige in the discipline; moreover, educational development is often seen as a low-status, quasi-academic activity to be treated with (polite) disdain; and that it is likely that the department actually needs to have more knowledge if they are to develop effectively but it is not easy to see how that knowledge might be put into colleagues' hands. Unfortunately, people with the skill and knowledge to be good at professional-development work are not in abundant supply.

Feeling, if not evidence, strongly inclines to the view that development work can be the most powerful route to professional learning. Given the foregoing discussion, it may be that it is not the highway: conferences, half-day seminars, day-long workshops and guest speakers are cheaper ways of reaching more people (Gibbs, 1995a) especially where the university requires a representative from each department to attend. Newsletters are a print-based alternative. Unfortunately, by themselves, there is little evidence that they are effective: certainly respondents to Wright and O'Neil's survey (1995) placed these activities very near the bottom of their rankings of teaching improvement activities. It may well be that the problem is that these activities are cheap but to be cheap they have to be brief, perhaps even superficial. Related to that is the idea that they may (and may not) fire people up to make changes but then leave them to face the very difficult task of selling the changes (which they may only partly understand) to colleagues, and then of managing the complexities of the change process itself.

The dilemma is that development work is reckoned to be a powerful route to professional learning, when certain conditions are met. It is expensive and success is not guaranteed. Cheaper approaches reach more people but appear likely to affect thinking rather than to lead to much action, let alone team- or department-wide action.

## Action research

The distinction between action research and development work is by no means a clear one. Angelo and Cross (1993) explain how their Classroom Assessment technique can be used to fuel what is to all intents and purposes, action research.

Zuber-Skerritt (1993: 47) has defined 'action research':

> as collaborative, critical (and self-critical) enquiry by reflective practitioners who are accountable to make the results of their enquiry public. They evaluate their own practice and engage in participative problem-solving and continuing professional development.

The differences between this and what might be expected to come out of development work might seem to be super-subtle but they are important. Action research starts with an unease, a feeling that something might be a problem. It is not often a response to an external stimulus but is rather something owned by the action researchers. Enquiries are then made and on the basis of that 'research' developments take place. These developments are evaluated, which is another form of research. In turn, this leads to further thinking and to further development. Action research is seen, ideally as a continuing cycle of enquiry, reflection, planning and action: it is a stance towards practice, whereas development work is often an event. One other element should be mentioned, although this too may be found in some development projects. Action research should be a confluence of theory and practice: research on the basis of common sense is not sufficient, since planning, doing, evaluating and reflecting should all be informed by the voices of theory and research (Gibbs, 1995b). The key point, then, is that action research should be serious research, since otherwise the 'action' in action research is based on preconceptions and flimsy self-confirming evidence that legitimates such preconceptions.

Professional and practical learning might confidently be expected to flow from action research. It faces the same problems as development work and has its own besides. Development work often commands participation but action research is voluntary, coming from a personal or group sense that here there is a problem or issue to investigate and act upon. While every action researcher has to do their first project, the ideal is that action researchers are committed to continuing professional enquiry, which may not match very well the rhythms of academic life. A development project may be accommodated this year but next year is to be dominated by research. Action research should be for life. It follows that there is a strong connection between a commitment to action research and an orientation to continuous quality improvement.

None of this is to deny the power that action research has as a model of continuous professional quality improvement. The main objection is that if it can be distinguished from development work, pure and simple, then it is distinguished on grounds that make it less potent as a vehicle for staff development.

## Appointment, appraisal, tenure and promotion

Appointment, appraisal, tenure and promotion are occasions that are increasingly likely to prompt faculty to take action to improve their skill at teaching and in the promotion of learning.

It has long been held that there is little incentive for academic staff to take teaching seriously since tenure and promotion decisions have not been based on teaching quality (whatever that might be). There has been change over the past ten years, so that in some British universities promotion to senior posts can be achieved through teaching achievement, although Fulton's evidence, summarized above, suggests that it is managerial responsibility that still dominates promotion in those universities that have traditionally claimed to give a high priority to teaching. However, there are few British universities that do not consider teaching skill to be an important element in promotion decisions and performance appraisals will normally examine the teaching performance of teaching staff. Appointments in the United Kingdom are also made with more attention to teaching quality and it is increasingly common for people applying for their first academic job to have followed a teaching orientation programme. Again, though, there are stories of appointments being made on the grounds of research rather than teaching in institutions that have no hope of achieving anything more than a research reputation of average, if that.

There are exceptions, as at the University of Otago (1995), where the promotion criteria for applicants for professorship are that candidates should demonstrate at least high level competence, and preferably outstanding leadership in teaching, assessment and curriculum development. The announcement of the American Association for Higher Education's 1996 Faculty Roles and Rewards conference avers that 'tenure and promotion guidelines across the country have been changed to recognize a broader range of faculty work', moving from the notion that scholarly excellence was tantamount to research excellence. The collection edited by Wright *et al.* (1995) contains a number of examples of programmes to prepare people for academic careers and detailed advice on preparing a teaching portfolio which will be useful, amongst other things, for promotion and tenure applications (O'Neil and Wright, 1995).

Where universities value teaching and the promotion of learning, then it follows that the centre should ensure that this value is reflected throughout the system. A very powerful way of doing this is by applying leverage at key points. Appointment, appraisal, tenure and promotion are such points. Where the value is proclaimed but the system is weak, then important opportunities for fostering improvements in student learning and faculty teaching are being lost. The survey by Wright and O'Neil (1995) showed that education-development personnel in four areas of the world thought that the second most important set of teaching improvement practices related to employment policies and practices.

## Validation events, quinquennial reviews, external audits and evaluations

Each of these events has the power to direct a department towards professional development for teaching. If new courses are validated or approved without scrutiny of the goals and the ways in which the learning and assessment methods are related to those goals, then there is no pressure from the system to give priority to professional development. Likewise with the five-year reviews that are now faced by many departments in Britain. If evidence of a learning policy, of its implementation and of its impact is not sought, then a valuable opportunity to foster a learning culture is lost.

External audits in Britain have sent a variety of messages about teaching quality and have been remarkably silent on learning quality, a theme that we explored in Chapter 5. This is probably a fair reflection of the difficulties that face bureaucracies when trying to treat teaching as a commodity. In the USA the process of regional accreditation is in disrepute and the National Policy Board on Higher Education Institutional Accreditation has proposed the creation of a Higher Education Accreditation Board. While it remains to be seen what will come of this ferment, it is interesting to speculate that state legislatures that have mandated assessment programmes in institutions receiving state funding may have had a bigger impact on the status of teaching and hence on the need for educational development activities. Since most states have followed the Virginia loose–tight coupling model (p. 144), requiring institutions to reform assessment to produce evidence of learning achievements while leaving institutions free to devise their own ways of complying, these initiatives have generally not forced institutions to compromise on their educational goals. The case of James Madison University in Chapter 8 illustrates this.

## Professional development experts

The case so far is that professional development for the propagation of transformative learning depends on system-wide direction, at least at the level of the university and preferably at a state level too. However, direction is not the same as control and within a loose–tight coupling model it has been argued that departments and teams should have freedom to choose how best to put transformative learning at the centre of their undergraduate work. However, teams and departments do need expert advice and help, whether they know it or not, since learning, assessment and teaching are complicated matters.

Assuming that there ought to be a team of educational development specialists in each university, questions arise about the size of the team, its location and rôle, its priorities and about the skills it needs to contain.

It sometimes seems as though every institution has found a different answer to these questions. Take size, for example. The size of a professional development unit will partly be decided by the proportion of its income from undergraduate teaching that the university chooses to spend on this form of research and development, in investment for the future. Comparisons with businesses with similar turnovers suggest that this figure will generally be too low. Whatever the figure, the university has to decide how much it spends on staff and how much goes on the provision of workshops, seminars and conferences; on incentives for people to attend them; and on money to generate and support research and developmental projects by academic staff. A great deal of activity may be generated with few educational development personnel but a lot of money going out in grants to support grass-roots work. The price may be that there is a paucity of good advice about development and that projects have little influence beyond those directly touched by them.

Location and rôle are again contentious. Should education-development professionals be a central team or should money be put into having expertise in every school or faculty? And is the best orientation of these professionals towards personnel, where the term 'staff development' might convey that here is an agency for carrying out university policies? Or might the term 'professional' or 'educational development' imply that here is a group of academic staff committed to the improvement of learning and teaching through engaging colleagues with the best research findings on these topics? Elton (1995: 186) has argued strongly that professional development work might be undertaken by 'a quite normal academic department' providing award bearing courses, doing research and providing staff development services. Unfortunately, this comes at a time when some universities are treating staff development as an administrative job of contracting for people to provide training sessions.

With rôle definition go questions about appropriate targets. How is success to be measured? By the number of people participating in (award-bearing) activities? By the number of successful projects? By records of the unit's activity? By publications? Each of these criteria has the power to lead educational development personnel away from promoting transformative learning across the university but what alternatives would be better, bearing in mind that a number of academics, perhaps even most, will prefer to plough on with other work?

As for priorities, in the absence of any firm knowledge about what works best (and it may be, as we noted above, that the only answer of value is one that is related to a particular context), how are priorities to be set? Is time best spent on development work with enthusiastic departments or in teasing shy departments out of hiding? Is it best spent on graduate assistants and teaching assistants, or with new staff, or with heads of department? There are, in fact, far more possibilities and far more needs for educational development work than could ever be satisfied, especially where professional development, in the spirit of transformative learning, is seen as a matter of *continuous* quality improvement. There seem to be three main ways of setting priorities and it is likely that all three come into play simultaneously. One is to let government and university policy make the running. A second is for the educational development practitioners to give priority to what their expertise tells them are pressing needs, while the third is where decisions are made on the basis of asking academic staff what they feel their needs are. There still remain questions about what is nicely called 'the methods of delivery', although in the United Kingdom there seems to be a trend to use a cascade model, that is to work with relatively senior people in each department and lead them to take the message back to their colleagues for action. This, as we have suggested in Chapter 6, should be based on responsible agenda setting by the team, who will identify their own professional development needs.

It should be clear from the argument of this book and from this chapter in particular, that the job specification for educational developers ought to be formidable. Interpersonal and management skills need to be of a high order and considerable commitment is needed. Resilience is also necessary, since the professional development officer, as an outsider in departmental development planning is an easy target for people's frustration at being asked to change not simply what they think and do but also, in a real sense, who they are. There are also considerable knowledge demands (Knight, 1994).

If educational development professionals are to play a significant role in the shift from transmission teaching to transformative learning, they need, we suggest, to know a lot about learning and teaching, to know about different theories of learning and teaching, about the research evidence and about what has happened elsewhere. Knowledge of the craft, or profession, of educational development is also needed and given that much of that knowledge rests on common sense, not on research evidence, a commitment to action research in their own practice is a reasonable, minimum expectation. Yet, a survey reported by Nicol (1992) found that educational developers in England were uninterested in further research on staff development, teaching and learning. More recently, Brew (1995: 1) said that 'staff developers are essentially pragmatists, concentrating on the next meeting or the next course or consultation'. Gibbs (1995b) develops a good case for this pragmatic approach where the thinking behind it represents a good knowledge of the research literature, as is the case with his work. The worry is that it might be too easy to accept the pragmatism and fail to appreciate the depth of understanding that ought to underpin it. In the United States educational developers and assessment officers seem to hold higher qualifications than their British counterparts and may not take the craft view of their British colleagues, recognizing that in an academic environment influence is related to academic credibility.

## Conclusion

Professional development should take the form of enabling academic staff to develop their own strategies for facilitating transformative learning, preferably through collegial work, often at departmental level, in keeping with the approach to CQI that we developed in Chapter 6. However, simply enabling is not enough, since without guidance on what is possible and about the range of desirable ways of working towards those possibilities, there is a distinct danger that they will be rearranging the deckchairs on the *Titanic*. This is where educational development professionals undoubtedly have a rôle, albeit a very fuzzy rôle based on craft common sense more than anything else. We have also insisted that initiatives at the team, individual and departmental levels depend considerably on the system within which they take place. Moreover, professional development personnel in four areas of the world have said that institutional practices have the greatest part to play in the improvement of teaching (Wright and O'Neil, 1995). Not only can the system encourage or marginalize them but, more importantly, the way the university operates deeply affects the importance that is attached to such reform of student learning.

# 11

## Conclusions

> Give a small boy a hammer, and he will find that everything he encounters needs pounding.
>
> (Kaplan, 1964: 28)

We have argued that many governments have found in the assessment of quality a hammer with which to pound higher education, as well as schools, police, social services and health providers. In the case of higher education, we have accepted that some pounding may have been necessary, which is to say that using measures of quality in the service of accountability has not been a completely sterile exercise.

However, when the proclaimed intention is to improve the quality of learning, then such accountability-driven approaches have their limitations. Hence, we have argued that the best ways of improving the quality of higher education involve attending to the processes of learning, teaching and assessment. Invariably, this demands serious attention to the professional development of academic staff, since what we have described is, in many cases, a transformation of higher education. This is doubly so if account is taken of the reference we have made to the non-cognitive outcomes of higher education. While these have been studied more seriously in the USA, and although there is, we believe, a growing interest in these non-cognitive benefits in the UK, this is very much '*terra incognita*: here be dragons'.

We wish to draw attention to one non-cognitive element in higher education that seems to us to be both crucial and rather neglected. Self-esteem is vital for learning, especially where we want learners to take risks, to take the initiative and to take responsibility. Pascarella and Terenzini (1991) have reported that higher education is associated with some growth in self-esteem but it is arguable that the degree of development is generally not as great as is needed if higher education is to be a transformative experience. This is not the same as saying that higher education should aim to promote arrogance, for while it might be thought that arrogance is important in certain work environments, it is confidence with flexibility that employers say they want, not arrogance (see Chapter 3). Self-esteem ought to be accompanied, for example, by the ability to work with others, to motivate them and to reflect upon oneself as well. Without self-esteem, it is hard to see how these abilities can grow.

This leads us to consider how university courses, which are intellectually demanding, as well as sometimes being quite draining, can contribute to the development of this esteem. We suggest that it is the experience of success and the recognition of achievement and of capability that are vital to the promotion of self-esteem. This takes us back to what we have said about good learning, good teaching and good assessment. Where learners know what is expected of them, where the quality of learning is a priority and where learners get useful feedback on their achievements, then there is fertile ground for the development of self-esteem. In contrast, where assessment is norm-referenced, so that failure for some is in-built, where students are expected to sink or swim, and where teaching is a ritual that staff go through, not a considered process of helping students to display their best achievements, then self-esteem is threatened.

However, it would be trite to imply that failure is something to be avoided at all costs. Through making mistakes, through failing, we can learn. Failing is a fact of learning. Trying to banish error and failure would be trying to banish information about the gap between what we understand, know and can do and what we could, understand and do. Banishing failure could be seen as tantamount to banishing the continuous willingness to learn that we have valued elsewhere in this book. If higher education and learners in it are to be transformed, we need to examine ways to reduce the fear of failure. Failure is harmful to self-esteem when we attribute it to our own stupidity, rather than to things that we can change, such as insufficient practice. Failure is harmful to self-esteem when it is seen as a terminal condition, a part of learned helplessness, rather than as a concomitant of learning. We suggest that students ought to learn to expect to get things wrong, to err and to fail *and* that their expectations should include the recognition that failing, or falling short of a goal, is a part of the process of learning. Gelb and Buzan (1994) illustrate this when they take the business of learning to juggle as a metaphor for the processes of human learning in general. They say that you have to learn to drop balls and to be prepared for times when, so far from progressing, skill seems to be being lost.

So as knowledge proliferates and mutates, it becomes more and more evident that education at any level ought to help learners to be able to continue to learn and to adapt. While developing good self-esteem is important to this orientation, it is not the whole story. Fostering the dispositions that go with this orientation to life-long, self-propelled learning is becoming a priority for educational systems, and it is a priority that takes many academic staff into new areas, facing them with redoubtable challenges.

There is a danger that in attending to these non-cognitive outcomes we might be seen to be extending the surveillance of the state over the lives of its citizens. One response to this is to acknowledge that any attempt to promote certain qualities does involve making decisions about the desirable manifestations of human capability. However, the particular non-cognitive outcomes that we have identified, especially in Chapters 1 and 3, might be described as 'open' qualities. People who have them are only locked into being open to change, to working with others, to tolerance and to the power of reason, for example. In democratic societies these non-cognitive outcomes seem to be uncontentious.

It might be fairly objected that this manifesto for transformation is idealistic, fit for Utopia (which is Latin for 'nowhere'). We accept the sentiments behind such responses. It may even be that the ideal is unattainable, especially when one considers the financial problems of higher education and the ways in which these financial problems increase faculty workloads, exacerbate rôle conflicts and compound stress. Just as financial pressures tend to lead academic staff to adopt coping strategies, so too with students. Yet, are ideals to be held only if they are attainable? Or is the purpose of ideals to give a direction, rather than the promise that a destination will be reached? We have taken the latter view and are clear that the direction that this ideal sets, a direction that involves concentrating on the processes of learning, teaching and assessment, is a direction that has a greater potential for improving the quality of higher education than does pounding the system through bureaucratic accountability in terms of performance indicators of dubious validity and with little power to prompt improvement. Indeed, what might appear to be idealistic is, we claim, a positive, and indeed necessary, requirement for higher education in the twenty-first century.

We have suggested that if higher education is to be transformed so as to be fit for the twenty-first century, then some common working practices will have to be transformed too. In particular, we have placed emphasis on responsive professional collegiality (Chapter 6), and on the importance of continuing professional learning (Chapter 10). Without such transformations, it is hard to see how academic staff will have both the freedom and the ability to promote transformative learning by students. Implicit in this argument is the view that the scholarship of teaching ought to be given greater respect in the higher education system.

This book has been about transforming higher education. Higher education has the potential to transform learners: enhance and empower them as knowledgeable, skilful, comprehending and critical people. The world needs people who are able to cope with and anticipate change, people who, for example, are able to take a part in the transformation of the organizations who employ them. Higher education is in a unique position to transform students to become transformative agents. To do this, though, we have argued that higher education must itself be transformed. Such transformation can only result from a critical exploration of the purposes and practices of higher education, through a process of deconstructing its heritage and current dilemmas and reconstructing a new system of higher education for the twenty-first century. Considered deconstruction and reconstruction is the essence of critical transformation. The last thing higher education needs right now is demolition with a big hammer!

# References

Acherman, H. (1995) 'Meeting quality requirements', abstract of paper, with additional comments, presented at the Organisation for Economic Co-operation and Development (OECD), Programme on Institutional Management in Higher Education (IMHE) Seminar, at OECD, Paris, 4–6 December 1995.

Adelman, C. (1990) *A College Course Map: Taxonomy and Transcript Data.* Washington DC: U.S. Government Printing Office.

Adelman, C. and Silver, H. (1990) *Accreditation: The American Experience,* discussion paper. London: CNAA.

Adey, P. and Shayer, M. (1994) *Really Raising Standards.* London: Falmer.

Alexander, D. and Morgan, J. (1992) 'Quality assurance in a European context', paper presented to the AETT conference on 'Quality in Education', University of York, 6–8 April 1992.

Allen, F. (1981) 'Selecting new graduates for administration and management', *BACIE Journal,* 36(1): 19–21.

Allen, M. J. and Scrams, D. J. (1991) 'Careers of undergraduate psychology alumni', paper to the 99th Annual Convention of the American Psychological Association, San Francisco, 16–20 August 1991.

Alverno College (1993) *The Proof is in the Performance.* Milwaukee, WI: Alverno College.

Alverno College Faculty (1992) *Liberal Learning at Alverno College.* Milwaukee, WI: Alverno College.

Alverno College Faculty (1995) *Alverno at a Glance.* Milwaukee, WI: Alverno College.

Amaral, A. (1995) 'The role of governments in institutions: the Portuguese and Brazilian cases', *Quality in Higher Education,* 1(3): 249–56.

Anderson, L. W. (1990) 'If schools matter, can they be improved?', *Educational Researcher,* 19(3): 39–40.

Anderson, L. W. and Burns, R. B. (1989) *Research in Classrooms: The Study of Teachers, Teaching and Instruction.* Oxford: Pergamon Press.

Angelo, T. A. and Cross, K. P. (1993) *Classroom Assessment Techniques: A Handbook for College Teachers,* second edition. San Francisco, CA: Jossey-Bass.

Annan, Lord (1993) Opening address on 'Universities'. In *Hansard,* 6 December 1993, 5.33 pm, p. 788.

Askling, B., Almén, E. and Karlsson, C. (1995) 'From a hierarchical line to an interactive triangle: a new model for institutional governance at Linköping University', paper presented at the 17th Annual EAIR Forum, 'Dynamics in Higher Education: Traditions Challenged by New Paradigms', Zurich, Switzerland, 27–30 August 1995.

Association of Graduate Recruiters (AGR) (1995) *Skills for the 21st Century.* Cambridge: AGR.

Astin, A. W. (1985) *Achieving Educational Excellence.* San Francisco, CA: Jossey-Bass.

Astin, A. W. (1990) 'Assessment as a tool for institutional renewal and reform', in American Association for Higher Education Assessment Forum (1990) *Assessment 1990: Accreditation and Renewal,* pp. 19–33. Washington, DC: AAHE.

Astin, A. W. (1991) *Assessment for Excellence: The Philosophy and Practice of Assessment and Evaluation in Higher Education.* New York: American Council on Education and Macmillan.

Astin, A. W. and Solomon, L. C. (1981) 'Are reputational ratings needed to measure quality?', *Change,* 13: 14–19.

Atkins, M. (1995) 'What should we be assessing?', in Knight, P. (ed.) *Assessment for Learning in Higher Education.* London: Kogan Page.

Ausubel, D. (1985) 'Learning as constructing meaning', in Entwistle, N. (ed.) *New Directions in Educational Psychology,* vol. 1. Lewes: Falmer Press.

Ayarza, E. H. (ed.) (1992) *Acreditación Universitaria en América Latina y El Caribe.* Based on the papers presented at the International Seminar on University Accreditation in Latin America and the Caribbean, organized by the Centre Interuniversitario de Desarrollo (CINDA) in Santiago, Chile, December 1991.

Ayarza, E. H. (1993) 'Quality assurance in Latin America: an overview of university accreditation', paper presented at the First Biennial Conference and General Conference of the International Network of Quality Assurance Agencies in Higher Education (INQAAHE), Montréal, Canada, 24–28 May 1993.

Bacon, C., Benton, D. and Gruneberg, M. M. (1979) 'Employers' opinions of university and polytechnic graduates', *The Vocational Aspect of Education,* 31: 95–102.

Bailey, A. (1990) 'Personal transferable skills for employment: the role of higher education', in Wright, P. W. G. (ed.) *Industry and Higher Education: Collaboration to Improve Students' Learning and Training,* pp. 68–72. Buckingham: Society for Research into Higher Education (SRHE)/Open University Press.

Baird, J. R. (1988) 'Quality: what should make higher education "higher"', *Higher Education Research and Development,* 7(2): 141–52.

Baldwin, G. (1995) 'An Australian approach to quality assessment', paper, with additional comments, presented at the Organisation for Economic Co-operation and Development (OECD), Programme on Institutional Management in Higher Education (IMHE) Seminar, at OECD, Paris, 4–6 December 1995.

Baldwin, P. J. (1992) *Higher Education Funding for the 1993–1995 Triennium.* Canberra: Australian Government Publishing Service.

Ball, C. J. E. (ed.) (1985) *Fitness for Purpose: Essays in Higher Education.* Guildford: SRHE and NFER/Nelson.

Ball, C. and Eggins, H. (eds) (1989) *Higher Education into the 1990s.* Buckingham: Society for Research into Higher Education/Open University Press.

Banta, T. *et al.* (1991) 'Critique of a method for surveying employers', paper to the 31st Association for Institutional Research (AIR) Annual Forum, San Francisco, 26–29 May 1991.

Banta, T. (1995) 'An assessment of some performance indicators used in funding: performance funding in Tennessee at age sixteen', paper presented at the 17th Annual EAIR Forum, 'Dynamics in Higher Education: Traditions Challenged by New Paradigms', Zurich, Switzerland, 27–30 August 1995.

Barblan, A. (1995) 'Management for quality: the CRE programme of institutional evaluation: issues encountered in the pilot phase – 1994–1995', paper submitted to the Organization for Economic Co-operation and Development (OECD),

Programme on Institutional Management in Higher Education (IMHE) Seminar, at OECD, Paris, 4–6 December 1995.

Barnett, R. (1988) 'Entry and exit performance indicators for higher education: some policy and research issues', *Assessment and Evaluation in Higher Education*, 13(1): 16–30.

Barnett, R. (1990) *Changing Patterns of Course Review*, a CNAA project report, June. London: CNAA.

Barnett, R. (1994) *The Limits of Competence: Knowledge, Higher Education and Society.* Buckingham: Society for Research into Higher Education/Open University Press.

Barnett, R., Parry, G., Cox, R., Loder, C. and Williams, G. (1994) *Assessment of the Quality of Higher Education: A Review and Evaluation*, report for the HEFCE. London: Centre for Higher Education Studies, Institute of Education, University of London.

Baseline Market Research (1991) *A Study of Employer Satisfaction with Services of the Department of Advanced Education and Training (DAET) and Community Colleges: Final Report.* Fredricton, New Brunswick: Department of Advanced Education, and Training, Planning Services.

Bauer, M. (1986) 'A commentary on the Northeast Missouri and Tennessee Evaluation Models', in Kogan, M. (ed.) *Evaluating Higher Education*, pp. 53–5. London: Jessica Kingsley.

Bauer, M. (1995) 'Demands on quality in a national reform of higher education and quality as viewed by university teachers and leadership', paper presented at the 17th Annual EAIR Forum, 'Dynamics in Higher Education: Traditions Challenged by New Paradigms', Zurich, Switzerland, 27–30 August 1995.

Bauer, M. and Franke-Wikberg, S. (1993) 'Quality assurance in Swedish higher education: shared responsibility', paper presented at the First Biennial Conference and General Conference of the International Network of Quality Assurance Agencies in Higher Education (INQAAHE), Montréal, Canada, 24–28 May 1993.

Bauer, M. and Kogan, M. (1995) 'Evaluation systems in the UK and Sweden: Successes and difficulties', paper for the Conference on 'Evaluating Universities', AF-Forum, Rome, 26–27 September 1995.

Bell, C. (1995) Introductory remarks of panel moderator on 'Preliminary lessons to be drawn from the case studies' at the Organisation for Economic Co-operation and Development (OECD), Programme on Institutional Management in Higher Education (IMHE) Seminar, at OECD, Paris, 4–6 December 1995.

Biggs, J. B. (1987) *Student Approaches to Learning and Studying.* Hawthorne, Victoria: Australian Council for Educational Research.

Biggs, J. B. (1993) 'From theory to practice: a cognitive systems approach', *Higher Education Research and Development*, 12(1): 73–85.

Binks, M., Grant, A. and Exley, K. (1993) 'Assessing the output of institutions of higher education: a pilot study', in Harvey, L. (ed.) (1994) *Proceedings of the Second QHE Quality Assessment Seminar, 16–17 December 1993*, pp. 18–28. Birmingham: QHE.

Birch, W. (1988) *The Challenge to Higher Education: Reconciling Responsibilities to Scholarship and Society.* London: Society for Research into Higher Education/Open University Press.

Bothams, J. (1995) 'Action learning as a way of helping professionals into a new management role', in Thomas, D. (ed.) *Flexible Learning Strategies in Higher and Further Education.* London: Cassell.

Boucher, A. (1993) 'Position statement prepared on behalf of group B2 who discussed employer satisfaction as a way of assessing quality', in Harvey, L. (ed.)

(1994) *Proceedings of the Second QHE Quality Assessment Seminar, 16–17 December, 1993*, pp. 44–5. Birmingham: QHE.

Boud, D. (1992) 'The role of self-assessment schedules in negotiated learning', *Studies in Higher Education*, 17(2): 185–200.

Boud, D. (1995a) 'Assessment and learning: contradictory or complementary?' in Knight, P. (ed.) *Assessment for Learning in Higher Education*. London: Kogan Page.

Boud, D. (1995b) *Enhancing Learning through Self Assessment*. London: Kogan Page.

Bourner, T. and Hamed, M. (1987) *Entry Qualifications and Degree Performance*, Publication 10. London: CNAA Development Services.

Bowtell, C. (1993) *Bulletin: Stop Work*. Academics' Federation of Victoria.

Boyatzis, R. E., Cowen, S. S., Kolb, D. A. *et al.* (1995) *Innovation in Professional Education*. San Francisco, CA: Jossey-Bass.

Boyer, E. L. (1990) *Scholarship Reconsidered. Priorities of the Professoriate*. Princetown, NJ: Carnegie Foundation for the Advancement of Learning.

Boys, C. (1995) 'National Vocational Qualifications: the outcomes-plus model of assessment', in Edwards, A. and Knight, P. (eds) *The Assessment of Competence in Higher Education*. London: Kogan Page.

Bråten, I. (1992) 'Vygotsky as precursor to metacognitive theory: III. Recent meta-cognitive research within a Vygotskian framework', *Scandinavian Journal of Educational Research*, 36(1): 3–19.

Brennan, J. and McGeevor, P. (1988) *Graduates at Work, Degree Courses and the Labour Market*. London: Jessica Kingsley.

Brew, A. (1995) 'Trends and influences', in Brew, A. (ed.) *Directions in Staff Development*. Buckingham: Society for Research into Higher Education/Open University Press.

British Telecom (BT) (1993) *Matching Skills: A Question of Demand and Supply*. London: BT.

Brown, S. and Knight, P. (1994) *Assessing Learners in Higher Education*. London: Kogan Page.

Bulmer, M. (1984) *The Chicago School of Sociology: Institutionalization, Diversity and the Rise of Sociological Research*. Chicago: University of Chicago Press.

Burgess, T. (ed.) (1986) *Education for Capability*. Windsor, NFER-Nelson.

Burrows, A., Harvey, L. and Green, D. (1992a) *Is Anybody Listening? Employers' Views on Quality in Higher Education*. Birmingham: QHE.

Burrows, A., Harvey, L. and Green, D. (1992b) *The Policy Background to the Quality Debate in Higher Education 1985–1992: A Summary of Key Documents*. Birmingham: QHE.

Buscaglia, L. (1982) *Living, Loving and Learning*. New York: Fawcett Columbine.

Business-Higher Education Round Table (1992) *Educating for Excellence: Business-Higher Education Round Table 1992 Education Surveys*. Camberwell, Victoria: Business-Higher Education Round Table.

Business and Technician Education Council (BTEC) (1991) *Common Skills: General Guidelines*. London: BTEC.

Cannon, T. (1986) 'View from industry' in Moodie, G. C. (ed.) *Standards and Criteria in Higher Education*, pp. 145–56. Milton Keynes: Society for Research into Higher Education/Open University Press. SRHE and NFER/Nelson.

Cannon, R. A. (1994) 'Quality and traditional university values: policy development through consultation', *The Australian Universities' Review*, 37(1): 26–30.

Carey, L. J. and Magennis, S. P. (1995) 'Using large-scale surveys to assess and change the student experience', paper presented to SRHE Conference 'Changing the Student Experience', Birmingham, July 4–5 1995.

Carter, C. L., Jr. (1978) *The Control and Assurance of Quality, Reliability, and Safety.* Milwaukee, WI: American Society for Quality Control.

Caswell, P. (1983) 'Graduate recruits: what do employers look for?', *Teaching News,* 18: 13–15.

Cave, M. and Kogan, M. (1990) 'Some concluding observations', in Cave, M., Kogan, M. and Smith, R. (eds) (1990) *Output and Performance Measurement in Government: The State of the Art,* pp. 179–87. London: Jessica Kingsley.

Cave, M., Hanney, S., Kogan, M. and Trevett, G. (1991) *The Use of Performance Indicators in Higher Education: A Critical Analysis of Developing Practice.* London: Jessica Kingsley.

Chan, I. and Sensicle, A. (1995) 'Institutional development following a major external review', in *Background Papers for the Third Meeting of the International Network of Quality Assurance Agencies in Higher Education,* 21–23 May 1995, pp. 125–8. Utrecht, Netherlands: VSNU/Inspectorate of Education.

Cheong, D. (1993) 'A system of quality assurance of courses at the Singapore Polytechnic', paper presented at the First Biennial Conference and General Conference of the International Network of Quality Assurance Agencies in Higher Education (INQAAHE), Montréal, Canada, 24–28 May 1993.

Church, C. H. (1988) 'The qualities of validation', *Studies in Higher Education,* 13: 27–43.

Clark, B. (1983) *The Higher Education System. Academic Organization in Cross-National Perspectives.* Berkeley: University of California Press.

Clark, C. and Peterson, P. L. (1986) 'Teachers' thought processes', in Wittrock, M. C. (ed.) *Handbook of Research on Teaching.* New York: Macmillan.

Commission of the European Communities (CEC) (1991) *Memorandum on Higher Education in the European Community.* Brussels: European Commission.

Committee for Quality Assurance in Higher Education (CQAHE) (1994) *Quality Review Report: Griffith University,* March 1994. Brisbane: CQAHE.

Committee of Vice-Chancellors and Principals of the Universities of the United Kingdom (CVCP) (1985) *Report of the Steering Committee for Efficiency Studies in Universities* (The Jarratt Report). London: CVCP.

Committee of Vice-Chancellors and Principals of the Universities of the United Kingdom (CVCP) (1986) *Academic Standards in Universities* (with an introduction by Prof. P. A. Reynolds). London: CVCP.

Committee of Vice-Chancellors and Principals of the Universities of the United Kingdom (CVCP) (1987) *Academic Staff Training – Code of Practice,* Circular, April. London: CVCP.

Committee of Vice-Chancellors and Principals of the Universities of the United Kingdom and Universities Grants Committee (CVCP/UGC) (1986) *Performance Indicators in Universities: A First Statement.* London: CVCP/UGC.

Committee of Vice-Chancellors and Principals of the Universities of the United Kingdom and Universities Grants Committee (CVCP/UGC) (1987a) *Performance Indicators in Universities: A Second Statement.* London: CVCP/UGC.

Committee of Vice-Chancellors and Principals of the Universities of the United Kingdom and the University Grants Committee (CVCP/UGC) (1987b) *University Management Statistics and Performance Indicators.* London: CVCP/UGC.

Committee of Vice-Chancellors and Principals of the Universities of the United Kingdom and the University Grants Committee (CVCP/UGC) (1988) *University Management Statistics and Performance Indicators in the UK,* second edition. London: CVCP/UGC.

Committee of Vice-Chancellors and Principals of the Universities of the United

Kingdom and the University Grants Committee (CVCP/UGC) (1989) *University Management Statistics and Performance Indicators in the UK*, third edition. London: CVCP/UGC.

Committee of Vice-Chancellors and Principals of the Universities of the United Kingdom and the University Grants Committee (CVCP/UGC) (1990) *University Management Statistics and Performance Indicators in the UK*, fourth edition. London: CVCP/UGC.

Committee on Higher Education (CHE) (1963) *Higher Education: Report of the Committee under the Chairmanship of Lord Robbins*, Cmnd. 2154. London: HMSO.

Commonwealth of Australia (1991) *Higher Education: Quality and Diversity in the 1990s*, policy statement by the Hon. Peter Baldwin MP, Minister for Higher Education and Employment Services, October. Canberra: Australian Government Publishing Service.

Confederation of British Industry (CBI) (1988) *Skills for Success: The 1988 CBI Training Presentation.* London: CBI.

Confederation of British Industry (CBI) (1989) *Towards a Skills Revolution.* London: CBI.

Confederation of British Industry (CBI) (1991) *Survey of Students' Attitudes: 17 and 18 Year Olds Going on to Higher Education.* London: CBI.

Council for Industry and Higher Education (CIHE) (1987) *Towards a Partnership: Higher Education – Government – Industry.* London: CIHE.

Council for Industry and Higher Education (CIHE) (1992) *Investing in Diversity: An Assessment of Higher Education Policy.* London: CIHE.

Council for National Academic Awards (CNAA) (1990a) *The Measurement of Value Added in Higher Education.* London: CNAA.

Council for National Academic Awards (CNAA) (1990b) *Handbook 1990–91.* London: CNAA.

Council for National Academic Awards (CNAA) (1992) *The External Examiner and Curriculum Change*, Discussion Paper, 7. London: CNAA.

Council for National Academic Awards and Department of Education and Science (CNAA/DES) (1989) *The Role of External Examiners: A Summary of the Principal Findings of a Project on the Role of the External Examiners in Undergraduate Courses in the United Kingdom During 1986.* Swindon: ESRC.

Council of State Decision (CoSD) (1986) Valtioneuvoston päätös korkeakoululaitoksen kehittämisestä vuosina, 1988–91 [Council of State Decision on the Development of Higher Education, 1988–91]. Helsinki, Finland.

Council of University Classical Departments (CUCD) (1990) *Classics in the Market Place: An Independent Research Study on Attitudes to the Employment of Classics Graduates.* Exeter: CUCD, Department of Classics, University of Exeter.

Crawford, F. W. (1991) *Total Quality Management*, CVCP Occasional Paper. London: CVCP.

Crosby, P. B. (1979) *Quality Is Free.* New York: McGraw-Hill.

Crosby, P. B. (1984) *Quality Without Tears: The Art of Hassle-Free Management.* New York: McGraw-Hill.

Crosby, P. B. (1986) *Running Things – The Art of Making Things Happen.* Milwaukee, WI: American Society for Quality Control.

Cross, K. P. (1990) 'Streams of thought about assessment', in AAHE Assessment Forum (1990) *Assessment 1990: Understanding the Implications* (Assessment Forum Resource), pp. 1–14. Washington, D.C.: American Association for Higher Education.

Cross, P. (1995) 'Improving teaching and learning through classroom assessment and classroom research', paper presented to Third International symposium, 'Improving Student Learning', Exeter, 11 September 1995.

Dall'alba, G. (1993) 'The role of teachers in higher education: enabling students to enter a field of study and practice', *Learning and Instruction*, 3, 299–313.

Danish Ministry of Education (DME) (1991) *Kompetence 2000, Hovedrapport.* Copenhagen: DME.

Darby, Sir Charles (1993) 'Quality assessment and employer satisfaction', keynote presentation at the *QHE* 24-Hour Seminar, Scarman House, University of Warwick, 16–17 December 1993, in Harvey, L. (ed.) (1994) *Proceedings of the Second QHE Quality Assessment Seminar, 16–17 December 1993*, pp. 36–8. Birmingham: QHE.

Davies, G. (1993) 'HEFCE quality assessment methodology: how it addresses employer-education links', in Harvey, L. (ed.) (1994) *Proceedings of the Second QHE Quality Assessment Seminar, 16–17 December 1993*, pp. 32–6. Birmingham: QHE.

De Boer, H. F. and Goedegebuure, L. (1995) *Decision-making in Higher Education: A Comparative Perspective.* Enschede: University of Twente, CHEPS. (A version of this paper entitled 'Institutional governance structures: a comparative perspective' was presented on behalf of the authors by Frans van Vught at the 17th Annual EAIR Forum, 'Dynamics in Higher Education: Traditions Challenged by New Paradigms', Zurich, Switzerland, 27–30 August 1995.)

De Winter Hebron, C. C. (1973) 'What employers think of graduates', *Newcastle Polytechnic Bulletin of Educational Research*, 6: 15–26.

Dearlove, J. (1995) 'Collegiality, managerialism and leadership in English universities', *Tertiary Education and Management*, 1(2): 161–9.

Debrock, M. (1995) 'Quality assessment in higher education: conditions and resources', paper presented at the Organisation for Economic Co-operation and Development (OECD), Programme on Institutional Management in Higher Education (IMHE) Seminar, at OECD, Paris, 4–6 December 1995.

Delphy, C. (1985) *Close to Home.* London: Hutchinson.

Deming, W. E. (1982) *Out of the Crisis: Quality, Productivity and Competitive Position.* Cambridge: Cambridge University Press.

Department of Education and Science (DES) (1985) *The Development of Higher Education into the 1990s*, Green Paper, Cmnd. 9524. London: HMSO.

Department of Education and Science (DES) (1987) *Higher Education: Meeting the Challenge*, White Paper, Cm. 114. London: HMSO.

Department of Education and Science (DES) (1991a) *Higher Education: A New Framework*, White Paper, Cm. 1541. London: HMSO.

Department of Education and Science (DES) (1991b) 'Clarke tells polytechnics to plan for changes next year', *The Department of Education and Science News*, 294/91, 17 September 1991.

Department of Trade and Industry and Council for Industry and Higher Education (DTI/CIHE) (1989) *Policy and Strategy for Companies.* London: HMSO.

Department of Trade and Industry and Council for Industry and Higher Education (DTI/CIHE) (1990) *Getting Good Graduates.* London: HMSO.

Dill, D. (1993) 'Quality by design: toward a framework for academic quality management', in Smart, J. (ed.) (1993) *Higher Education: The Handbook of Theory and Research.*

Dill, D. (1995) 'Through Deming's eyes: a cross-national analysis of quality assurance policies in higher education', *Quality in Higher Education*, 1(2): 95–110.

Dillon, P. A. (1992) 'What business expects from higher education', *College Board Review*, 164: 22–5.

Dowell, D. and Neal, J. (1982) 'A selective review of the validity of student ratings of teaching', *Journal of Higher Education*, 53(1): 51–62.

Drucker, P. F. (1993) *Post-Capitalist Society*. Oxford: Butterworth-Heinemann.

Education Commission of the States (1986) *Transforming the State Role in Undergraduate Education*, no. PS-86-3. Denver, CO: Education Commission of the States.

Edwards, A. and Knight, P. (1994) *Effective Early Years Education*. Buckingham: Open University Press.

Elton, L. (1992) 'University teaching: a professional model for quality and excellence', paper to the 'Quality by Degrees' Conference at Aston University, 8 June 1992.

Elton, L. (1993) 'Enterprise in Higher Education: an agent for change', in Knight, P. T. (ed.) (1994) *University-Wide Change, Staff and Curriculum Development*, Staff and Educational Development Association, SEDA Paper, 83, May 1994, pp. 7–14. Birmingham: SEDA.

Elton, L. (1995) 'An institutional framework', in Brew, A. (ed.) *Directions in Staff Development*. Buckingham: Society for Research into Higher Education/Open University Press.

Emanuel, R. (1994) Presentation during the final plenary session of Lancaster University's 'Hunting the Snark: The Pursuit of Quality' Conference at Scarman House, Warwick University, 24–25 February 1994.

Employment Department Group, Training, Enterprise and Education Directorate. (ED TEED) (1990) *Higher Education Developments – The Skills Link*. Sheffield: Employment Department Group.

Employment Department Group, Training, Enterprise and Education Directorate (ED TEED) (1991) *Enterprise in Higher Education. Key Features of Enterprise in Higher Education, 1990–91*. Sheffield: Employment Department Group.

Employment Policy Institute (EPI) (1995) *The Skills Mirage: Is Training the Key to Lower Unemployment?* London: EPI.

Engwall, L. (1995) 'A Swedish appoach to quality in education: the case of Uppsala University', paper, with additional comments, presented at the Organisation for Economic Co-operation and Development (OECD), Programme on Institutional Management in Higher Education (IMHE) Seminar, at OECD, Paris, 4–6 December 1995.

Entwistle, N. (1994) 'Recent research on student learning and the learning environment', paper presented to the International Symposium 'Independent Study and Flexible Learning', Cambridge, 6 September 1994.

Entwistle, N. and Ramsden, P. (1983) *Understanding Student Learning*. London: Croom Helm.

Eraut, M. (1994) *Developing Professional Knowledge and Competence*. London: Falmer.

Erwin, T. D. and Knight, P. (1995) 'A transatlantic view of assessment and higher education', *Quality in Higher Education*, 1(2): 179–88.

Escudero, T. (1995) 'Evaluation fever at the Spanish University: a critical analysis', paper presented at the 17th Annual EAIR Forum, 'Dynamics in Higher Education: Traditions Challenged by New Paradigms', Zurich, Switzerland, 27–30 August 1995.

European Commission (EC) (1991) *Memorandum on Higher Education in the European Community*, 5 November 1991. Brussels: Commission of the European Communities, Task Force, Human Resources, Education, Training, Youth.

Fairclough, P. G. (1993) 'Quality of teaching and universities', in Radloff, A. and Latchem, C. (eds) *Quality Teaching – The Institutional Context: Seminar Proceedings,*

24 February 1993, Fremantle, Australia. A DEET National Priority (Reserve) Fund Project, Curtin University, pp. 13–16.

Fay, B. (1993) 'The elements of critical social science', in Hammersley, M. (ed.) (1993) *Social Research: Philosophy, Politics and Practice*. London: Sage.

Feldman, K. A. (1976) 'Grades and college students' evaluations of their courses and teachers', *Research in Higher Education*, 4, 69–111.

Fergus, A. (1981) 'Selecting new graduates for administration and management', *BACIE Journal*, 36(1): 19–21.

Ferguson-Hessler, M. G. M. (1993) 'Meta-knowledge and the development of expertise in complex domains', *Tijdshrift voor Onderwijsresearch*, 18(3): 175–85.

Fidler, K. (1993) 'Let's start a movement', *Times Higher Education Supplement*, 15 October 1993, p. 14.

Filteau, C. H. (1993) 'Evaluating the evaluators: does the Ontario Council on Graduate Studies appraisal process work?', paper presented at the Fifth International Conference on 'Assessing Quality in Higher Education', Bonn, Germany, July 1993.

Fisher, P. (1994) 'Some degrees of coercion', *Guardian*, 3 March 1994, pp. 14–15 of the Special Supplement to mark Human Resources Development Week.

Flavell, J. H., Miller, P. H. and Miller, S. A. (1993) *Cognitive Development*, third edition. Englewood Cliffs, NJ: Prentice-Hall.

Folds, T. H. *et al.* (1990) 'When children mean to remember', in Bjorklund D. F. (ed.) *Children's Strategies*. Hillsdale, NJ: Erlbaum.

Fong, B. (1988) 'Old wineskins: the AAC external examiner project', *Liberal Education*, 74: 12–16.

Fontana, D. (1981) *Psychology for Teachers*. London: The British Psychological Society and Macmillan.

Frazer, M. (1995) 'Ten papers on national developments', in *Proceedings of the Third Meeting of the International Network for Quality Assurance Agencies in Higher Education, 21–23 May 1995*, pp. 55–71. Utrecht, Holland: VSNU/Inspectorate of Education.

Frederiks, M. M. H., Westerheijden, D. F. and Weusthof, P. J. M. (1993) 'Self-evaluations and visiting committees: effects on quality assessment in Dutch higher education', paper presented to the 15th EAIR Forum, University of Türkü, 15–18 August 1993.

Fulton, O. (1995) 'Mass access and the end of diversity? The academic profession in England on the eve of structural reform', in Altbach, P. (ed.) *The Academic Profession in Comparative Perspective*. Princeton, NJ: Carnegie Foundation for the Advancement of Learning.

Further Education Unit (FEU) (1990) *The Core Skills Initiative*. London: FEU.

Gallagher, A. (1991) 'Comparative value added as a performance indicator', *Higher Education Review*, 23(3): 19–29.

Garnham, A. and Oakhill, J. (1994) *Thinking and Reasoning*. Oxford: Blackwell.

Garvin, D. A. (1988) *Managing Quality: The Strategic and Competitive Edge*. London: Collier Macmillan.

Geddes, T. (1992) 'The total quality initiative at South Bank University', paper presented at the Centre for Higher Education Studies Seminar on Implementing Total Quality Management in Higher Education at the Institute of Education, London, 3 December 1992. (Subsequently published in *Higher Education*.)

Gedge, P. S. and Louden, L. M. R. (1994) *S. Martin's College, 1964–1989*. Lancaster: Centre for North-West Regional Studies.

Gelb, M. and Buzan, T. (1994) *Lessons from the Art of Juggling*. London: Aurum Press.

Gibbs, G. (1992) *Teaching More Students: No. 3. Discussion with More Students*. Oxford: Oxford Centre for Staff Development.

Gibbs, G. (1995a) 'National-scale faculty development for teaching large classes', in Wright, W. A. *et al.*, *Teaching Improvement Practices*. Bolton, MA: Anker.

Gibbs, G. (1995b) 'Changing lecturers' conceptions of teaching and learning through action research', in Brew, A. (ed.) *Directions in Staff Development*. Buckingham: Society for Research into Higher Education/Open University Press.

Girdwood, A. (1995) 'Evolving roles and responsibilities: the university in Africa', in Schuller, T. (ed.) *The Changing University?*, pp. 93–104. Buckingham: Society for Research into Higher Education/Open University Press.

Goedegebuure, L. C. J., Maassen, P. A. M. and Westerheijden, D. F. (eds) (1990) *Peer Review and Performance Indicators: Quality Assessment in British and Dutch Higher Education*. Culemborg: Lemma.

Goodlad, S. (1995) *The Quest for Quality. Sixteen Forms of Heresy in Higher Education*. Buckingham: Society for Research into Higher Education/Open University Press.

Gordon, A. (1983) 'Attitudes of employers to the recruitment of graduates', *Educational Studies*, 9(1): 45–64.

Gorospe, F. L. (1995) 'The role of the government in sustaining quality education in higher education in the Philippines', unpublished paper, made available to delegates at the Third Meeting of the International Network for Quality Assurance Agencies in Higher Education at Utrecht, 21–23 May 1995.

Green, D. (1990) 'Student satisfaction: assessing quality in HE from the customer's view', in *Proceedings of the Second International Conference on Assessing Quality in H.E.* Tennessee: University of Tennessee.

Green, D. (ed.) (1993) *What is Quality in Higher Education?* Buckingham: Society for Research into Higher Education/Open University Press.

Green, D. and Harvey, L. (1993) 'Quality assurance in Western Europe: trends, practices and issues', paper presented at the Fifth International Conference on 'Assessing Quality in Higher Education', Bonn, 21 July 1993.

Green, S. (1990) *Analysis of Transferable Personal Skills Requested by Employers in Graduate Recruitment Advertisements in June 1989*. Sheffield: University of Sheffield.

Greenwood, R. G., Edge, A. G. and Hodgetts, M. (1987) 'How managers rank the characteristics expected of business graduates', *Business Education*, 8(3): 30–4.

Grover, P. R. (1989) 'Enterprise, culture and anarchy', *Higher Education Review*, 21(3): 7–20.

Gungwu, W. (1992) 'Universities in transition in Asia', *Oxford Review of Education*, 18(1): 17–27.

H.M. Government (1991) *Further and Higher Education Bill*, HL Bill 4 50/5. London: HMSO.

H.M. Government (1992) *Further and Higher Education Act*. London: HMSO.

H.M. Inspectorate (HMI) (1989a) 'In pursuit of quality – an HMI view', in *Quality in Higher Education: An HMI Invitation Conference*, at Heythrop Park, 16–18 June 1989, pp. 3–15. London: HMI. Reprinted in Polytechnics and Colleges Funding Council (1990) *Recurrent Funding and Equipment Allocations of 1990–91*. Bristol: PCFC.

H.M. Inspectorate (HMI) (1989b) 'Conference conclusions', in *Quality in Higher Education: An HMI Invitation Conference*, at Heythrop Park, 16–18 June 1989, pp. 24–25. London: HMI.

H.M. Inspectorate (HMI) (1990) *Performance Indicators in Higher Education. A Report by HMI*, Reference 14/91/NS. January–April 1990. London: DES.

H.M. Inspectorate (HMI) (1993) *A Survey of the Enterprise in Higher Education Initia-*

*tive in Fifteen Polytechnic and Colleges of Higher Education: September 1989–March 1991*. London: DFE.

Halpin, J. (1966) *Zero Defects: A New Dimension in Quality Assurance*. New York: McGraw Hill.

Hamilton, J. (1995) 'Thinking skills in higher education: the MENO Project', in Edwards, A. and Knight, P. (eds) (1995) *The Assessment of Competence in Higher Education*. London: Kogan Page.

Handy, C. (1994) *The Empty Raincoat: Making Sense of the Future*. London: Hutchinson.

Hansen, R. (1991) 'The congruence between industry demand and professional school response in architecture', paper to the Annual Meeting of the American Educational Research Association, Chicago, April 1991.

Harrington, H. J. (1988) *Excellence – The IBM Way*. Milwaukee, WI: American Society for Quality Control.

Harrison, D. (1991) 'Challenges and opportunities for institutions', paper to the CBI Conference on 'Higher Education in the 1990s', 21 November 1991.

Harvey, L. (1987) *Myths of the Chicago School*. Aldershot: Avebury.

Harvey, L. (1990) *Critical Social Research*. London: Routledge.

Harvey, L. (ed.) (1993a) *Quality Assessment in Higher Education: Collected Papers of the QHE Project*. Birmingham: QHE.

Harvey, L. (1993b) 'An integrated approach to student assessment (with appendix)', paper to the 'Measure for Measure: Act II: Reassessing Student Assessment' Conference at Warwick University Conference Centre, 6–8 September 1993.

Harvey, L. with Green, D. (1994) *Employer Satisfaction*. Birmingham: QHE.

Harvey, L. (1994a) 'Quality assurance in higher education in the UK: current situation and issues', in New Zealand Qualifications Authority (NZQA) *Quality Assurance in Education and Training: Conference Papers*, 3 volumes for a conference held in Wellington, 10–12 May 1994. Wellington, NZQA, volume 1, pp. 143–54.

Harvey, L. (1994b) 'Continuous quality improvement: A system-wide view of quality in higher education', in Knight, P. T. (ed.) (1994) *University-Wide Change, Staff and Curriculum Development*, Staff and Educational Development Association, SEDA Paper 83, pp. 47–70, May 1994.

Harvey, L. (1994c) 'Total student experience', in *QHE Update*, No. 7, May 1994, p. 1. Birmingham: QHE.

Harvey, L. (1995a) *Quality Assurance Systems, TQM and the New Collegialism*. Birmingham: QHE.

Harvey, L. (1995b) 'Beyond TQM', *Quality in Higher Education*, 1(2): 123–46.

Harvey, L. (1995c) 'The new collegialism: improvement with accountability', *Tertiary Education and Management*, 2(2): 153–60.

Harvey, L. (1995d) *Editorial in Quality in Higher Education*, 1, 1.

Harvey, L. and Burrows, A. (1992) 'Empowering students', *New Academic*, Summer, p. 1ff.

Harvey, L. and Green, D. (1993) 'Defining quality', *Assessment and Evaluation in Higher Education: An International Journal*, 18(1): 9–34.

Harvey, L. and Mason, S. (1995) *The Role of Professional Bodies in Higher Education Quality Monitoring*. Birmingham: QHE.

Harvey, L., Burrows, A. and Green, D. (1992a) *Someone Who Can Make an Impression: Report of the Employers' Survey of Qualities of Higher Education Graduates*. Birmingham: QHE. Also in Harvey (1993a).

Harvey, L., Burrows, A. and Green, D. (1992b) *Total Student Experience: A First Report of the QHE National Survey of Staff and Students' Views of the Important Criteria for Assessing the Quality of Higher Education*. Birmingham: QHE. Also in Harvey (1993a).

Harvey, L., Burrows, A. and Green, D. (1992c) *Criteria of Quality*. Birmingham: QHE.

Harvey, L., Geall, V., Mazelan, P., Moon, S. and Plimmer, L. (1995) *The 1995 Report on the Student Experience at UCE*. Birmingham: UCE, Centre for Research into Quality.

Hazel, E. (1995) 'Improving laboratory teaching', in Wright, W. A. *et al.* (eds) *Teaching Improvement Practices*. Bolton, MA: Anker.

Heath, T. (1988) 'Communication skills and veterinary education', *Higher Education Research and Development*, 7(2): 111–17.

Higher Education Funding Council for England (HEFCE) (1992) 'New Funding Council to review library provision in higher education: and to decide in July on a funding method for teaching', press release, HEFCE 1/92, 17 June 1992. Bristol: HEFCE.

Higher Education Funding Council for England (HEFCE) (1993a) *Assessment of the Quality of Education*, Circular 3/93, February. Bristol: HEFCE.

Higher Education Funding Council for England (HEFCE) (1993b) *Assessment of the Quality of Education: Self-Assessments*, letter to Heads of HEFCE institutions and Heads of Further Education Funding Council institutions with HEFCE-funded education from Professor Graeme Davies, 2 July 1993, with Annex 'Description of the template used in June 1993 to analyse the self-assessments and claims for excellence received in May 1993'. Bristol: HEFCE.

Higher Education Funding Council for England (HEFCE) (1994a) *The Quality Assessment Method from April 1995*, HEFCE Circular, 39/94. Bristol: HEFCE.

Higher Education Funding Council for England (HEFCE) (1994b) *Quality Assessment Report, Q77/94, University of East Anglia, History, November, 1993*. Bristol: HEFCE.

Higher Education Funding Council for Wales (HEFCW) (1994) *The Assessment of Quality in the Higher Education Sector in Wales: Future Directions*, Circular W941/36HE, 31 May 1994. Cardiff: HEFCW.

Higher Education Quality Council (HEQC) (1995a) *The Future Development of the External Examiner System*, HEQC Consultative Document, June. London: HEQC.

Higher Education Quality Council (HEQC) (1995b) *Graduate Standards Programme: Progress Report*, June. London: HEQC.

Higher Education Quality Council, Division of Quality Audit (HEQC DQA) (1993) *Notes for Guidance of Auditors*, January. Birmingham: HEQC.

Higher Education Funding Council for England, Scottish Higher Education Funding Council, Higher Education Funding Council for Wales (HEFCE/SHEFC/HEFCW) (1993) *A Report for the Universities Funding Council on the Conduct of the 1992 Research Assessment Exercise*, June. Bristol: HEFCE.

Holmes, G. (1993) 'Quality assurance in further and higher education: a sacrificial lamb on the altar of managerialism', *Quality Assurance in Education*, 1(1): 4.

Hounsell, D. (1984) 'Students' conceptions of essay-writing', PhD thesis. University of Lancaster.

Hutchings, P. and Marchese, T. (1990) 'Watching assessment: questions, stories, prospects', *Change*, September/October 12–38.

Ifrim, M. (1995) 'Accreditation and quality assurance in higher education institutions in Romania', *QA*, 8: 14–19.

Industrial Research and Development Advisory Committee of the Commission of the European Communities (IRDAC) (1990) *Skills Shortages in Europe: IRDAC Opinion*, November. Brussels: EC.

Industrial Research and Development Advisory Committee of the Commission of the European Communities (IRDAC) (1994) *Quality and Relevance: Unlocking Europe's Human Potential*, March. Brussels: EC.

Ingle, S. (1985) *In Search of Perfection: How to Create/Maintain/Improve Quality*. Englewood Cliffs: Prentice-Hall.

Inspectie Hoger Onderwijs (IHO) (1992) *De bestuulijk hantering van de resultaten van der externe kwaliteitszorg 1989 in het wettenschappenlijk onderwijs*, report 1992–8. Zoetermeer: Ministerie van Onderwijs en Wetenschappen.

Institute of Directors (IOD) (1991) *Performance and Potential: Education and Training for a Market Economy*. London: Institute of Directors.

Institute of Manpower Studies and the Association of Graduate Recruiters (IMS/ AGR) (1991) *Graduate Salaries and Vacancies: 1991 Summer Update Survey*. Falmer, Sussex: IMS/AGR.

International Network of Quality Assurance Agencies in Higher Education (INQAAHE) (1995) *Background Papers for the Third Meeting of the International Network of Quality Assurance Agencies in Higher Education*, 21–23 May. Utrecht, Netherlands: VSNU/Inspectorate of Education.

Ishikawa, K. (1985) *What Is Total Quality Control? The Japanese Way*. Englewood Cliffs: Prentice-Hall.

Jacobi, M., Astin, A. and Ayala, F. (1987) *College Student Outcomes Assessment: A Talent Development Perspective*. Washington DC: Association for the Study of Higher Education.

Jacobs, R. and Floyd, M. (1995) 'A bumper crop of insights', *People Management*, 9 February 1995.

Jenkins, A. (1995a) 'The Research Assessment Exercise: funding and teaching quality', *Quality Assurance in Education*, 3(2): 4–12.

Jenkins, A. (1995b) 'The impact of the Research Assessment Exercise on teaching in selected geography departments in England and Wales', *Geography*, 80(4): 367–74.

Jennings, E. T., Jr. (1989) 'Accountability, program quality, outcome assessment, and graduate education for public affairs and administration', *Public Administration Review*, 49: 5.

Johnes, J. and Taylor, J. (1990) *Performance Indicators in Higher Education*. Buckingham: Society for Research into Higher Education/Open University Press.

Johnson, D. and Pere-Vergé, L. (1993) 'Attitudes towards graduate employment in the SME sector', *International Small Business Journal*, 11(4): 65–70.

Johnson, D., Pere-Vergé, L. and Hanage, R. (1993) 'Graduate retention and the regional economy', *Entrepreneurship and Regional Development*, 5: 85–97.

Jones, A. (1994) 'Keynote address' at the Coventry Showcase, 17 March 1994, at the Coventry Motor Vehicle Museum.

Joseph, K. (1986) *Degree courses in the public sector: quality and validation*, Circular. London: DES.

Kaplan, A. (1964) *The Conduct of Inquiry*. San Francisco, CA: Chandler.

Karlsen, R. and Stensaker, B. (1995) 'Between governmental demands and institutional needs: peer discretion in external evaluations – what is it used for?', paper presented at the 17th Annual EAIR Forum, 'Dynamics in Higher Education: Traditions Challenged by New Paradigms', Zurich, Switzerland, 27–30 August 1995.

Kells, H. R. (1992) *Self-Regulation in Higher Education: A Multinational Perspective on Collaborative Systems of Quality Assurance and Control.* London: Jessica Kingsley.

Khawaja, S. *et al.* (1991) *Technical Education: Its Relevance to Job Market. A Research Report,* AEPAM Research Study, no. 90. Islamabad: Ministry of Education, Academy of Educational Planning and Management.

Kivinen, O. and Rinne, R. (1992) *Educational Strategies in Finland in the 1990's.* Türkü: University of Türkü, Research Unit for the Sociology of Education.

Knight, P. (ed.) (1993) *The Audit and Assessment of Teaching Quality.* Birmingham: SCED/SRHE (SD).

Knight, P. (ed.) (1994) *University-wide Change, Staff and Curriculum Development,* Paper 83, May. Birmingham: Staff and Educational Development Association.

Knight, P. (ed.) (1995) *Assessment for Learning in Higher Education.* London: Kogan Page.

Knight, P. (1996) 'Independent study, independent studies and "core skills" in higher education', in Tait, J. and Knight, P. (eds) *The Management of Independent Learning.* London: Kogan Page.

Kogan, M. (ed.) (1986) *Evaluating Higher Education: Papers from the Journal of Institutional Management in Higher Education.* London: Jessica Kingsley.

Kolb, D. A. (1984) *Experiential Learning: Experience as the Source of Learning and Development.* Englewood Cliffs, NJ: Prentice-Hall.

Kuhn, T. (1970) *The Structure of Scientific Revolutions,* second edition. Chicago: University of Chicago Press.

Larrain, J. (1979) *The Concept of Ideology.* London: Hutchinson.

Laurillard, D. (1993) *Rethinking University Teaching.* London: Routledge.

Lindley, R. (ed.) (1981) *Higher Education and the Labour Market.* Guildford: Society for Research into Higher Education (SRHE).

Lindop, N. (1985) *Academic Validation in Public Sector Higher Education.* London: HMSO.

Lloyd, R. (1992) Foreword in Roberts and Higgins (1992) *Higher Education: The Student Experience: The Findings of a Research Programme into Student Decision Making and Consumer Satisfaction.* Leeds: HEIST.

Lobo, P. (1993) 'Thoughts about institutional evaluation', paper presented at the First Biennial Conference and General Conference of the International Network of Quality Assurance Agencies in Higher Education (INQAAHE), Montréal, Canada, 24–28 May 1993.

Lowe, R. (1990) 'Education for industry: the historical role of higher education in England', in Wright, P. W. G. (ed.) (1990) *Industry and Higher Education: Collaboration to Improve Students' Learning and Training,* pp. 9–17. Buckingham: Society for Research into Higher Education/Open University Press.

Luukkonen, T. and Ståhle, B. (1990) 'Quality evaluations in the management of basic and applied research', *Research Policy,* 19: 357–68.

MacNamara, D. (1988) 'Do the grounds for claiming that schools matter matter?', *British Journal of Educational Psychology,* 58(3): 356–60.

Mansergh, T. P. (1990) 'The relationship of occupational skills and attributes in work situations to salary and occupation', MEd thesis, University of New England.

Marchese, T. (1989) 'Summary comments' at the FIPSE Conference, Sante Fé, New Mexico, 7 December 1989, in *Proceedings: Assessment and Accountability in Higher Education,* p. 17. Denver: Education Commission of the States.

Marquis, C. (1995) 'Achievements and difficulties in the creation of a national system of assessment and accreditation: the Argentine case', paper presented at the 17th Annual EAIR Forum, 'Dynamics in Higher Education: Traditions Challenged by New Paradigms', Zurich, Switzerland, 27–30 August 1995.

Marsh, H. W. (1982) 'SEEQ: a reliable, valid, and useful instrument for collecting student evaluations of university teaching', *British Journal of Educational Psychology*, 52: 77–95.

Marton, F., Hounsell, D. J. and Entwistle, N. J. (eds) (1984) *The Experience of Learning*. Edinburgh: Scottish Academic Press.

Maslen, G. (1995) 'Canberra overhauls assessment' (including quotations from Professor Brian Wilson, Chairman of the Quality Committee), *Times Higher Education Supplement*, 3 November 1995, p. 8.

Massaro, V. (1995) 'Developing diversity', paper, with additional comments, presented at the Organisation for Economic Co-operation and Development (OECD), Programme on Institutional Management in Higher Education (IMHE) Seminar, at OECD, Paris, 4–6 December 1995.

McClain, C. J., Krueger, D. W. and Taylor, T. (1986) 'Northeast Missouri State University value-added assessment program: a model for educational accountability', in Kogan, M. (ed.) *Evaluating Higher Education*, pp. 33–42. London: Jessica Kingsley.

Meade, P. (1993) 'Recent development in quality assurance in Australian higher education: strategies for professional development', paper presented at the First Biennial Conference and General Conference of the International Network of Quality Assurance Agencies in Higher Education (INQAAHE), Montréal, Canada, 24–28 May 1993.

Meanwell, R. J. and Barrington, G. V. (1991) *Senior Executive Views on Education in Alberta*. Edmonton: Alberta Education.

Meikle, J. (1991) 'A higher flying kite-mark', *Guardian*, 15 October 1991, p. 25.

Mentkowski, M. and Doherty, A. (1984) 'Abilities that last a lifetime: outcomes of the Alverno experience', *AAHE Bulletin*, 36(6): 5–14.

Mercaddo del Collado, R. (1993) 'The advancements and limitations experienced in the four years of operation of a national evaluation system for higher education: the case of Mexico', paper presented at the First Biennial Conference and General Conference of the International Network of Quality Assurance Agencies in Higher Education (INQAAHE), Montréal, Canada, 24–28 May 1993.

Meyer-Dohm, P. (1990) 'Graduates of higher education: what do employers expect in the 1990s?', in Wright, P. W. G. (ed.) (1990) *Industry and Higher Education: Collaboration to Improve Students' Learning and Training*, pp. 61–7. Buckingham: Society for Research into Higher Education/Open University Press.

Middlehurst, R. (1993) *Leading Academics*. Buckingham: Society for Research into Higher Education/Open University Press.

Middlehurst, R. and Gordon, G. (1995) 'Leadership, quality and institutional effectiveness', *Higher Education Quarterly*, 49: 265–85.

Middlehurst, R. and Woodhouse, D. (1995) 'Coherent systems for external quality assurance', *Quality in Higher Education*, 1(3): 257–68.

Millard, R. M. (1991) 'Governance, quality and equity in the United States', in Berdahl, R. O., Moodie, G. C. and Spitzberg, I. J. (eds), *Quality and Access in Higher Education: Comparing Britain and the United States*, pp. 42–57. Buckingham: Society for Research into Higher Education/Open University Press.

Miller, H. D. R. (1994) *The Management of Change in Universities: Universities, State and Economy in Australia, Canada and the United Kingdom*. Buckingham: Society for Research into Higher Education/Open University Press.

Miller, L. H. (1990) 'Hubris in the academy: can teaching survive the overweaning quest for excellence?', *Change*, September/October, 9ff.

Millis, B. (1995) 'Introducing faculty to cooperative learning', in Wright, W. A. *et al.* (eds) *Teaching Improvement Practices.* Bolton, MA: Anker.

Ministry for Education and Science [Dutch] (1985) *Hoger Onderwijs, Autonomie en Kwaliteit* [Higher Education, Autonomy and Quality]. Den Haag: SDU.

Ministry of Education (1991) *Financial Reporting For Tertiary Institutions.* Wellington: New Zealand Government.

Minogue, K. R. (1973) *The Concept of a University.* London: Weidenfeld & Nicolson.

Mockiene, B. and Vengris, S. (1995) 'Quality assurance in higher education in the Republic of Lithuania: implications and considerations', in *Background Papers for the Third Meeting of the International Network of Quality Assurance Agencies in Higher Education* (INQAAHE), 21–23 May 1995, pp. 204–8, Utrecht, Netherlands: VSNU/Inspectorate of Education.

Moodie, G. C. (ed.) (1986a) *Standards and Criteria in Higher Education.* Milton Keynes: Society for Research into Higher Education/Open University Press.

Moodie, G. C. (1986b) 'Fitness for what?' in Moodie, G. C. (ed.), *Standards and Criteria in Higher Education*, pp. 1–8. Milton Keynes: Society for Research into Higher Education/Open University Press.

Moodie, G. C. (1988) 'The debates about higher education quality in Britain and the USA', *Studies in Higher Education*, 13: 5–13.

Moon, S. (1995) 'Student survey boosts satisfaction', *The Chronicle of CQI*, 1(8), November, Florida, USA.

Moore, I. (1995) 'Staff and educational development for assessment reform: a case study', in Knight, P. (ed.) *Assessment for Learning in Higher Education.* London: Kogan Page.

Moore, J. W. and Langknecht, L. F. (1986) 'Academic planning in a political system', *Planning for Higher Education*, 14(1).

Mulgan, G. (1995) 'Trust me, they owe it to us', *Times Higher Education Supplement*, 17 November 1995, p. 14.

Murphy, J. (1993a) 'A degree of waste: the economic benefits of educational expansion', *Oxford Review of Education*, 19(1): 9–31.

Murphy, J. (1993b) 'A degree of waste: a reply to Johnes', *Oxford Review of Education*, 20(1): 81–92.

Murphy, P. (1994) 'Research quality, peer review and performance indicators', *The Australian Universities' Review*, 37(1): 14–18.

Murray, H. (1984) 'The impact of formative and summative evaluation of teaching in North American Universities', *Assessment and Evaluation in Higher Education*, 9(2): 117–32.

Murray, H. G. (1991) 'Effective teaching behaviors in the college classroom' in Smart, J. C. (ed.) *Higher Education: A Handbook of Theory and Research*, Volume VII. New York: Agathon Press.

Nadeau, G. (1993) 'Criteria and indicators of quality and excellence for colleges and universities in Canada: report on a national Delphi study', paper presented at the First Biennial Conference and General Conference of the International Network of Quality Assurance Agencies in Higher Education (INQAAHE), Montréal, Canada, 24–28 May 1993.

National Advisory Body and University Grants Committee (NAB/UGC) (1984) *A Strategy for Higher Education in the Late 1980s and Beyond.* London: NAB.

National Board of Employment, Education and Training (NBEET) (1992) *Skills Required of Graduates: One Test of Quality in Australian Higher Education.* Canberra:

Australian Government Publishing Service. (Also referred to as *Skills Sought by Employers of Graduates* on front cover of published report.)

National Board of Employment, Education and Training Higher Education Council (NBEET HEC) (1992) *Higher Education: Achieving Quality*. Canberra: Australian Government Publishing Service.

National Governors' Association (NGA) (1986) *Time for Results: The Governors' 1991 Report on Education*. Washington, DC: NGA.

National Governors' Association Task Force (NGATF) (1986) 'Task force on college quality', in *Time for Results: The Governors' 1991 Report on Education*, pp. 153–71. Washington, DC: NGA.

National Policy Board on Higher Education Institutional Accreditation (NPB) (1994) *Independence, Accreditation and the Public Trust*. Washington, DC: NPB.

National Union of Students (NUS) (1993) 'What is quality?', NUS Training *Handout*. London: NUS.

Newstead, S. E. (1992) 'A study of two "quick and easy" methods of assessing individual differences in student learning', *British Journal of Educational Psychology*, 63: 229–312.

Nicol, D. J. (1992) 'The support needs of staff developers', *Education and Training Technology International*, 29(2): 152–63.

Norman, D. (1978) 'Notes towards a complex theory of learning', in Lesgold, A. M., Pollegrino, J. W., Fokkema, S. D. and Glaser, R. (eds) *Cognitive Psychology and Instruction*. New York: Plenum Press.

O'Leary, J. (1981) 'A crisis of our own manufacturing', *Times Higher Education Supplement*, no. 450, p. 8.

O'Neil, C. and Wright, W. (1995) *Recording Teaching Achievement*. Halifax, NS: Dalhousie University.

Oakland, J. S. (1992) 'A TQM model for education and training', keynote speech to the AETT conference on 'Quality in Education', University of York, 6–8 April 1992.

Ontario Council on University Affairs (OCUA) (1992) *Academic Quality Reviews for Public Accountability: A Working Paper for Discussion at the 1992 OCUA Fall Hearings*, 29 September 1992.

Ontario Council on University Affairs (OCUA) (1994) *Sustaining Quality in Changing Times: Funding Ontario Universities – A Discussion Paper*. Toronto: OCUA.

Otter, S. (1992) 'Learning outcomes: a quality strategy for higher education', paper to the 'Quality by Degrees' Conference at Aston University, 8 June 1992.

Pascarella, E. T. and Terenzini, P. T. (1991) *How College Affects Students*. San Francisco, CA: Jossey-Bass.

Pascarella, E. T. *et al.* (1994) *What have we Learned from the First Year of the National Study of Student Learning?* Pennsylvania: National Center on Postsecondary Teaching, Learning and Assessment.

Paskow, J. (ed.) (1990) *Assessment Programs and Projects: A Directory*. (Updated by Francis, E.) Washington, DC: American Association for Higher Education.

Peace Lenn, M. (1995) 'Toward common educational standards for North America: a case study in trade agreements, the professions and higher education', in *Background Papers for the Third Meeting of the International Network of Quality Assurance Agencies in Higher Education* (INQAAHE), 21–23 May 1995, pp. 209–13. Utrecht, Netherlands: VSNU/Inspectorate of Education.

Pechar, H. (1993) 'New ways of quality management in Austrian higher education', paper presented at the 15th Annual EAIR Forum, Türkü, Finland, 15–18 August 1993.

Percy, K. and Ramsden, P. (1980) *Independent Study: Two Examples from English Higher Education*. Guildford: Society for Research into Higher Education.

Perkins, D. N. and Salomon, G. (1989) 'Are cognitive skills context-bound?', *Educational Researcher*, 18(1): 16–25.

Perry, R. P. (1991) 'Perceived control in college students: implications for instruction', in Smart, J. C. (ed.) *Higher Education: Handbook of Theory and Research*, Volume VII. New York: Agathon Press.

Peters, T. (1992) *Liberation Management: Necessary Disorganisation for the Nanosecond Nineties*. London: BCA.

Peters, T. (1994) *The Pursuit of WOW!* London: Pan Books.

Peters, T. J. and Waterman, R. H. (1982) *In Search of Excellence: Lessons from America's Best-Run Companies*. New York: Harper and Row.

Petersen, J. C. (1995) 'Report proposes accreditation changes in US', *QA*, 8: 6–7, February.

Pfeffer, N. and Coote, A. (1991) *Is Quality Good for You? A Critical Review of Quality Assurance in the Welfare Services*. London: Institute of Public Policy Research.

Pierce, D. (1993) 'Position statement prepared on behalf of group C2 who discussed integrating and assessing transferable skills', in Harvey, L. (ed.) (1994) *Proceedings of the Second QHE Quality Assessment Seminar, 16–17 December, 1993*, p. 48. Birmingham: QHE.

Pike, G. R., Phillippi, R. H., Banta, T. W., Bensey, M. W., Milbourne, C. C. and Columbus, P. J. (1991) *Freshman to Senior Gains at the University of Tennessee, Knoxville*. Knoxville: The University of Tennessee, Center for Assessment Research and Development.

Pirsig, R. M. (1976) *Zen and the Art of Motorcycle Maintenance: An Enquiry into Values*. London: Corgi.

Policy Studies Institute (PSI) (1990) *Britain's Real Skills Shortage*. London: PSI.

Pollitt, C. (1990) 'Measuring university performance: never mind the quality, never mind the width', *Higher Education Quarterly*, 44(1): 60–81.

Polytechnics and Colleges Funding Council (PCFC) (1989) *Recurrent Funding Methodology 1990–91: Guidance for Institutions*, Circular. London: PCFC.

Polytechnics and Colleges Funding Council (PCFC) (1990a) *Teaching Quality*, Report of the Committee of Enquiry Appointed by the Council, October. London: PCFC.

Polytechnics and Colleges Funding Council (PCFC) (1990b) *Performance Indicators: Report of a Committee of Enquiry chaired by Mr. Alfred Morris*, June. London: PCFC.

Polytechnics and Colleges Funding Council (PCFC) (1990c) *Recurrent Funding and Equipment Allocations 1990–91*, London: PCFC.

Polytechnics and Colleges Funding Council (PCFC) (1990d) *Research in the PCFC Sector: Report of the Committee of Enquiry Appointed by the Council*, September. London: PCFC.

Polytechnics and Colleges Funding Council and Universities Funding Council (PCFC/UFC) (1992a) *The Funding of Teaching in Higher Education*. Bristol: PCFC.

Polytechnics and Colleges Funding Council and Universities Funding Council (PCFC/UFC) (1992b) *A Funding Methodology for Teaching in Higher Education*. Bristol: PCFC.

Polytechnics and Colleges Funding Council (PCFC) (1992) *Macro Performance Indicators*, May. Bristol: PCFC.

Porrer, R. (1984) *Higher Education and Employment*. London: Association of Graduate Careers Advisory Services.

Porter, L. J. and Oakland, J. S. (1992) 'Developing the European Quality Model: the implementation of total quality management at the Management Centre, University of Bradford', paper presented at the AETT conference on 'Quality in Education', University of York, 6–8 April 1992.

President's Work Group on Accreditation (PWGA) (1995) *The Council for Higher Education Accreditation.* Urbana, IL: University of Illinois.

Prosser, M. (1993) 'Phenomenography and the principles and practices of learning', *Higher Education Research and Development,* 12(1): 21–31.

Race, P. (1995) 'What has assessment done for us – and to us?', in Knight, P. (ed.) *Assessment for Learning in Higher Education.* London: Kogan Page.

Ramsden, P. (1986) 'Students and quality', in Moodie, G. C. (ed.) (1986) *Standards and Criteria in Higher Education,* pp. 157–70. Milton Keynes: Society for Research into Higher Education/Open University Press.

Ramsden, P. (ed.) (1988) *Improving Learning: New Perspectives.* London: Kogan Page.

Ramsden, P. (1991) 'A performance indicator of teaching quality in higher education: the Course Experience Questionnaire', *Studies in Higher Education,* 16(2): 129–50.

Ramsden, P. (1995) Personal correspondence, November, 1995.

Rasmussen, P. (1995) 'A Danish approach to quality in education: the case of Aalborg University', paper, with additional comments, presented at the Organisation for Economic Co-operation and Development (OECD), Programme on Institutional Management in Higher Education (IMHE) Seminar, at OECD, Paris, 4–6 December 1995.

Ratcliff, J. L. (1995) 'Building effective learning communities', keynote paper presented to SRHE Conference 'Changing the Student Experience', Birmingham, 4–5 July 1995.

Ratcliff, J. L. and associates (1995) *Realizing the Potential: Improving Postsecondary Teaching, Learning and Assessment.* Pennsylvania: National Center on Postsecondary Teaching, Learning and Assessment.

Rear, J. (1994a) 'Defenders of academic faith', *Times Higher Education Supplement,* 21 October 1994, p. 15.

Rear, J. (1994b) 'Freedom with responsibility', *Times Higher Education Supplement,* 2 December 1994, p. 12.

Rear, J. (1994c) 'Institutional responses in British higher education' in Westerheijden, D., Brennan, J. and Maasen, P. (eds) *Changing Contexts of Quality Assessment: Recent Trends in West European Higher Education,* pp. 75–94. Utrecht: Lemma.

Reeves, M. (1988) *The Crisis in Higher Education: Competence, Delight and the Common Good.* Milton Keynes: Society for Research into Higher Education/Open University Press.

Ribier, R. (1995) 'The role of governments vis-à-vis the evaluation agencies', in *Background Papers for the Third Meeting of the International Network of Quality Assurance Agencies in Higher Education* (INQAAHE), 21–23 May 1995, pp. 214–15. Utrecht, Netherlands: VSNU/Inspectorate of Education.

Richards, H. (1992) 'University opt-out call', *Times Higher Education Supplement,* no. 1020, 22 May 1986.

Richardson, D. M. (1989) 'Perceptions of Employers of Northern Alberta Institute of Technology (NAIT) Marketing Management Graduates: A Follow-up Study'. MEd thesis, University of Alberta.

Richardson, R. C., Jr. (1992) 'Quality in undergraduate education: a conceptual framework', draft paper for consideration by the Education Commission of the States' dinner meeting, 22nd June 1992, Fontainebleau Hilton, Miami Beach.

Rigg, M. *et al.* (1990) *An Overview of the Demand for Graduates.* London: HMSO.

Robbins, D. (1988) *The Rise of Independent Study*. Milton Keynes: Society for Research into Higher Education/Open University Press.

Ross, L. (1981) 'The "intuitive scientist" formulation and its developmental implications', in Flavell, J. H. and Ross, L. (eds) *Social Cognitive Development: Frontiers and Possible Futures*. Cambridge: Cambridge University Press.

Rothblatt, S. (1992) 'National standards or local interests?', *Times Higher Education Supplement*, 7 Febuary 1992, p. 14.

Rovio-Johansson, A. and Ling, J. (1995) Comments on the experiences of one university in the CRE programme of institutional evaluation at the Organisation for Economic Co-operation and Development (OECD), Programme on Institutional Management in Higher Education (IMHE) Seminar, at OECD, Paris, 4–6 December 1995.

Saarinen, T. (1995) 'Systematic higher education assessment and departmental impacts: translating the effort to meet the need', *Quality in Higher Education*, 1(3): 223–34.

Sachs, J. (1994) 'Strange yet compatible bedfellows; quality assurance and quality improvement', *The Australian Universities' Review*, 37(1): 22–5.

Sallis, E. and Hingley, P. (1992) 'Total quality management', *Coombe Lodge Report*, 23(1). Blagdon: The Staff College.

Schein, E. H. (1992) *Organizational Culture and Leadership*, second edition. San Francisco, CA: Jossey-Bass.

Schrock, E. M. and Lefevre, H. L. (eds) (1988) *The Good and Bad News About Quality*. Milwaukee, WI: American Society for Quality Control, ASQC Quality Management Division.

Scottish Higher Education Funding Council (SHEFC) (1992a) *Assessment of Quality of Provision of Education in Higher Education Institutions*, August. Edinburgh: SHEFC.

Scottish Higher Education Funding Council (SHEFC) (1992b) *Quality Assessment: The SHEFC Approach* (Report in four sections), October. Edinburgh: SHEFC.

Secretary of State for Education (1988) Letter to the Chairman of the PCFC, Circular, 1 November 1988. London: DES.

Semler, R. (1993) *Maverick: The Story Behind the World's Most Unusual Workplace*. London: Century.

Shores, A. R. (1988) *Survival of the Fittest: Total Quality Control and Management Evolution*. Milwaukee, WI: American Society for Quality Control.

Silver, H. (1993) *External Examiners: Changing Roles?* London: CNAA.

Silver, H., Skennett, A. and Williams, R. (1995) *External Examiner System: Possible Futures*, report of a project commissioned by HEQC, May. London: QSC.

Sims, R. R. (1986) *The Politics of Multiracial Education*. London: Routledge.

Smith, L. (1993) *Necessary Knowledge*. Hove: Lawrence Erlbaum Associates.

Springer, L. *et al.* (1994) 'Influences on college students' orientations towards learning for self-understanding', *Journal of College Student Development*, 36(1): 5–18.

Standing Conference of Employers of Graduates (SCOEG) (1985) *What Employers Look for in their Graduate Recruits*. London: SCOEG.

Standing Conference of Rectors, Presidents and Vice-Chancellors of the European Universities (CRE) (1995) *Institutional Audit of the University of Oporto: CRE Auditors' Report*, March. Geneva: CRE.

Staropoli, A. (1991) 'Quality assurance in France', paper presented to the Hong Kong Council for Academic Accreditation Conference on 'Quality Assurance in Higher Education', Hong Kong, 15–17 July.

Stensaker, B. and Karlsen, R. (1994) *Judging quality? A study of the external evaluation of business administration education*, Report 10/94. Oslo: Institute for Studies in Research and Higher Education.

Su, Jin-Li (1995) 'The effects of the trial implementation of a departmental evaluation project in Taiwan', *Quality in Higher Education*, 1(2): 159–72.

Tait, J. and Knight, P. (1995) 'Assessment and continuous quality improvement: a North American case study', *Innovations in Education and Training International*, 32(4).

Targett, S. (1993) 'Danger in hit and miss approach to skills', *Times Higher Education Supplement*, 10 December 1993, p. 2.

Targett, S. (1995) 'Shephard rounds on CBI', *Times Higher Education Supplement*, 17 November 1995, p. 2.

Tavistock Institute of Human Relations (TIHR) (1990) *The First Year of Enterprise in Higher Education. Final Report of the Case Study Evaluation of EHE*. Sheffield: Employment Department Group.

Teichler, U. (1989) 'Research on higher education and work in Europe', *European Journal of Education*, 24(3): 223–47.

Thune, C. (1993) 'The experience with establishing procedures for evaluation and quality assurance of higher education in Denmark', paper presented at the First Biennial Conference and General Conference of the International Network of Quality Assurance Agencies in Higher Education (INAAQHE), Montréal, Canada, 24–28 May 1993.

Thune, C. (1995) 'Danish experiences with evaluation of higher education', *QA*, 8: 10–14 February.

Tomlinson, P. and Saunders, S. (1995) 'The current possibilities for teacher profiling in teacher education', in Edwards, A. and Knight, P. (eds) *The Assessment of Competence in Higher Education*. London: Kogan Page.

Trades Union Congress (TUC) (1989) *Skills 2000*. London: TUC.

Trageton, S. and Utne, E. (1995) 'Evaluation as an institutional enterprise', paper presented at the 17th Annual EAIR Forum, 'Dynamics in Higher Education: Traditions Challenged by New Paradigms', Zurich, Switzerland, 27–30 August 1995.

Trigwell, K. (1995) 'Increasing faculty understanding of teaching' in Wright, W. A. *et al.* (eds) *Teaching Improvement Practices*. Bolton, MA: Anker.

Trigwell, K. and Prosser, M. (1991) 'Improving the quality of student learning: the influence of learning context and student approaches to learning on learning outcomes', *Higher Education*, 22: 251–66.

Trow, M. (1993) 'Managerialism and the academic profession: the case of England', paper presented to the 'Quality Debate Conference', Milton Keynes, 24 September 1993.

United Nations Educational, Scientific and Cultural Organization (UNESCO) (1995) *Policy Paper for Change and Development in Higher Education*. Paris: UNESCO.

University of Otago (1995) *Academic Staff Promotions, 1996*, Memorandum to Assistant Vice-Chancellors, Deans and Heads of Departments from Stephen Gray, Staff Registrar, Appendix 1, *Criteria for Staff Promotion*, Schedule 11, 15 May. Dunedin: University of Otago.

van Schaik, M. and Köllen, E. (1995) *Quality Management at the Hogeschool Holland: Towards a Policy of Systematic Quality Assessment*. Hogeschool Holland: AG Diemen.

van Vught, F. (1991) 'Higher education quality assessment in Europe: the next step', *CRE-Action*, 96(4): 61–82.

van Vught, F. (1992) 'Towards a European higher education quality assessment system', paper to the 4th International Conference on Assessing Quality, Twente University, Enschede, Netherlands, 28–30 July.

van Vught, F. and Westerheijden, D. F. (1992) 'Quality management and quality assurance in European higher education: methods and mechanisms', draft paper, 31 August 1992.

Volet, S. E. (1991) 'Modelling and coaching of relevant metracognitive strategies for enhancing university students' learning', *Learning and Instruction*, 1(4): 315–36.

Vroeijenstijn, T. I. (1991) 'External quality assessment: servant of two masters?', paper presented to the Hong Kong Council for Academic Accreditation Conference on 'Quality Assurance in Higher Education', Hong Kong, 15–17 July.

Vroeijenstijn, T. I. (1995) 'Improvement and accountability', in *Proceedings of the Third Meeting of the International Network for Quality Assurance Agencies in Higher Education, 21–23 May, 1995*, pp. 25–35, Utrecht, Holland: VSNU/Inspectorate of Education.

Vroeijenstijn, T. I. and Acherman, H. (1990) 'Control-oriented versus improvement-oriented quality assessment', in Goedegebuure, L. C. J., Maassen, P. A. M. and Westerheijden, D. F. (eds) *Peer Review and Performance Indicators: Quality Assessment in British and Dutch Higher Education*, pp. 81–101. Utrecht: Lemma.

Walsh, K. (1991) 'Quality and Public Services', *Public Administration*, 69(4): 503–14.

Wang, Zonglie and Li, Jianmin (1993) 'Academic degree accreditation and evaluation in China', paper presented at the First Biennial Conference and General Conference of the International Network of Quality Assurance Agencies in Higher Education (INQAAHE), Montréal, Canada, 24–28 May 1993.

Ward, P. (1995) 'A 360-degree turn for the better', *People Management*, 9 February 1995.

Warnock, Baroness M. (1989) *Universities: Knowing Our Minds*. London: Chatto and Windus.

Warren Piper, D. J. (1994) *Are Professors Professional? The Organisation of University Examinations*. London: Jessica Kingsley.

Warren Piper, D. J. (1995) 'Assuring the quality of awards' *Quality in Higher Education*, 1(3): 197–210.

Wei, Runbai and Gui, Shuide (1995) 'Shanghai Higher Education Quality Assurance Committee', *QA*, 8: 8–9, February.

Weimer, M. and Lenze, L. F. (1991) 'Instructional interventions: a review of the literature on efforts to improve instruction', in Smart, J. C. (ed.) *Higher Education: Handbook of Theory and Research*, volume VII. New York: Agathon Press.

Widdecomb, A. (1993) 'After-dinner speech', in Harvey, L. (ed.) (1994), *Proceedings of the Second QHE Quality Assessment Seminar, 16–17 December 1993*, pp. 29–31. Birmingham: QHE.

Wiggins, G. (1990) 'The truth may make you free but the test may keep you imprisoned: towards assessment worthy of the liberal arts', in AAHE Assessment Forum (1990) *Assessment 1990: Understanding the Implications*, pp. 15–32. Washington, DC: American Association for Higher Education (Assessment Forum Resource).

Wilkins, J. (1994) 'Letter to the editor', *Times Higher Education Supplement*, 28 October 1994, p. 10.

Wingrove, J. and Herriot, P. (1984a) 'Graduate pre-selection: some findings and their guidance implications', *British Journal of Guidance Counselling*, 12(2): 166–74.

Wingrove, J. and Herriot, P. (1984b) 'Decision in graduate pre-selection', *Journal of Occupational Psychology*, 57(4): 269–75.

Winter, R. (1995) 'The assessment of professional competences: the importance of general criteria', in Edwards, A. and Knight, P. (eds) *The Assessment of Competence in Higher Education*. London: Kogan Page.

Woodhead, M. (1989) 'Is early education effective?, in Desforges, C. (ed.) *Early Childhood Education*. Edinburgh: Scottish Academic Press.

Wright, W. A. and O'Neil, M. C. (1995) 'Teaching improvement practices: international perspectives', in Wright, W. A. *et al.* (eds) *Teaching Improvement Practices*. Bolton, MA: Anker.

Yorke, M. (1993) 'Total quality higher education?', paper at the 15th EAIR Forum, University of Türkü, 15 August 1993.

Yorke, M. (1995a) 'Shouldn't quality be enhanced rather than assessed?', paper presented at the 17th Annual EAIR Forum, 'Dynamics in Higher Education: Traditions Challenged by New Paradigms', Zurich, Switzerland, 27–30 August 1995.

Yorke, M. (1995b) 'Siamese twins? Performance indicators in the service of accountability and enhancement', *Quality in Higher Education*, 1(1): 13–30.

Zuber-Skerritt, O. (1993) 'Improving learning and teaching through action learning and action research', *Higher Education Research and Development*, 12(1): 45–58.

# Index

# The Society for Research into Higher Education

The Society for Research into Higher Education exists to stimulate and coordinate research into all aspects of higher education. It aims to improve the quality of higher education through the encouragement of debate and publication on issues of policy, on the organization and management of higher education institutions, and on the curriculum and teaching methods.

The Society's income is derived from subscriptions, sales of its books and journals, conference fees and grants. It receives no subsidies, and is wholly independent. Its individual members include teachers, researchers, managers and students. Its corporate members are institutions of higher education, research institutes, professional, industrial and governmental bodies. Members are not only from the UK, but from elsewhere in Europe, from America, Canada and Australasia, and it regards its international work as among its most important activities.

Under the imprint *SRHE & Open University Press*, the Society is a specialist publisher of research, having some 60 titles in print. The Editorial Board of the Society's Imprint seeks authoritative research or study in the above fields. It offers competitive royalties, a highly recognizable format in both hardback and paperback and the world-wide reputation of the Open University Press.

The Society also publishes *Studies in Higher Education* (three times a year), which is mainly concerned with academic issues, *Higher Education Quarterly* (formerly *Universities Quarterly*), mainly concerned with policy issues, *Research into Higher Education Abstracts* (three times a year), and *SRHE News* (four times a year).

The Society holds a major annual conference in December, jointly with an institution of higher education. In 1993, the topic was 'Governments and the Higher Education Curriculum: Evolving Partnerships' at the University of Sussex in Brighton. In 1994, it was 'The Student Experience' at the University of York and in 1995, 'The Changing University' at Heriot-Watt University in Edinburgh. Conferences in 1996 include 'Working in Higher Education' at Cardiff Institute of Higher Education.

The Society's committees, study groups and branches are run by the members. The groups at present include:

Teacher Education Study Group
Continuing Education Group
Staff Development Group
Excellence in Teaching and Learning

# Benefits to members

## Individual

Individual members receive:

- *SRHE News*, the Society's publications list, conference details and other material included in mailings.
- Greatly reduced rates for *Studies in Higher Education* and *Higher Education Quarterly*.
- A 35 per cent discount on all SRHE & Open University Press publications.
- Free copies of the Proceedings – commissioned papers on the theme of the Annual Conference.
- Free copies of *Research into Higher Education Abstracts*.
- Reduced rates for conferences.
- Extensive contacts and scope for facilitating initiatives.
- Reduced reciprocal memberships.
- Free copies of the *Register of Members' Research Interests*.

## Corporate

Corporate members receive:

- All benefits of individual members, plus.
- Free copies of *Studies in Higher Education*.
- Unlimited copies of the Society's publications at reduced rates.
- Special rates for its members, e.g. to the Annual Conference.
- The right to submit application for the Society's research grants.

 *Membership details*: SRHE, 3 Devonshire Street, London WIN 2BA, UK. Tel: 0171 637 2766. Fax: 0171 637 2781 *Catalogue*: SRHE & Open University Press, Celtic Court, 22 Ballmoor, Buckingham MK18 1XW. Tel: (01280) 823388.

**THE LIMITS OF COMPETENCE**
KNOWLEDGE, HIGHER EDUCATION AND SOCIETY

**Ronald Barnett**

Competence is a term which is making its entrance in the university. How might it be understood at this level? *The Limits of Competence* takes an uncompromising line, providing a sustained critique of the notion of competence as wholly inadequate for higher education.

Currently, we are seeing the displacement for one limited version of competence by another even more limited interpretation. In the older definition – one of academic competence – notions of disciplines, objectivity and truth have been central. In the new version, competence is given an operational twist and is marked out by know-how, competence and skills. In this operationalism, the key question is not 'What do students understand?' but 'What can students do?'

The book develops an alternative view, suggesting that, for our universities, a third and heretical conception of human being is worth considering. Our curricula might, instead, offer an education for life.

*Contents*

222pp     0 335 19341 2 (Paperback)     0 335 19070 7 (Hardback)

## WHAT IS QUALITY IN HIGHER EDUCATION?

**Diana Green (ed.)**

In the UK, the absence of any agreed definition of quality is problematic in the wake of the changes set in train by the 1988 Education Reform Act. Pressure for greater accountability in the use of public funds and changes to the structure and funding of higher education (designed to increase competition for students and resources) provided the initial rationale for giving quality a higher profile than in the past. The Government's commitment to a higher participation rate, together with the decision to overtly tie quality assessment to funding decisions, sharpened the concern. However, a fundamental dilemma remains: if there is no consensus about what quality is in higher education, how can it be assessed?

This book was stimulated by, and reflects some of the debate following the publication of the 1991 Further and Higher Education Bill and its subsequent enactment. It also draws on the preliminary findings of a major national research project funded by a partnership of government, business and higher education, designed to develop and test methods for systematically assessing quality.

The focus here is on the quality of teaching and learning. The book illustrates the extent to which quality has overtaken efficiency as the key challenge facing higher education in the 1990s. It underlines the growing awareness that institutions are accountable not only to the government which funds them but also, in an increasingly competitive higher education market, to the customers – the students. The book therefore signals the early stages of what threatens to be cultural revolution as profound as that which has transformed the behaviour of organizations in the manufacturing and commercial sectors.

### Contents

*Part 1: What is quality in higher education? – Concepts, policy and practice – Quality in higher education: a funding council perspective – Part 2: Models from within British higher education – Defining and measuring the quality of teaching – Inspecting quality in the classroom: an HMI perspective – Quality audit in the universities – Part 3: Models from beyond British higher education – Quality and its measurement: a business perspective – Royal Mail: developing a total quality organization – Quality in higher education: an international perspective – Looking ahead – Index.*

### Contributors

Jim Finch, Malcolm Frazer, Diana Green, Terry Melia, Baroness Pauline Perry, Ian Raisbeck, William H. Stubbs, Carole Webb.

160pp     0 335 15740 8 (Paperback)

# THE MEANINGS OF MASS HIGHER EDUCATION

**Peter Scott**

This book is the first systematic attempt to analyse the growth of mass higher education in a specifically British context, while seeking to develop more theoretical perspectives on this transformation of elite university systems into open post-secondary education systems. It is divided into three main sections. The first examines the evolution of British higher education and the development of universities and other institutions. The second explores the political, social and economic context within which mass systems are developing. What are the links between post-industrial society, a post-Fordist economy and the mass university? The third section discusses the links between massification and wider currents in intellectual and scientific culture.

### Contents

*Preface – Introduction – Structure and institutions – State and society – Science and culture – Understanding mass higher education – Notes – Index.*

208pp     0 335 19442 7 (Paperback)     0 335 19443 5 (Hardback)